Adopting Large Sibling Groups:
The experience of adopters and adoption agencies

Adopting Large Sibling Groups:
The experience of adopters and adoption agencies

Hilary Saunders and
Julie Selwyn

Published by British Association
for Adoption & Fostering
(BAAF)
Saffron House
3rd Floor, 6–10 Kirby Street
London EC1N 8TS
www.baaf.org.uk

Charity registration 275689 (England and Wales)
and SC039337 (Scotland)

British Library Cataloguing in Publication Data
A catalogue record for this book is available
from the British Library

ISBN 978 1 907585 44 9

Editorial project management by Shaila Shah,
BAAF Publications
Designed by Helen Joubert Associates
Typeset by Avon DataSet Ltd, Bidford on Avon
Printed in Great Britain by TJ International Ltd
Trade distribution by Turnaround Publisher Services,
Unit 3, Olympia Trading Estate, Coburg Road,
London N22 6TZ

BAAF is the leading UK-wide membership
organisation for all those concerned with
adoption, fostering and child care issues.

Contents

List of tables

List of figures

Acknowledgements

We are very grateful to the Sir Halley Stewart Trust for recognising the need for this research and providing the funding that made it possible.

In particular, we want to thank all the sibling group adopters who took part in the study and described their experiences so vividly. Their candid views on adoption services, and the warmth and compassion they expressed for their children, made the interviews not only fascinating but also enjoyable. It was a pleasure to meet people with such generosity of spirit.

We also want to express our gratitude to all the staff in local authority and voluntary adoption agencies who helped us to contact sibling group adopters, took part in the interviews and provided numerous examples of good practice. It is important also to acknowledge the invaluable help provided by staff at the Consortium of Voluntary Adoption Agencies, the Adoption Register, *Be My Parent* and Adoption UK in enabling us to find adoption agencies and adopters for our sample.

We are especially grateful to the members of our advisory group for all their helpful suggestions and comments: Cherilyn Dance (University of Bedfordshire), Mo O'Reilly (British Association for Adoption and Fostering), Lindsay Wright (London Borough of Islington), Jadwiga Ball (Clifton Children's Society), Delma Hughes (Siblings Together), Sue Dromey (Post-Adoption Centre, London) and Alison Jones (adopter of siblings).

Any errors or deficiencies in this study are the sole responsibility of the researchers and should not be attributed to any of the advisers or to the Sir Halley Stewart Trust.

1 Introduction

After 50 years, Sonia Lamb (aged 64) finally met her younger brother Chris on 8 August 2010. Her two brothers had been adopted because her mother could not afford to support four children. Sonia had found out about her brothers when she was ten years old and 'never stopped thinking about them from that day'. She could not ask her mother, because her mother 'kept it all inside' and never spoke about the boys. Chris had discovered his hidden adoption certificate when he was 15 and eventually used the adoption records to track down his sister. An elated Sonia commented, 'I've done nothing but cry since I found out, it's been so emotional . . . He's lovely and we're so alike – we have the same colour eyes and our mannerisms are identical. It's like we've never been apart.' The two are now desperately trying to find their other brother (*Hemel Hempstead Gazette*, 17.8.10).

All over the UK there are brothers and sisters in similar circumstances. Siblings matter to each other, whether they share a history or not. After birth mothers, siblings are the next largest group of relatives putting their names on the Adoption Contact Register[1] in the hope of finding "lost" sisters and brothers (Mullender and Kearn, 1997). Their motivation for searching includes a sense of loss and grief, a notion of the sibling as part of themselves, and just wanting to know if their sibling is all right.

The importance of maintaining sibling relationships is now widely recognised in policy and legislation. An amendment to the Children Act 1989 (S22(c)) states that a placement should enable the child to live together with a sibling. Moreover, Adoption Statutory Guidance (Department for Education, 2011) states that in relation to domestic adoption, siblings should be adopted by the same adopter unless there

---

1 The Adoption Contact Register enables adoptees and their birth relatives to make contact with each other, after the adoptee reaches age 18 and both parties have registered a wish to be contacted.

is good reason why not. Where it is not possible for siblings to be placed together, the agency should consider carefully the need for the children to remain in contact with each other and the need for adoption support (paragraph 4.12).

While legislation and guidance state that it is preferable to place siblings together, in practice it can be difficult to meet these obligations. Children being adopted today are, on average, three years and 11 months old and often have multiple special needs (Department for Education, 2010). They have usually suffered abuse or neglect, or were born to mothers who misused substances and/or alcohol during pregnancy and/or have a history of mental health problems. Consequently, children's developmental prognosis is often uncertain. Adoptive parenting brings many rewards but also many challenges, especially when siblings have different and sometimes competing needs.

Attempts to find families for large sibling groups are frequently unsuccessful. The Adoption Register for England and Wales suggests matches for waiting children with suitable adopters from any part of the country. Although the Register has managed to find suitable matches for many children, they still have difficulty finding adopters for more than two siblings. The Adoption Register 2009/10 annual report shows that out of 186 children referred to the Register for placement in sibling groups of three or four, only 34 were placed (ten sibling groups of three children and one sibling group of four) as a result of suggested matches made by the Register. The expertise of voluntary adoption agencies (VAAs) in placing larger sibling groups is reflected in the fact that ten of these sibling groups were placed with adopters approved by VAAs, while only one was placed with adopters approved by a local authority adoption agency (LA). It is not known whether the remaining 152 siblings were eventually placed together by their local authorities, but it is likely that many were not.

While difficulties in finding a family willing to take a sibling group are recognised, some practitioners question whether LAs do enough to find joint placements for sibling groups. One example is contained in the evidence (Hughes, 2009) submitted to the National Institute for Health and Clinical Excellence to inform the development of guidance aimed at improving the quality of life for looked after children. Having been separated from her six siblings in the care system, Delma Hughes later founded the voluntary organisation Siblings Together. In her evidence statement, she urged social workers to think again and ask themselves if any of the following reasons given for separating siblings in care would be acceptable for separating brothers and sisters living in families in the community:

- 'They fight all the time.'
- 'They are a bad influence on each other.'
- 'This placement is not appropriate to meet his or her needs.'
- 'This placement does not take that type of child.'
- 'We would like to keep them together but there isn't the funding for it.'
- 'We have to focus on the needs of the individual.'
- 'He or she has become too old to stay in this placement.'
- 'He or she needs to be moving on to independence.'

Anecdotal evidence from staff in voluntary adoption agencies also suggests that local authority social workers can sometimes be very pessimistic about the chances of finding an adoptive placement for sibling groups, and this leads to weak and indecisive family-finding. It is also worth noting that social workers' pessimism was found to lead to reduced family-finding efforts in a study of minority ethnic children with adoption recommendations (Selwyn *et al*, 2010).

There is no research specifically looking at the practices and policies that help to create happy and enduring adoptive placements for sibling groups of three children or more. Indeed, there is not a large amount of research into sibling placements in the UK. Studies have focused mainly on the decision-making process, particularly the assessment as to whether siblings should be placed together or apart and the potential benefits and disadvantages of doing so.

The British Association for Adoption and Fostering (BAAF) has produced a helpful guide focusing on assessment: *Together or Apart? Assessing brothers and sisters for adoption* (Lord and Borthwick, 2008). While this includes advice on the recruitment, assessment and training of prospective adopters and on introductions, placement and support, it does not explore these issues in depth, nor does it consider these issues from the perspective of adopters and adoption staff.

This study is, therefore, the first to examine adopters' experiences of parenting a large sibling group and the views of staff in adoption agencies who need to recruit and support adopters willing to take siblings. To place this study in context, the next chapter reviews the research literature on siblings generally, on siblings in the care system, and on adopted siblings.

2 Research on siblings and sibling placements

This chapter reviews the research on siblings and sibling relationships, with an emphasis on larger families with three or more children, siblings who have faced adversity, siblings who are looked after, and adopted siblings. There is a considerable body of research on siblings but much less on large sibling groups. Caution is needed in comparing the findings of these studies, because the term "sibling" is often defined differently with some studies including half-siblings and others not. It should also be noted that most of these studies focus on sibling pairs, so the findings may not be valid for larger sibling groups.

As there are numerous studies on siblings, we focus on those which we consider to be the most significant, particularly with regard to understanding the needs of large sibling groups. We begin this literature review by considering how couples in the general population decide how many children to have, the effects of family size on children's progress, and attitudes towards larger families.

Siblings in the general population

Family size – preferences, effects and attitudes

Family size has been steadily decreasing in the UK, and it has become the norm for families in the UK to have only one or two children. Data from the 2001 Population Census (ONS, 2001) found that the average number of dependent children in a family was less than two (1.8). However, family size varied by the ethnicity of the parent, with minority ethnic families being larger than white families. About a third of Pakistani and Bangladeshi households, 11 per cent of black households, and ten per cent of Indian households contained three or more children in comparison with only five per cent of white households (Platt, 2002). A study of attitudes towards ideal family size (Penn and Lambert, 2002) found that: adults who came from large families preferred to have more children; in Britain, both Christians and Muslims wanted larger families than non-religious respondents; and family size preferences were not determined by gender, socio-economic factors or educational levels. The desire for at least one child of each sex also influenced the decision to have more than two children (Stansfield et al, 2007).

Families with four or more dependent children make up less than five per cent of all families but more than 20 per cent of children living in poverty, and mothers who first give birth at age 15 or 16 have a greater than 50 per cent chance of going on to have four or more children (Iacovou and Berthoud, 2006). This is one of many studies showing that children in larger families are disadvantaged. For example, the National Child Development Study found that, compared to children from small families, children in large families were at a disadvantage with regard to reading attainment, arithmetic attainment, social adjustment and height (Fogelman, 1975). Child bearing in close succession may also have long-term negative effects on children, for example low levels of literacy (Baydar et al, 1993). Most of the inverse relationship between the number of siblings and children's educational attainment can be explained by parental resources (time, energy and money) being "diluted" among children as the number of siblings increases (Downey, 1995). However, a large-scale study (Zill, 1996) showed that parents' own level of education is often a stronger predictor of child well-being than family income or family size.

This is clearly a class issue and large families living on welfare benefits have been singled out for criticism, not only by the media but also by government ministers (*Spectator* 6.10.10; *Daily Mail* 8.10.10). Couples with more than two children have also been accused of being "irresponsible" by creating an unbearable burden on the environment (*Sunday Times* 1.2.09). As these negative views are common, it would be surprising if they did not have some impact on the attitudes of adoption social workers. For example, social workers may be suspicious of the motivations of prospective adopters who express a wish to have a large family or they may be very pessimistic about the likelihood of finding adopters willing to take a large sibling group.

There is a danger that such attitudes could lead not only to inaction but also to a failure to appreciate the importance of sibling relationships.

The importance of siblings

Sibling relationships are likely to last a lifetime. They form an integral part of a child's sense of identity, while potentially providing support, companionship, continuity, annoyance, competition and conflict (Edwards *et al*, 2006). Siblings play formative roles in each others' social and emotional development, for better or for worse (Deater-Deckard and Dunn, 2002; Kramer and Conger, 2009). They may also provide invaluable support in later life (Cicirelli, 1989; Connidis and Campbell, 1995).

Warmth and affection

Sibling relationships are an important influence on the growing child, because children understand their siblings so well and feel very strongly about them. From as early as 16–18 months of age, children develop a practical understanding of how to annoy or collude with a sibling (Dunn, 1987). Fantasy play with an affectionate sibling enables the development of a sense of humour and an understanding of social and moral rules (Dunn, 1987; Herrera and Dunn, 1997; Howe *et al*, 2005). Feelings of warmth and closeness are greater in same-sex pairs than opposite-sex pairs (Furman and Buhrmester, 1985), and sisters tend to be more affectionate and less antagonistic than brothers (Dunn *et al*, 1999; Hetherington *et al*, 1999). Sibling affection is linked to the development of pro-social behaviour and high self-esteem. Strong bonds can develop between brothers and sisters, especially when they are involved in caring for each other (Dunn, 1993). Twins, in particular, are more likely than non-twin siblings to use their sibling as an attachment figure (Tancredy and Fraley, 2006).

Conflict

The highest level of sibling conflict in families in the general population is reported when siblings are near in age (Furman and

Buhrmester, 1985; Beckett *et al*, 1998). This finding is interesting because social workers are often concerned about the impact on adoptive families of placing children who are near in age. Although they tend to have closer relationships, it is clear that such children are likely to argue more and social workers should prepare adopters for this.

Sibling conflict is not always negative. It has an important function in helping children to learn about managing disputes, resolving arguments, and sharing. Children who experience high warmth from *and* moderate conflict with their siblings have been found to be more socially competent and emotionally controlled than their peers (Stormshak *et al*, 1999). In contrast, single children are more likely to be victimised and aggressive in their peer group (Kitzmann *et al*, 2002). However, if conflict between siblings is very high, there is a greater likelihood of children developing antisocial behaviour (Yeh and Lempers, 2004; Padilla-Walker *et al*, 2010) and this can lead to child maladjustment (Brody, 1998). Fortunately, the intensity and frequency of negative interactions between siblings decrease as children grow older (Buhrmester and Furman, 1990; Kim *et al*, 2006).

Relationships may also be ambivalent, switching rapidly between warmth and conflict (Pike *et al*, 2006). Children often perceive older siblings within pairs as having greater status and power, particularly when the difference in age is great, but older siblings may also nurture a younger sibling (Furman and Buhrmester, 1985). However, some children try to establish their own identity by amplifying differences and minimising similarities with their siblings (Edwards *et al*, 2006; Vivona, 2007).

It has been argued that birth order and gender affect personality and social behaviour (Toman, 1993), and that later born siblings are more likely to be risk-takers and innovative thinkers, while firstborns are more conservative (Sulloway, 1996). These claims are not widely supported by other research, but some studies suggest that the youngest sibling tends to be more favoured (Furman and Buhrmester, 1985; Harris and Howard, 1985). From a family therapy perspective, each member of the family has a recognised role to play in common interactions and scenarios. Family script theory can be used to explore or modify the ways in which beliefs about family life based on shared experiences can influence and sustain behaviour patterns between siblings (Byng-Hall, 1995). Similarly, family systems theory views the family as an emotional unit, and suggests that individuals cannot be understood in isolation from their family and that the influence of sibling relationships will continue throughout the life span (Cox, 2010).

Why are siblings so different?

Numerous studies have tried to determine to what extent similarities and differences between siblings are due to genetic factors or to upbringing. A review of the research evidence on siblings (Dunn and Plomin, 1990) reached some surprising conclusions. Heredity accounts for more differences than similarities, because siblings (with the exception of twins) have a 50/50 chance of inheriting a different chromosome within each pair of chromosomes. Being raised in the same family (having a "shared environment") affects IQ in childhood and also physical aggression and delinquency. However, children in the same family do not experience events in the same way. For example, siblings of different ages and stages of development will respond very differently to domestic violence (Cunningham and Baker, 2004). Children also perceive that they are treated differently by their parents (Brody and Stoneman, 1994; McGuire et al, 1995), and parents do treat siblings differently according to their age, gender and temperament. Moreover, siblings are likely to have many non-shared environments too, and they will have different friends, move in different circles at school, and experience different events and influences beyond the family. So actually, they lead separate lives despite living in the same family. Because "non-shared environment" is crucial for understanding the differences between siblings, Dunn and Plomin recommend that clinicians should 'shift from a family-by-family frame of reference to an individual-by-individual perspective within the family' (p 165).

How the quality of parenting affects sibling relationships

Even very young children monitor their parents' behaviour toward themselves and their siblings to detect any potentially inequitable treatment (Dunn and Stocker, 1989). This is a fundamental issue, as many studies show that the quality of sibling relationships is inversely associated with the extent to which parents treat siblings differently (Stocker *et al*, 1989; McHale *et al*, 2000). More positive sibling relationships are associated with differential treatment being perceived as fair, but *controlling* behaviours are often perceived as unfair (Kowal *et al*, 2006). Boys show more aggression to their siblings if mothers have restrained or punished a high proportion of their quarrelsome behaviours (Kendrick and Dunn, 1983). Therefore, it might be better to ignore low-level bickering than to intervene too quickly when quarrels begin. The perception of favouritism (particularly by the mother) has also been associated with vandalism and violence in boys and with theft in girls (Scholte *et al*, 2007), and with mental health problems in children and adolescents (Yahav, 2007). Indeed, recollections of maternal favouritism also predict tensions among adult siblings (Suitor *et al*, 2009).

Dunn's (1993) classic studies of siblings show that family difficulties can escalate with the birth of a second child. She found that when parents helped their first child to understand that the baby had *feelings and needs*, the transition to having more than one child went more smoothly. In these families, parents vocalised feelings and needs, for example, by saying to the first child, 'Oh look! The baby is hungry, he is crying. What shall we do?' Dunn's research (1993) shows that children under two years of age are especially sensitive to *how* people are talking (tone, facial expression, mood), and families where feelings and needs are recognised are more likely to promote pro-social behaviour in their children. Children's socialisation is shaped by the extent to which their parents exert parental authority and are warm, rational and receptive to what children say (Baumrind, 1971), and sibling relationships can improve over time if differential treatment is reduced (Richmond *et al*, 2005).

Sibling responses to marital conflict and divorce

Research on the impact of marital conflict on sibling relationships has produced mixed findings. Some studies (Conger and Conger, 1996; Stocker and Youngblade, 1999) show that children living with parental conflict are likely to experience hostile sibling relationships. However, a meta-analysis of 53 studies (Kunz, 2001) found that children from divorced homes had more positive sibling relationships than children from intact homes. It appears that sibling relationships during parental separation and divorce are more likely to be high in both warmth and hostility (Sheehan et al, 2004; Noller, 2005). There is evidence that a supportive sibling relationship can act as a buffer during the stress of divorce and remarriage (Hetherington, 1988; Kempton et al, 1991; Jenkins, 1992), and that sisters provide more comfort to their siblings than brothers do (Gass et al, 2007).

Sibling caretaking and "parentification"

Intense sibling loyalties tend to exist where the parents have been weak, absent, hostile, or died during the siblings' formative years (Bank and Kahn, 1982). Siblings often respond to parental unavailability by becoming more responsible and nurturing (Bryant and Crockenberg, 1980), and when severe life events occur, older siblings tend to behave more positively to their younger siblings (Dunn et al, 1994). If parents are neglectful, siblings may take over some parental roles (Cicirelli, 1980) and, remarkably, an analysis of 2001 Census micro-data (Nandy and Selwyn, 2011) found that in the UK between one-fifth and one-half of children being brought up by relatives without a parent present were being cared for by a sibling. In large, low-income, immigrant or single-parent families and non-industrialised societies, older siblings are frequently expected to take care of younger siblings (Weisner and Gallimore, 1977; Zukow-Goldring, 2002; Hafford, 2010). Shlonsky and his colleagues (2005) note that 'sibling caregiving behaviors may not necessarily be negative, can be normative in many cultures, and may be an indicator of a strong commitment to sibling ties' (p 3). Indeed, such arrangements are mostly viewed positively by caretaking and cared for children

(Kosonen, 1996b). However, sibling caretaking does pose risks, as siblings can be more punitive than parents (Weisner and Gallimore, 1977). Moreover, children who are expected to provide emotional care and to fulfil excessive, developmentally inappropriate responsibilities may later suffer from psychopathology (Jurkovic, 1997). Although a "parentified child" may become the primary attachment figure for younger siblings, sibling bonds developing in traumatic conditions can be fearful, ambivalent or violently negative (Bank and Kahn, 1982).

Parental abuse or neglect of siblings

When parents are neglectful or abusive, siblings do not always experience trauma equally. A study (Hamilton-Giachritsis and Browne, 2005) of 795 siblings of 400 children, who had been referred to child protection units in England, found that in 44 per cent of families the referred child had been scapegoated, in 37 per cent all the siblings were maltreated, and in 20 per cent abuse was directed at some siblings but not all. Although siblings report similar *neglectful* parenting behaviours, boys report more parental neglect than girls (Hines *et al*, 2006). Having older siblings can be a protective factor for children subjected to multiple victimisation, but paradoxically this can also be a risk factor for children who are *not* repeatedly victimised, probably by bringing them into contact with bigger, older friends and dangerous situations (Finkelhor *et al*, 2007). Unfortunately, siblings can also be abusive to each other.

Sibling abuse of other siblings

An NSPCC prevalence study of child maltreatment in the UK (Radford *et al*, 2011) found that 21 per cent of children and young people under the age of 18 in a random probability sample reported that they had been victimised by a sibling during the past year. This was associated with significantly reduced emotional well-being and higher levels of delinquent behaviour, particularly in children aged 5–10. Nearly all of this victimisation involved physical violence, but siblings also perpetrated three per cent of the reported sexual abuse.

Bullying is very common among siblings. First findings from *Understanding Society*, a longitudinal social survey involving 40,000 households in Britain, show that more than half of all siblings (54%) were involved in bullying in one form or another, which is a rate higher than has been reported in the USA, Israel or Italy using similar measures (Wolke and Skew, 2011). This study also found that sibling bullying was frequent; a third of all adolescents both bullied their siblings and were bullied by their siblings; and children who were bullied both at home and at school were 14 times more likely to report severe behavioural problems. Although sibling abuse (physical, sexual, emotional and psychological) is under-reported (Whipple and Finton, 1995; Caffaro and Conn-Caffaro, 2005) and often defined differently by child protection workers (Kominkiewicz, 2004), it can have long-lasting effects (Laviola, 1992; Wiehe, 1996). Younger and older children have similar trauma symptom levels associated with sibling victimisation (Finkelhor and Turner, 2006).

Siblings in the care system

In 2010, Children's Care Monitor (a national annual survey of the views of children in care) reported that most looked after children (55%) thought that siblings in care should always be placed together, while 29 per cent said it would depend on the circumstances, nine per cent said no and seven per cent were not sure (Ofsted, 2010). Of the 768 children who responded to a question about siblings, 58 per cent had at least one brother or sister who was also in care and 74 per cent were living separately from one or more siblings. The vast majority (89%) of the 114 children placed with their siblings thought this was the right decision for them. Forty-one per cent of the separated siblings thought it was the wrong decision, 21 per cent were not sure, and 37 per cent thought it was the right decision. Surprisingly, this survey also found that children living in children's homes were more likely than children in foster homes to have been separated from their siblings (94% compared to 71% in foster care). This echoes the findings of a recent study in Scotland (McPheat *et al*, 2007) that substantial numbers of sibling groups were still being separated and admitted to different residential care settings due to a reluctance to plan for and use children's homes as a positive choice.

The frequency with which siblings are separated was also highlighted in a study of looked after and adopted siblings in England (Rushton *et al*, 2001). Of the 133 children featured in this study, 40 per cent had siblings living with a birth parent (usually half-siblings born later) and 38 per cent had siblings living elsewhere in the care system. It should also be noted that children in foster care tend to have more siblings than families in the general population (Kosonen, 1999).

What determines whether siblings are placed together or apart?

Children are most likely to be separated from siblings when entering or leaving care (Kosonen, 1996a; Shlonsky *et al*, 2003), and often this happens as a consequence of children being removed serially (Maclean, 1991; Rushton *et al*, 2001). In her Scottish study, Kosonen found that over half of the 337 children were separated because their siblings were not in care or had left care to return to their parents, to live independently or to be adopted. Furthermore, their social workers lacked information about siblings, and often did not make plans to reunite separated siblings within the care system. Other factors associated with separation were: being part of a large sibling group (Shlonsky *et al*, 2003), being a teenager, and having wide age gaps between siblings (Staff and Fein, 1992; Drapeau *et al*, 2000; Wulczyn and Zimmerman, 2005). Two US studies (Shlonsky *et al*, 2003; Wulczyn and Zimmerman, 2005) are particularly significant as they involved the quantitative analysis of very large sets of administrative data.

According to foster carers and social workers, the main reasons for separating siblings were lack of space and children's behavioural problems (Smith, 1996; Leathers, 2005). Moreover, social workers were often highly pessimistic about finding shared placements for siblings (Hegar, 1986) and may have limited their efforts accordingly. A phenomenological analysis of five cases involving large sibling groups (Hollows and Nelson, 2006) also found a tendency for short-term "holding" decisions to become long-term realities if the individual social worker was not highly committed to maintaining sibling relationships. As a consequence, four years after placement, 79 per cent of sibling groups entering care on the same day remained intact (Wulczyn and Zimmerman, 2005), while most siblings who were initially separated remained apart (Staff and Fein, 1992; Drapeau *et al*, 2000; Wulczyn and Zimmerman, 2005).

However, reasons for foster carers *agreeing* to accept a sibling group included: belief in the importance of keeping siblings together (77%); willingness to take siblings to avoid losing a child already placed (26%); available space (19%); and easier scheduling when children were related (19%) (Smith, 1996). Rushton and his colleagues (2001) found 'evidence of a good deal of thought being given to keeping siblings together' (p162), and if children were placed singly it was often because they had more severe personal problems (Aldridge and Cautley, 1976; Rushton *et al*, 2001). Foster children were at high risk of perpetrating and being victims of sibling aggression and violence (Linares, 2006), and it might be necessary to place siblings apart if there was a risk of one child physically or sexually abusing another (Farmer and Pollock, 1998; Lowe *et al*, 1999). Small-scale studies of sexually abused children have found that most were sexually abusive to other children (Head and Elgar, 1999) and that high levels of supervision were needed due to a real risk of sexual activity, sometimes involving the birth children of foster carers (Farmer and Pollock, 1998).

How do looked after children feel about their siblings?

When children are removed from their birth parents, they experience many emotions such as fear, bewilderment, and a sense of loss and abandonment (Folman, 1998). They may blame themselves for what has happened, or feel relief or anger (Winter, 2010). A sibling may be the only familiar source of comfort and sometimes a child's main attachment figure. An overview (Hegar, 1988) of studies of siblings in foster care concluded that sibling ties are highly important to many foster children. Foster children also perceive their siblings as being very important to them in the future (Kosonen, 1999). It has been suggested (Heptinstall *et al*, 2001) that siblings take on 'almost symbolic importance' for foster children, because full and half-siblings almost always appeared when children were asked to place important people on a relationship map. This was the case whether the children had met their siblings or not. The importance of brothers and sisters was highlighted in an example given by the researchers of a boy putting the postman in his inner circle of important people, because the postman brought letters from his siblings, with whom he had lived previously.

Being separated from their siblings as well as their parents could be shocking for children, especially if they were not given sufficient information and an opportunity to express their feelings about the decision (Timberlake and Hamlin, 1982; Folman, 1998). This could lead to heightened anxiety, depression, and behavioural problems (Timberlake and Hamlin, 1982), especially if a sibling had previously been a source of companionship and emotional security (Linares *et al*, 2007). Qualitative research with over 200 pre-adolescent foster children (Whiting and Lee, 2003) revealed their reliance on siblings, stories of suffering together, and being dismayed about being separated. Interviews with nine looked after young people also found that they felt guilty that they had escaped maltreatment, while their siblings had not (Harrison, 1999).

Contact arrangements for siblings in foster care

Nearly 400 looked after children and young people took part in the Blueprint Project, organised by the charity Voice, to improve the lives of children in care. Feeling connected to siblings was identified as having special importance for children in care, 'even when it was recognised that they might not get on well at that particular time' (p 37). Placing brothers and sisters apart was seen as a barrier to providing a child-centred service. A key recommendation in the charity's main publication (Voice, 2004) was that all looked after children should be helped to maintain a link with at least one member of their birth family, and that children should be encouraged to identify who is important to them within their network so that links can be strengthened and renewed.

Previous research shows why such changes are necessary. A study of 1,068 children in care or accommodation (Bilson and Barker, 1992–93) found that only two-fifths had regular contact with separately placed siblings. Half of the placements in another study (Rushton *et al*, 2001) were made without any plan for sibling contact, although contact was viewed positively by the families and had positive outcomes. Contact with siblings also enabled care leavers to have a sense of belonging and identification with their families (Biehal and Wade, 1996). The carer's views on the feasibility or desirability of sibling contact sometimes influenced such decisions (James *et al*, 2008). Other studies (Zimmerman, 1982; Knipe and Warren, 1990) have found that separated siblings continually asked for increased contact and information about their siblings, but often faced so many obstacles that they gave up (Harrison, 1999).

Outcomes of sibling placements in foster care

Better child outcomes and more stable placements have been a consistent finding in child care research on children placed with siblings in foster care (e.g. Berridge and Cleaver, 1987; Staff and Fein, 1992; Drapeau *et al*, 2000; Rushton *et al*, 2001; Hegar, 2005; Washington, 2007). As long ago as World War II, a study of 587 children (Isaacs, 1941) separated from their parents and evacuated from London to Cambridge found that significantly more children adapted well to their foster placements if they were accompanied by siblings. This report stated:

> *The presence of the child's own brothers or sisters in the foster home is, therefore, clearly favourable to ease of adjustment to the new home, while, as our figures show, the presence of other evacuated children or of [local] Cambridge children has no such effect. This suggests that it is not the presence of other children but the continuance of part of the child's own family life that is important. (p 61)*

More recent research has confirmed those findings. If separated and placed singly into an established family, children had an increased risk of poor outcomes (Boer *et al*, 1995; Quinton *et al*, 1998; Leathers, 2005) and separated siblings also experienced more placement changes (Thorpe and Swart, 1992; Drapeau *et al*, 2000).

Split placements are associated with behaviour problems (Aldridge and Cautley, 1976; Smith, 1996). Furthermore, an Australian study (Tarren-Sweeny and Hazell, 2005) found that girls fostered separately from their siblings had poorer mental health and socialisation than girls living with at least one sibling. Young people were also less likely to run away if placed with their siblings (Courtney *et al*, 2005). In Canada, however, siblings placed separately were found to have better school attainment in foster care and fewer symptoms at discharge than siblings who stayed together (Thorpe and Swart, 1992).

However, adolescents placed with a *consistent* number of siblings while in foster care had a stronger sense of integration and belonging and a higher chance of adoption than those who were separated from all their siblings (Leathers, 2005). Foster children who were placed with some or all of their siblings were also more likely to be reunified with their birth family than siblings placed separately (Farmer and Parker, 1991; Webster *et al*, 2005).

Several studies link kinship care to a greater likelihood of keeping siblings together (e.g. Kosonen, 1996a; Shlonsky *et al*, 2003; Wulczyn and Zimmerman, 2005). Children at risk who were placed with one or more siblings were significantly more likely than others to feel emotionally supported and close to their carer, and to like the people they lived with – and this response was initially much higher for siblings in kinship care than for those in long-term foster care (Hegar and Rosenthal, 2009).

While these findings suggest that joint sibling placements have considerable benefits, it is important to remember that siblings who had been placed individually were much more likely to have significant emotional and behavioural difficulties to begin with (Quinton *et al*, 1998; Rushton *et al*, 2001).

Siblings placed for adoption

Most of the literature focusing on the adoption of large sibling groups consists of practitioners' reflections on a few cases (Jones and Niblett, 1985; Kaniuk, 1988; O'Leary and Schofield, 1994; Hollows and Nelson, 2006) or recommendations for practice (Ward, 1984, 1987). However, large sibling groups sometimes make up a sizable part of the sample in other studies. For example, in the first British study of sibling adoptions (Wedge and Mantel, 1991), 30 per cent of the 642 children were in sibling groups of three or more.

Unsurprisingly, many siblings were separated in adoption, as they had been in the care system. In 1998–99, a comprehensive analysis of adoptions in 116 local authorities in England (Ivaldi, 2000) found that 80 per cent of adopted children had birth siblings but only 37 per cent were placed with siblings. This survey also found that more adopters were initially willing to take sibling pairs or larger sibling groups than those who eventually had siblings placed with them. As this finding clearly reflected local authority practice, the researcher suggested that panels might not approve families for two or more siblings, or local authorities might choose to place siblings singly with their own adopters rather than placing them together through another agency.

Recruiting and choosing adopters for large sibling groups

A survey of adoption agencies in England and Wales (Dance et al, 2010) found that about a quarter did not appear to operate targeted recruitment drives to find adopters for children with additional needs. Moreover, in 14 per cent of the responding agencies the family-finder rarely or never saw the children. As sibling group adopters are in short supply, it is important not to rule out categories of applicants. Foster carers, for example, are often successful adopters of siblings (Rosenthal et al, 1988; Crea et al, 2008). Lesbian mothers are as loving, child focused and responsive as their heterosexual counterparts (Miller et al, 1981; Golombok et al, 1983; Tasker and Golombok, 1995), and the research on gay fathers is also positive (Bigner and Jacobsen, 1989). Although a study comparing heterosexual and gay/lesbian adoptions (Leung et al, 2004) found lower family functioning in sibling adoptions,

19

this was attributed not to the parents' sexual orientation but to inadequate support services. Similarly, a large-scale study (Averett *et al*, 2009) found that children's behavioural problems were not linked to the sexual orientation of their adopters.

Enabling adopters to choose their own children
Although 90 per cent of adoption agencies studied by Dance and her colleagues (2010) used the family-finding services of *Be My Parent* and *Children Who Wait*, this accounted for a relatively small proportion of the placements made. This study also found that reluctance to pay the inter-agency fee for a voluntary adoption agency placement was a barrier to matching children with suitable adopters. There can be significant benefits in enabling prospective adopters to find children who are right for them, not least because adopters sometimes take more children than they originally intended. A large-scale study (Avery and Butler, 2001) of children photolisted for adoption in New York state found that belonging to a sibling group being jointly placed for adoption *increased* the probability of adoption, and each additional child in the sibling group speeded up the adoption by approximately 3.2 months. Interestingly, women have been found to have a significant preference for children who look like them, but this recognition was unconscious and was not found in men (Bressan *et al*, 2009).

Differential policies and practices on separating and placing siblings
The survey by Dance and her colleagues (2010) found that the proportion of children placed for adoption with a sibling varied from 14 to 80 per cent of placed children, suggesting differential policies on the separation of siblings and on the speed with which children are removed and placed for adoption. Detailed examination of the reasons given for separating 176 siblings in Bradford (Maclean, 1991) revealed: a "positive choice" in 75 cases; 36 children coming into care serially (some not being born when their siblings were removed); 25 children disrupting from sibling group placements; joint placements not being available for 30 siblings who entered care simultaneously (although

two-thirds were placed with at least one sibling); and reasons un-known in ten longstanding cases (p 35). As practical and financial considerations often come to the fore when placing large sibling groups (Hollows and Nelson, 2006), social workers need to be committed to finding the best solution for the children, not just the least detrimental arrangement.

Outcomes of sibling adoptions

It can be difficult to specify the outcomes of sibling adoptions. This is because studies on siblings often consider fostering and adoption together (e.g. Rushton *et al*, 2001; Hegar, 2005), include sibling groups under the heading of "special needs adoptions" (e.g. Rosenthal *et al*, 1988; McRoy, 1999), or compare sibling placements with those of single children as well as single separated siblings (e.g. Rushton *et al*, 2001; Boer *et al*, 1994).

Families who adopt two siblings and have no birth children in the home have been found to have surprisingly successful outcomes in an American study with a sample of 1,155 children (Barth *et al*, 1988). An overview (Hegar, 2005) of 17 studies on sibling placements (of which only five focused solely on adoption) supported 'the tentative conclusion that joint sibling placements are as stable as or more stable than placements of single children or separated siblings, and several studies suggest that children do as well or better when placed with their brothers and sisters' (paragraph 5.3). Yet some of these studies show that substantial majorities of the children studied were placed alone with no information presented about separation from siblings (Barth *et al*, 1988; Holloway, 1997).

While generally sibling placements appear to have better outcomes, this does not mean that everything will go smoothly. A study (Logan *et al*, 1998) of risk factors for psychological disturbance in 97 adopted children found that the presence of siblings was associated with high problem scores. Sanders (2004) suggests that sibling adopters need to be clear about the potential long-term benefits if they are to persevere when the going gets tough.

Educational and behavioural outcomes

A meta-analysis (van IJzendoorn *et al*, 2005) of 62 studies of adopted children found that they had a higher IQ and better school performance than siblings remaining in the birth family or in institutional care. However, they lagged behind birth children in their adoptive home with regard to school performance and language abilities, and more adopted children developed learning problems.

A major British study on sibling placements (Rushton *et al*, 2001) found that roughly one-third of the children showed conduct and emotional difficulties, problems with siblings, and difficulties at school. About one-fifth had ongoing problems with peer relationships and play, and other common difficulties included lack of concentration, restlessness, defiance to parents, fears and tempers. However, around three-quarters of placements were classified as having a satisfactory or good outcome after a year. Recent findings from a study of Romanian adoptees (Beckett *et al*, 2008) have led the researchers to hypothesise that one reason why sibling placements have better outcomes is that children feel more able to talk about adoption with siblings and with their adoptive parents, and this appears to boost their self-esteem.

When relatives adopt sibling groups, the outcomes can be less positive. Research examining 397 kin placements in the United States (Ryan *et al*, 2010) found that the adoption of sibling groups by kin 'exerted a negative influence' on willingness to adopt (if they could make that choice again) and on relationship satisfaction (p 1,636). One possible explanation suggested by the researchers was that 'kin families may have felt more obligated to take on additional family members, despite unpreparedness or ambivalence' (p 1,637).

Outcomes when adopters already have birth children

Several studies suggest that sibling placements may be contraindicated for adopters who already have birth children living at home (e.g. Nelson, 1985; Groze, 1986; Barth and Brooks, 1997). The presence of birth children has been associated with higher disruption rates (Kadushin and Seidl, 1971; Boneh, 1979; Wedge and Mantel, 1991;

McRoy, 1999). Parents might view an adopted child more negatively compared to a birth child (Glover et al, 2010) or might feel closer to a biological child (Loehlin et al, 2010). Difficulties reported by birth children included a sense that the adoptee was invading their "turf" and interfering with parent–child relationships (Ward and Lewko, 1988), and birth children sometimes experienced quite significant problems (Rushton et al, 2001), especially if the adopted child was older (Nix, 1983). However, Wedge and Mantle (1991) found no disruptions when there was a gap of at least three years between the placed child and the stepsibling closest in age, while there was a 52 per cent disruption rate among 27 children placed with new stepsiblings when they were not the youngest or the youngest by at least three years. As there is a high risk of conflict if an adopted child and a birth child are close in age (Rosenthal and Groze, 1992; Beckett et al, 1998), placement decisions need to take age gaps into account, especially when placing a sibling group.

Risk and protective factors

Research on risk and protective factors for sibling groups has produced mixed findings. Various studies have found no relationship between sibling adoption and disruption (Groze, 1986; Barth et al, 1988; Holloway, 1997; Rushton et al, 2001). For example, a study in a local authority in England (Holloway, 1997) found that only two per cent of adoptions broke down compared to 51 per cent of long-term fostering placements, and being placed with siblings was not a risk factor. Indeed, some studies (Festinger, 1986; Kagan and Reid, 1986) show lower disruption rates for sibling adoptions. In contrast, three studies (Kadushin and Seidl, 1971; Boneh, 1979; Benton et al, 1985) found that sibling adoptions disrupted more frequently, although Hegar (2005) suggests that these findings may be due to small or biased samples. Surprisingly, an adoption disruption study in the United States (Smith et al, 2006), which analysed administrative data on 15,947 children, identified adoptions of up to four children as being at higher risk, while placements of four or more siblings were less likely to disrupt. The positive outcomes for the nine per cent of children living in very large families in this research were echoed in another study (Glidden *et al*, 2000) which found that adoptive parents of five or more children were functioning as well or better than adoptive parents of more conventional-sized families.

An American study of 54 placements (Rosenthal *et al*, 1988) identified factors predicting intact rather than disrupted special needs adoption and those included younger age at time of placement, adoption by foster carer, placement with siblings, and social worker assessments of parenting skills, particularly the capacity to deal with an emotionally unresponsive child. Another factor strongly related to placement stability was children's styles of interaction with both new parents and each other, and placements of children who showed a high conflict level in combination with a relative lack of care towards siblings were more likely to be classified as unstable (Rushton *et al*, 2001). Attachment and behavioural difficulties came high on the list of reasons for disruption along with agency failings, such as poor preparation or lack of post-placement support (Wedge and Mantel, 1991). Unease during introductions and social workers persuading adopters to take on children who differed from their "ideal" were also identified as early warning signs (Rushton *et al*, 2001).

However, joint sibling placements appeared to offer protection in situations where difficulties might be expected. Children who are older at placement are commonly recognised as being likely to have more difficult behaviour and a higher risk of disruption (e.g. Fratter *et al*, 1991; Selwyn *et al*, 2006). However, a study (Boer *et al*, 1994) of international adoption outcomes after ten years found that although the 399 children adopted with siblings were on average older at arrival they did *not* show a tendency to have a higher disruption rate and higher problem scores. Similarly, children singled out for rejection by birth parents were found to have a higher risk of placement disruption and poor outcomes (Quinton *et al*, 1998; Rushton *et al*, 2001), but not if they were placed with their siblings (Rushton *et al*, 2001). Even in a sample of high-risk Romanian siblings who had suffered severe deprivation, and often been adopted into families with birth children close to them in age, only two out of 165 adoptions had broken down (Beckett et al, 1998).

Contact with siblings

As already noted (p 2), many siblings put their names on the Adoption Contact Register in the hope of finding "lost" sisters and brothers, and often they have strong feelings about the loss of this relationship. Even when adoption takes place in infancy and siblings have no contact during childhood, birth siblings feel very connected to their adopted siblings (Ludvigsen and Parnham, 2004). Similarly, when adopted children learn that they have siblings, they often want contact with them (Brodzinsky et al, 1992) and are keen to find them in adulthood (Schechter and Bertocci, 1990; Brodzinsky et al, 1992). However, a study of adopted adolescents (Wrobel et al, 2004) found that 34 per cent did not want to search for birth relatives. Moreover, the number of successful contacts facilitated by the Adoption Contact Register is relatively small compared to the number of names on the register, suggesting that in many cases only one party wants to make contact (Haskey and Errington, 2001).

As most countries do not place children in public care for adoption, the findings from international research on contact often do not apply here. In Britain, sibling contact involves a complex renegotiation of roles and relationships, is likely to be unsupervised, and can help to reassure adopted children about their siblings' welfare (Neil et al, 2010). One study (Thomas et al, 1999) found that almost two-thirds of adopted children had contact with their birth siblings, but some children expressed feelings of sadness, loss and loneliness, and wanted to know more about their birth family. Adopters often had difficulties arranging contact with foster carers or other adopters, and more contact support or supervision may be needed (Lowe et al, 1999; Neil et al, 2010). Macaskill (2002) found that successful direct contact between siblings depended on adoptive families sharing similar values and finding each other's company mutually rewarding. A longitudinal study including 126 adopted adults (Triseliotis et al, 2005) found that over two-thirds of adoptees who had direct contact with birth relatives formed the closest relationship with their siblings and particularly valued this relationship.

Therapeutic interventions

At some stage, most adopted children and their families will encounter the challenge of dealing with unresolved attachment issues or previous traumatic experiences. Unfortunately, Child and Adolescent Mental Health Services (CAMHS) are not always targeted on the looked after children with the highest level of mental health needs (Stanley *et al*, 2005). Moreover, recent research (Rao *et al*, 2010) has found that while referrals of looked after and adopted children were accepted when there were indications of a mental disorder, there was less consistency on decisions relating to attachment and behavioural problems – and this led to considerable service variation. CAMHS professionals sometimes refused to provide a service for foster children who were not yet in a secure placement, and it could be extremely difficult to plan mental health services for children who were moving to a placement in another area (BAAF, 2008).

As the 'immediate primary therapeutic agent', foster carers should ideally be offered therapeutic support to provide a home environment in which children can develop a sense of trust and security, but foster carers tend to be 'marginalised in terms of status, support training and reward' (Simmonds, 2010, p 609). Similarly, adopters frequently say they want practical parenting strategies to help them meet the specific needs of their child(ren), but this is not always provided (Quinton *et al*, 1998; Lowe *et al*, 1999; Rushton and Monck, 2009). These are worrying findings, as the long-term outcomes for a significant proportion of children with conduct disorders are poor if effective intervention is not provided (Baker, 2006).

Although the focus of social work still tends to be on the parent–child relationship, Sanders advocates maximising 'the potential of siblings to act as therapeutic agents' when siblings have a strong and positive bond, building relationships when siblings do not have a strong relationship, and working to resolve abusive sibling relationships' (Sanders, 2004, p 210). He highlights the value of assessing siblings jointly, using tools such as the Strengths and Difficulties Questionnaire (Goodman, 1997) and the Sibling Relationship Checklists (Lord and Borthwick, 2001), and he suggests using genograms with children to clarify complex family relationships and to help them understand their history.

Other researchers and practitioners have also emphasised the value of working with siblings together. Even very young siblings in foster care can be helped to provide each other with a stable emotional bond through taking part in play therapy sessions with their carer (Norris-Shortle *et al*, 1995). Play therapy can also help the siblings of sexually abused children, particularly boys, to develop a coherent narrative about the abuse so that it does not have an adverse effect on their developing sense of masculine identity (Hill, 2003). A review of intervention strategies (Stormshak *et al*, 2009) found that supportive sibling relationships can build competence in self-regulation and emotional understanding, and this is perhaps best achieved through family-centred approaches that build pro-social sibling interactions, curtail behaviour problems, and strengthen parenting. Involving siblings in family therapy can be effective in reducing children's symptoms (Gustafsson *et al*, 1995), including destructive levels of aggression and faulty self-other differentiation in sibling relationships (Gnaulati, 2002). Art therapy can also be used to help siblings work through difficulties in their attachment relationship to each other (Boronska, 2000).

As always, the problem is how to provide an integrated and consistent response for all looked after and adopted children with mental health difficulties. It has been argued (Tarren-Sweeney, 2010) that in order to achieve this there needs to be a dedicated clinical workforce with specialised knowledge and skills, a clinical psychosocial-developmental scope (as opposed to traditional clinical practice), and a strong advocacy role.

However, as we will see in this study, other childcare professionals also have significant roles to play in enabling large sibling groups to remain together, settle into their adoptive home and begin to trust their new parents.

3 Method

This exploratory study was funded by the Sir Halley Stewart Trust to understand more about adopters' experiences of parenting three or more siblings and to consider what constituted good social work practice in placing large sibling groups for adoption. Specifically, it set out to:

- understand what motivates adopters to take a large sibling group;
- examine the support made available to the adoptive families and whether they thought it was sufficient;
- explore the challenges and rewards from the adopters' perspective;
- examine different agency practices in the recruitment, assessment and preparation of sibling group adopters;
- compare different practices in moving siblings from foster care to the adopters' home and the impact of these practices from the adopters' perspective.

The sample of adoption agencies

In order to understand differences in social work practice, the challenges faced in family-finding for large sibling groups, and the support offered by agencies, a sample of local authority (LA) adoption teams and voluntary adoption agencies (VAAs) was sought. In total, the agency sample was five local authorities and nine VAAs from England, Wales and the Isle of Man.

The sample of voluntary adoption agencies (n=9)

At our request, the Consortium of Voluntary Adoption Agencies (CVAA) sent an email to all VAAs in England and Wales describing the study and inviting participation. CVAA then sent letters to 17 specific VAAs which were known to have had sibling groups placed with their approved adopters. In total, 11 of the 17 VAAs responded: a

65 per cent response rate. However, one responded too late to be included and, after discussion, another agency dropped out because so few sibling group placements had been made. Nine VAAs participated in the study.

The sample of local authorities (n = 5)

We specifically wanted to contact local authority adoption agencies (LAs) which had recruited and approved adopters who subsequently had large sibling groups placed with them. As national statistics are not available on the number of sibling groups placed for adoption, we contacted the Adoption Register (managed by BAAF) to ask for help in identifying these LAs. The manager of the Register identified five LAs in England and Wales that had had large sibling groups placed with their adopters between 1 January 2005 and 31 December 2008. In addition, a further 19 LAs were identified that had had sibling groups placed with their adopters through *Be My Parent*, making a total of 24 local authorities. This represents about 14 per cent of all local authorities in England and Wales and suggests that comparatively few LAs are placing large sibling groups for adoption.

Letters requesting co-operation were sent by BAAF to adoption team managers in the 24 local authorities. Six LAs responded to the invitation to participate, but one responded too late to be included. Five local authorities took part in the study (two London borough councils and three county councils).

The sample of adoptive parents (n = 37)

The main focus of this study was on adopters' experiences of the adoption process and parenting a large group of adopted siblings. While adoption agency staff could describe practice, it was only through interviewing adopters that we could gain more understanding about whether practices were helpful or otherwise.

Criteria for selection of VAA-approved adopters

We wanted to interview adopters who had taken large sibling groups in recent years so that they would be able to recall the adoption process more accurately. We decided to exclude adopters with children placed in the previous six months, as this is a time when adopters and children are forming bonds and attachments and we did not want to disrupt this. Therefore, criteria for entry to the study were restricted to VAA-approved adopters who had had a sibling group of three or more children placed with them in the three-year period between 1 January 2006 and 31 December 2008.

The nine VAAs were asked to forward letters from the research team to the 41 adopters they identified as being eligible to join the study. The letter asked adopters to forward a signed "consent to participate" sheet to the researchers; 17 (41%) replied and were interviewed.

Criteria for selection of LA-approved adopters

We expected to have more difficulty in contacting LA adopters and therefore set a wider eligibility period. Criteria for entry to the study specified LA-approved adopters who had had a sibling group of three or more children placed with them in the four-year period between 1 January 2005 and 31 December 2008.

The five LAs were asked to forward letters to the 23 adopters they identified as being eligible to join the study; 11 (48%) replied and were interviewed.

Contacting adopters through Adoption UK

As the initial response from adopters was very slow (a difficulty exacerbated by the start of the school summer holidays), information about the study was placed on the Adoption UK[2] message board and in their magazine *Adoption Today* in order to reach more adoptive parents. As a result of this publicity, we were contacted by 18 sibling group adopters, of whom ten met the criteria and seven were later interviewed. Although the Adoption UK publicity had specified the eligibility criteria, we also received positive responses from eight

---

2   Adoption UK is the only national self-help charity run by and for adoptive parents, offering support before, during and after adoption. It also provides support for foster carers.

adopters who had taken a sibling group before the eligible period. We were concerned about the low response rate at that time and so we decided to include two of these families in the interviews, specifically because one family had taken five siblings and one had experienced a disruption. We thought it unlikely that we would receive responses from other families with these characteristics. In total, nine adoptive families were interviewed because of the Adoption UK publicity: six of these were LA approved and three VAA approved.

It is important to note that the inclusion of adopters recruited through the Adoption UK publicity had an added advantage, as these adopters had been approved by other adoption agencies from all over England and Wales. For this reason, readers should not assume that comments made by adopters during the interviews are referring only to those agencies that directly participated in the research.

In total the participating families included 20 adopters approved by VAAs and 17 adopters approved by local authorities (see Table 3.1).

Table 3.1
The study sample by type of adoption agency

	Local authority	Voluntary adoption agency	Total
	n	*n*	*n*
Number of agencies	5	9	14
Adopters	17	20	37

Interview consent forms from adopters continued to arrive after the cut-off point, and 55 sibling group adopters responded altogether. We were unable to interview 18 adopters due to late replies and the timescale and budget for this study.

Data collection

Interviews with adoption agency staff
Prior to interview, a questionnaire was sent to all the adoption agencies asking for data on the total number of children placed for

adoption, the number of adopters approved, and the number of large sibling groups placed with their own adopters since 1 April 2006. We also asked LAs about the number of large sibling groups they had placed with adoptive families approved by other agencies. In addition, all agencies were asked if they had any policy documents, manuals or guidance for social workers with regard to sibling placements.

Face-to-face semi-structured interviews were conducted with senior social workers or adoption team managers in the workplace. Usually only one person was interviewed, but two of the VAA interviews involved two social work staff and one involved three. The interviews focused on how the agency recruited, assessed and prepared adopters who were willing to take sibling groups; how they managed the introductions and the placement; and the provision of support. In addition, we questioned LA staff about how decisions were made to separate siblings or place sibling groups together.

Interviews with adopters

We developed the interview schedule from the issues identified during the literature review and from our previous work in adoption (Selwyn et al, 2006, 2010). The initial drafts of the interview schedules were discussed with an advisory group, who suggested many helpful amendments.

The interviews took place throughout England, Wales and the Isle of Man, and they were all conducted in the adopters' home by the same interviewer. Most interviews involved one parent, but in 12 families (32%) both parents took part and, as they often discussed their responses with each other, these interviews sometimes took more than two hours.

Questions focused on the adopters' reasons for wanting to adopt a sibling group; why they felt able to do this; their experience of different aspects of the adoption process; what they found most helpful and most problematic; whether they had difficulties with the children; how the children were getting on; how they rated the service they had received; and whether they would recommend adopting a sibling group. At the end of each interview, after leaving the home, the researcher rated the stability of the placement, taking into account the whole content of the interview. A similar researcher rating was made of the warmth with which the adopter(s) had spoken about each child.

Standardised measures

Before the interview, we sent two questionnaires to adopters for completion and all were returned. The questionnaires asked for details of everyone living in the household, and contained two standardised measures:

- The General Health Questionnaire (GHQ28) is used to detect psychiatric disorders in the general population and within community or non-psychiatric clinical settings such as primary care or general medical outpatients. It assesses the respondent's current mental state and whether this is different from his or her usual state. It is, therefore, sensitive to short-term psychiatric disorders but not to long-standing attributes of the respondent. It has been used in many general population studies and in foster care, kinship care and adoption studies. It contains 28 items divided into four sub-scales: somatic symptoms, anxiety/insomnia, social dysfunction, and severe depression. In this study, the items were scored using the method advocated by the test author – binary (0–0–1–1) – and had a maximum score of 28.
- The Strengths and Difficulties Questionnaire (Goodman, 1997) is a widely used measure of children's emotional and behavioural adjustment, derived from the Rutter A&B scales. There are 25 items divided into five equal subscales covering: emotional difficulties, conduct problems, hyperactivity, peer problems, and pro-social behaviour. The scale yields scores in dimensional and categorical form and scores for each dimension. The pro-social scores are not included in the overall score. Nine additional questions cover the extent to which any difficulties interfere with the child's everyday life and put a burden on others. These questions give a more complete picture of the level of difficulties and provide information on the determinants of service use.

Limitations of the study

This was a small-scale exploratory study, and for this reason the findings cannot be considered as the answer to all we might want to know about large sibling groups. It is important to acknowledge that the adopters taking part in this study should not be viewed as representative of sibling group adopters, as the total numbers and characteristics of such adopters are unknown. Nor can we offer any authoritative statements linking good practice to children's outcomes.

Another considerable limitation, which needs to be addressed in future studies, was the fact that we did not have the time and resources to interview the siblings. While most of the adopters believed that the siblings had benefited from being adopted together, it is to be hoped that future research will include the views of adopted siblings on this and other issues.

Data analysis

Numerical data were entered onto an SPSS database, and bivariate analyses (e.g. Chi-square, Fishers exact, biserial correlations) were undertaken. A detailed summary of each family's circumstances was written immediately after the interview. The interviews were transcribed and the transcripts were read and re-read to become familiar with the data and to identify emerging themes. The qualitative data were entered into NVivo for analysis and coded into themes, which were developed from our previous knowledge, the interview framework and the transcripts. We completed the quantitative analysis first and then integrated the thematic analysis. This enabled any new or unexpected themes to become evident.

We now turn to the findings and will begin by describing the adoptive families and the agencies that took part in the study.

4 The adopters and the adoption agencies

This chapter provides demographic information about the 37 adoptive families who participated in the study. It also briefly describes the five local authority (LA) adoption agencies and the nine voluntary adoption agencies (VAAs) which took part. Together they make up the sample for this study.

The adoptive families (n = 37)

The adoptive parents were sent a questionnaire prior to interview that asked for basic details about themselves and their families. Figure 4.1 illustrates the number of families and children, and the size of sibling groups in the study.

Figure 4.1
Number of families and children, size of sibling groups

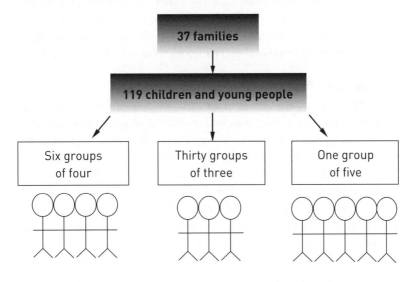

The adoptive parents

All of the children had been placed with two parents, including one placement with female same-sex partners. Although our sample included two London boroughs, all of the adopters were white. At the time of the interview, none of the adults had any physical disabilities. The average age of adoptive mothers was 41 years old, and for fathers 42. In most families the adoptive mother was the main carer, although in three families the main carer was the adoptive father.

Only two of the adoptive families had previous experience of parenting before the sibling group was placed. One family had two birth children who were now adults and had left home. Another family had previously adopted a sibling group of four, all of whom were still living at home when they took another group of four, so they were now parenting eight children. Therefore, only one sibling group moved into a home where other children were present.

Seventeen (46%) of the adopters had been approved by a local authority and 20 (54%) by a VAA.

Since the children had been placed, two couples had separated (one mother had remarried and the other was currently a single parent), but the majority (97%) of children were living in a two-parent family at the time of the interview. Most families (86%) had obtained an adoption order, but five (14%) had not yet had an adoption hearing.

The sibling groups

The adopters provided details of all their adopted children, including three children whose adoptions had recently disrupted – two children in one family had returned to foster care (leaving one child with the adopters) and one child in another family had returned to care (leaving two children with the adopters).

The sample comprised 37 sibling groups, which included 30 groups of three children, six groups of four and one group of five. Altogether, there were 119 children, of which 70 were girls and 49 were boys. The preponderance of girls may reflect a belief, expressed by one adopter, that girls would be "easier to manage". All the children were white. Most (26) of the sibling groups were a mix of boys and girls, although there were nine all-female groups and two all-male groups. There were also five sets of twins – a fairly high number given that the twinning rate for England and Wales is about 15 births in every 1,000 (ONS, 2007). Seven out of the ten twins were male, and research (McKay, 2010) shows that male twins in particular are at greater risk of becoming looked after than single-born children.

Surprisingly, children in 17 (46%) of the sibling groups had been living separately in foster care and had been subsequently re-united in their adoptive placement. None of the children had any physical disabilities, but 16 children (13%) were described as having learning difficulties.

Three-quarters of the children were being brought up as Christian, while the others were described by their parents as having "no religion".

Length of time in placement

Three-quarters of all children placed for adoption in England are under the age of three (Department for Children, Schools and Families (DCSF), 2009). As a consequence of being placed as a sibling group, the children in this sample were older at placement (see Figure 4.2). Children had been placed when they were, on average, 4.5 years old: age at placement ranged from shortly after birth to nearly 11 years old. In four sibling groups, all the children had been under age five when they were placed for adoption, and this included three families with twins. On average,[3] most children had been living with their adoptive families for 28 months (range 10 months to 11 years).

Age at placement

It has previously been noted that children placed with adopters approved by VAAs tend to be older (Deloitte, 2006), and this was the case with this sample. Nearly twice as many children were older than four years of age when placed with VAA approved adopters than those placed with LA adopters, and this was statistically significant (p<0.01).[4]

---

3 Average = mean
4 $\chi 2$ (1) = 4.291, p<0.01

Figure 4.2
Age at placement in months

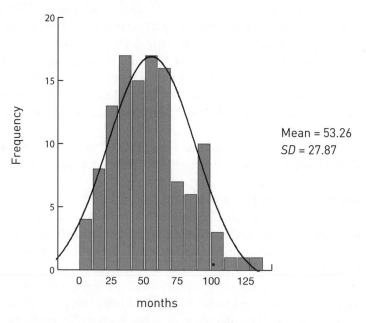

Mean = 53.26
SD = 27.87

months

Age of the children at the time of the interview

At the time of the interview with adoptive parents, most children were over five years of age, but the majority were still under ten years old (see Table 4.1 below).

Two families had been caring for the children for over nine years and all of their children were now over the age of ten. They were also the only adopters who had begun by fostering the children before adopting them.

Many studies of siblings in the general population (Furman and Buhrmester, 1985; Kramer and Baron, 1995; Volling, 2003) have noted the impact of age differences between siblings on the quality of their relationships. It is known that the narrower the age gap the more likely it is for there to be closeness but also conflict between siblings, expressed in quarrelling and competitiveness (Furman and Buhrmester, 1985). It was striking how many of the sibling groups in our study were very narrowly spaced. In 59 per cent of the sibling groups, all the children had been born within four years of the birth of the eldest child. A common pattern was a spacing of only 10–12 months between each child. Only two sibling groups had wide spacing (more than four years) between each sibling.

Table 4.1
Age of the children at the time of the interview

	Mean age in years	*Range in years*
Eldest sibling	8.9	3–18
Second sibling	7.1	2–15
Third sibling	5.4	2–14
Fourth sibling	6.3	2–13
Fifth sibling	11 (actual age)	–

The adoption agencies

We collected statistical information on the practice of the adoption agencies in our sample, which comprised five local authority and nine voluntary adoption agencies.

Local authority adoption agencies

The managers in the LA adoption agencies were asked to provide adoption data covering a three-year period. On average, two of the LA agencies placed fewer than 22 children a year for adoption, two placed about 30 children, and the fifth placed more than 50 children each year. The LA adoption agencies placed very few groups of three or more siblings, and these made up only 2–3 per cent of adoptions (see Table 4.2). However, in one LA adoption agency, sibling group adoptions comprised nearly six per cent of all adoptions.

The LAs in the sample placed a very low number of sibling groups with VAA-approved adopters during this three-year period. A likely reason for this is that these LAs were sampled because they were known to have in-house sibling group adopters, and they would have

Table 4.2
Local authority adoption agency activity (n = 5) over a three-year period from 1 April 2006 to 31 March 2009

	Total number
Children placed for adoption by the five LAs	554
Large sibling groups (three or more children) placed for adoption with LA-approved adopters	13
Large sibling groups placed with VAA-approved adopters	3
Own adopters taking a large sibling group from another LA	10
Adopters approved	523

been keen to use their own adopters whenever possible to avoid incurring additional costs. However, some LA-approved adopters in the sample had been matched with children from other areas, and these children had moved into the LA area.

Voluntary adoption agencies

All of the VAAs in the sample were based in England with the exception of one, which was on the Isle of Man. One VAA worked specifically with families in the armed forces, both in England and abroad. We asked agencies to supply data on the number of placements made and adopters approved over a three-year period. The agencies were a mix of small agencies providing placements for about 12 children a year, medium-sized agencies family-finding for about 25 children a year, and large agencies finding families for about 50 children annually. One agency was unable to provide the statistics requested. Eight VAAs had found families for 535 children over a three-year period.

Like the LA adoption agencies, the VAAs differed in the proportion of adoptive placements involving sibling groups. Two VAAs were very similar to the majority of the LA agencies, with 2–3 per cent of all placements involving large sibling groups; in three VAAs, sibling groups accounted for 5–7 per cent of all placements, while ten per cent of all placements in two VAAs were sibling-group placements.

Table 4.3
Voluntary adoption agency (n = 8) activity 1 April 2006–31 March 2009

	Total number
Children placed with the VAA's approved adopters	582
Large sibling groups placed with the VAA's approved adopters	39
Adopters approved	435

This chapter has described the characteristics of the adoptive families and the adoption agencies that took part in this study. Before children are placed for adoption, decisions have to be made about whether they should be placed with their siblings or separated. The next chapter considers how children's social workers make these very difficult judgements.

Summary

- The sample comprised 37 sibling groups (30 groups of three children, six groups of four, and one group of five). One family had adopted a second group of four siblings and were now caring for eight children. The 119 children included 70 girls and 49 boys. Two placements had partially disrupted, with three children returning to foster care.
- Children in 17 (46%) of the sibling groups had been placed separately in foster care and were subsequently re-united by adoption. All the children had been placed with two adoptive parents, including one female same-sex couple, and nearly all were placed into childless households.
- The sibling groups had been placed on average a year later than most adopted children in England. Children placed with a VAA adopter were significantly older than those placed with an LA adopter.
- Most (26) of the sibling groups were a mix of boys and girls, but there were nine all-female sibling groups and two all-male sibling groups.

- Children in four sibling groups were all under five years old when placed, and this included three sets of twins.
- At the time of the study, the children had been living on average with their adoptive parents for 28 months.
- All the adopters were white and nearly all were under age 50.
- The age gap between siblings was very narrow. It is known that children who are closely spaced quarrel and compete more often but are also likely to be closer than siblings who have wide age gaps.
- Adoption agencies in the sample varied in their size, the number of placements made and adopters approved, and in the proportion of placements involving sibling groups. The variation was not only between LAs and VAAs but also within the agency samples. Sibling-group placements made up 2–10 per cent of all children placed for adoption in these agencies.

5 Decision-making: should siblings be placed for adoption together or apart?

The decision to separate or keep siblings together is made by social workers and managers in the children's local authority, often in conjunction with the courts. This decision is not the responsibility of voluntary adoption agencies (VAAs). Respondents in the five participating local authorities (LAs) were asked how decisions were made to separate or keep siblings together and the factors that influenced those decisions. Although there were some differences, the ways in which adoption staff said they approached these issues appeared to be consistent.

Making decisions about sibling groups

LA staff stated that there was great reluctance to separate siblings with adoption plans, and decisions to do that had to be well evidenced. They said that decisions to place siblings together or to separate the group were generally made in a permanency planning meeting involving the children's social worker, the team manager and a senior member of the adoption team. All the LA respondents stated that the decision to place siblings separately was never or rarely made by a social worker alone and would have to be confirmed by the team leader. Sibling group issues were also discussed by adoption panels and in Looked After Children Reviews. In some cases, social workers also involved CAMHS professionals or medical advisers to ensure that the needs of each child were thoroughly assessed before making the decision. However, social work staff acknowledged that their strong belief that siblings should be kept together often had to give way when no suitable adopters could be found. Sometimes there were also concerns that adopters might be overwhelmed by the children's needs and so a decision was made to split the group.

LA staff thought that placing a sibling group for adoption was time consuming and that the needs of the siblings had to be balanced against the risks of delay. Some thought that pressure to split the siblings increased as time went on and that concerns about delay needed to be resisted, as one manager explained:

It takes time to do this and we need to counter arguments [about delay] so we don't get them going off into foster care, or we don't get them off into perhaps special guardianship placements with family members, which are really not going to last. (LA 3)

We did not ask VAA respondents for their views on whether siblings should be placed together or apart. However, two VAA managers suggested that in some cases it might be easier to promote good sibling relationships by placing siblings separately but establishing frequent contact. One agency was working with three adoptive families to develop the concept of a "clan family". Siblings would be placed separately but the three families would agree to be connected closely together. The manager explained this as follows:

. . . they need to create an artificial part of their family that allows them to help these kids understand that they are siblings. (. . .) They're going to see each other often enough to go through the arguments and the fallings out, and the not liking and get back together again, that you will never get even if you get regular monthly contact between siblings in separate homes, because you haven't helped the adults relate to each other well enough. (VAA 9)

Children's social workers have to account for their decisions in the children's care plan. This is a key document and is put before the court when care orders and placement orders are being considered.

The influence of the courts on decision-making

All the LA staff thought that courts and children's guardians had a considerable influence on decisions involving siblings. While managers were sometimes required to explain to the court why adopters were not available, most local courts were reported as allowing the LA time to find a suitable family. Experienced guardians were also thought to be helpful in pointing out contraindications to keeping siblings together or ensuring that enough consideration had been given in the adoption support plan to the needs of an adoptive family taking a large sibling group. However, some guardians were said to have opposed the care plan, because they did not believe it was possible to find adopters for a large sibling group or thought that such a placement would be unsuccessful. One LA manager stated that in one case, the court had prioritised keeping the siblings together and for this reason they were fostered instead of being placed in separate adoptive homes. However, she said that finding a long-term foster care placement could be just as difficult as finding an adoptive placement, because experienced foster carers usually had other children already in their care and did not have room for three or four siblings. Moreover, it was considered risky to place a large sibling group with new foster carers due to their inexperience and the children's need for stability.

Two LA managers expressed frustration that difficulties in placing sibling groups were compounded by delays in legal proceedings. Both attributed these problems to recent changes in the legislation on adoption:

> . . . we are increasingly being hit now by children who have care orders and placement orders, where we will select a family (. . .) and then the parents will be advised by their legal team to contest the care order or the placement order, and that has happened I think in the last three placements. (. . .) So you identify a family, and then they're told that this is on hold, and they move on to another child or sibling group, where that isn't the case. (. . .) In the days of freeing orders that didn't happen, but placement orders are so insecure. (LA 2)

> A child may be through panel but still in court for several months, so we know about some siblings (. . .) but we can't place them until everything is legally secure. Sometimes we know

about them for a very long time, because proceedings are taking
longer and longer since the legislation changed. (LA 5)

Factors identified by agency staff as influencing decisions about siblings

LA staff thought that a number of factors can influence decisions about whether siblings are separated or not. Assessments of the children sometimes recommended that their individual needs were so great that it would be preferable to separate them. Attachment difficulties or sexual abuse between siblings were sometimes seen as contraindications to keeping the group together. However, difficulty in finding suitable adopters was the most frequent concern.

LA managers stated that usually three to six months was spent searching for suitable adopters. If the search proved fruitless, social workers would have to decide whether to go on searching or to look for the most practical alternative placement. The reality of finding a placement for a sibling group was often highly problematic. One LA manager said that they currently had no adopters who were willing to take a sibling group and there were very few available through the regional consortium. However, widening the search had financial implications as it would entail paying an inter-agency fee to the VAA or LA that approved the adopters. Not all LA adoption teams had a budget that was sufficient to meet these costs.

Agency staff also said that it was difficult to place a sibling group with relatives for adoption, especially if the children had different birth fathers. In these circumstances, the different grandparents sometimes insisted that the siblings should be split.

Avoidance of decision-making

Some LA managers reported tensions in the way social workers planned for sibling groups. They thought that social workers sometimes found it difficult to manage the strong emotions that tended to accompany the separation of siblings. Avoiding difficult decisions has been identified previously as an issue for social work practitioners (Jones and Niblett, 1985). In our study, one respondent described this in the following terms:

You get huge emotional pain about splitting siblings and you get a lot of subjective views feeding into it (. . .) and we have to go back to people and say, "What is it about these siblings that makes you think we have to split them or keep them together?" (. . .) There are offices where there has been delay, and you know part of it is nobody wants to make that decision. (LA 5)

Staff found it particularly painful to tell siblings they were going to be separated, and they stressed the importance of being clear about what they tell children. Social workers sometimes struggled to find the right words so that children would not get the wrong message (e.g. believing that the separation was because they were naughty or unattractive). One manager gave the following example:

[For one sibling group] the explanation we worked out with the psychotherapist was, "The people who know you best think you need to live in different houses." (. . .) We did a representation as part of preparation, where we had different houses – ClipArt houses – and figures that represented the children, and we kept those figures through all their preparation materials and the children did identify with these figures. And two of them lived together and one lived in a different house with the car in the middle, and they have a lot of contact – five times a year . . . (LA 5)

Adopters' comments on decision-making

At the end of the interview, we asked the sibling-group adopters whether they thought that placing the children together was the right thing to do. Their replies are recorded on page 224. We did not ask the adopters for their views on the practice of court professionals such as children's guardians, but some commented on this spontaneously. In one case, the guardian apparently did not believe that anyone could adopt four children, even though prospective adopters had already been matched with this sibling group. This created uncertainty as to whether the siblings should be placed together for adoption, and the adopter was not impressed by the guardian's intervention:

I cannot think for a second that [the children] could have been apart, and to think that the guardian was suggesting that the two little ones possibly got adopted and the two older ones stayed in foster care because of [child's] age, to me is just a sackable offence! (. . .) If you knew the children, to think of them apart – it's just awful. (Adopter 21)

However, there were also positive comments about children's guardians. One adopter claimed that the adoption had disrupted due to insufficient support, but she felt vindicated by a comment that was apparently made by the guardian during the care proceedings, that the children and their adopters would need all the help they could get. In another case, where one child did not form a relationship with the adoptive mother, the couple had a "eureka moment" when they learned from the CAFCASS[5] report that this boy had never formed a relationship with his birth mother and had an issue with "female hierarchy".

Having described the decision-making process for placing siblings together or apart, we can now move on to look at the adoption process and how it was shaped by the adoption agencies and experienced by the sibling-group adopters. In the next chapter, we will consider how agencies recruited adopters who might be willing to take sibling groups.

Summary

- Respondents from five local authorities were interviewed about their policies and practices in relation to placing sibling groups. Although the benefits of keeping sibling groups together were recognised, various factors often made this difficult.
- Barriers to sibling-group placements included: a shortage of adopters willing to take three or more siblings; limited financial resources to pay the inter-agency fee; difficulties in finding foster carers who could take a large sibling group; relatives wanting to

---

5   Children and Family Court Advisory and Support Service

separate siblings; concerns that adopters would be overwhelmed by the children's needs; and delays in court proceedings.

- Decisions to keep siblings together or to separate them were generally made during a permanency planning meeting. Sometimes expert assessments were used in this process. LAs usually searched for three to six months for adopters who were willing and able to take all the children before they considered other options. LA staff stated that there was great reluctance to separate siblings, and decisions to do that had to be well evidenced.
- Some social workers avoided telling siblings that they were to be split because of the intense emotion this provoked, and this led to delays in planning. Careful wording was needed so that siblings did not misunderstand the reason why they were being separated.
- Sometimes local courts opposed the adoption plan. Examples were given of guardians who did not believe it was feasible to place large sibling groups for adoption and of a court opposing adoption plans involving separate placements because of a wish to keep siblings together. Staff in two LAs attributed increasing delays in court proceedings to a recent change in legislation.

6   Recruiting adoptive parents

This chapter looks at the way in which the local authorities (LAs) and voluntary adoption agencies (VAAs) in this study recruited adopters for sibling groups, the information provided in their recruitment materials, and their use of the media.

The adoption agencies' recruitment methods

All the adoption staff stated that their general recruitment materials drew attention to the number of sibling groups needing an adoptive placement. Information packs for prospective adopters described in general terms the kinds of children who were waiting to be adopted and mentioned the need to keep brothers and sisters together. However, most of the written recruitment materials supplied by the agencies mentioned siblings very briefly, and none had a leaflet specifically on siblings. Only occasionally did an information pack contain a personal account from a sibling-group adopter or a case study to highlight the needs of siblings (see example below):

One, two, three or more?
Where possible we try to keep brothers and sisters together and welcome applications from people with room in their lives to adopt more than one child.

James, aged three, John, aged six and Mary, aged seven, have always lived together. Their parents abuse drugs and are unable to care for them. Mary often took over the role of her parents. The three children need to be together with adopters who are able to manage their insecurities and loss. This can be extremely challenging.
Extract from adoption information pack (LA 1)

Two LA adoption agencies emphasised in their recruitment information that adopters applying for certain groups of children would be given "higher priority". This meant that applications would be dealt with more quickly, although one of these agencies said this approach had not been effective in recruiting adopters for large sibling groups. We noted that one LA had a policy of expecting separate bedrooms to be provided for each child – a requirement that might pose a considerable obstacle for sibling-group adopters.

Other methods used to recruit adopters who were willing to take sibling groups included adoption information days, open evenings, advertising in the media and using publicity opportunities such as National Adoption Week. Some adoption agency staff stressed the importance of having a rolling programme of recruitment, encouraging referrals from other agencies and taking enquiries from a wide geographical area. They thought it was crucial not to limit recruitment to adopters who were willing to take particular categories of children. One manager stated that her LA had made the mistake of only recruiting people who were willing at the outset to take older children and sibling groups. This policy had apparently deterred many prospective adopters and decimated their usual recruitment levels and, as a result, the agency was planning a more general advertising campaign to try to rectify the situation.

Advertising and the media

The adoption agencies did not make extensive use of advertising because of the costs involved and a reported lack of response. Three managers said they hardly ever used advertising because their service was well known and word of mouth was more effective:

However, they frequently sought media coverage, sometimes in very innovative ways. One VAA was currently planning a "5–4–3–2–1" campaign – a road show that would involve adopters speaking about their experiences of taking siblings. A LA adoption manager commented:

We haven't had to advertise for a long time because we have built up a good reputation. A local celebrity chef who was adopted has worked with the local authority, and he helped us to get lots of publicity when he came and spoke about his own adoption. When we did advertise, we targeted older people and put ads in magazines with the heading "Empty nest? We can fill it!" We also sent a flyer out in every payslip for [local authority employees], and social workers put flyers on cars at public events. (LA 1)

Whatever recruitment methods they used, adoption agency staff stressed the importance of remembering that prospective adopters often 'respond to children outside of their approval', and the idea of taking a sibling group can 'take quite a long time to germinate in people's minds' before they feel ready to explore the possibility. A VAA manager also emphasised the importance of being positive:

What we try and do is to make [taking sibling groups] feel possible and manageable and enjoyable! (VAA 6)

VAA and LA staff knew that adopters who were willing to take sibling groups were desperately needed, so they were usually keen to recruit, assess and prepare potential sibling-group adopters before any specific sibling group had been identified. VAA staff were confident that these adopters would not be waiting long for a placement and that LAs would be willing to pay the inter-agency fee.

Finding adopters for specific sibling groups

When a sibling group had been identified as needing a new family, LA staff used web-based family-finding sites, adoption exchange days and adoption consortiums as ways of notifying other agencies and approved/prospective adopters that a sibling group was waiting for a family. One LA manager emphasised that a good way of reducing delay (a problem experienced by many sibling groups) was to match adopters and children through local "mini in-house exchanges":

We just book a community centre, fairly central, and then beg the children and families workers to come and talk about their children for about five or six minutes (children who are ready) and then they are available to speak to adopters directly. It gets out of all this delay you get with advertising and adoption exchanges, and then we can deal with any proximity issues immediately rather then letting things rumble on and then discovering they all live in the same town. (LA 5)

Featuring children in publications such as *Be My Parent* could lead to many requests for further information. However, sometimes those who responded to these features were at an early stage of the adoption process and their timescale for being approved and the children's need for a speedy placement did not always coincide.

The Adoption Register was much appreciated by all agencies because it enabled LA staff to locate adopters quickly all over the country and had the advantage of only containing the details of approved adopters. However, one LA manager stated that they could only use the Adoption Register when they had enough funding to cover the inter-agency fee. It was also suggested that the inter-agency fee had prevented the implementation of an innovative scheme to recruit sibling-group adopters in a region where four VAAs had come together to put a specific proposal to LAs in their consortium. As a manager explained:

We did try to engage our local authorities (. . .) in a project. The most recent figures that we had at the time (. . .) showed that there were 168 children waiting where they were in a sibling group, and some of those had been waiting for up to 30 months. (. . .) And we made a proposal that four voluntary agencies would work together to recruit and assess and prepare families for those children who had been waiting longest, if they would give us some funding – pump priming – to try and get it off the ground. (. . .) But the local authorities couldn't agree amongst themselves (. . .) . . . it's this issue with the inter-agency fee . . . (VAA 3)

Sometimes VAAs were commissioned to find suitable families for sibling groups. For example, the VAA working with families in the armed forces had been approached by an LA that wanted to place a sibling group 'as far away out of the country as possible' for security reasons. Two VAAs had been commissioned to find families for very large sibling groups and as a result of their efforts successful adoptive placements had apparently been found for three groups of five siblings. In one of these cases, the children ('five very pretty little girls') were featured on television and over 200 people responded. The agency drew up a shortlist of about 40 families, and two social workers checked out families within a 100-mile radius. They each identified five possible families and then chose two, with one becoming "the back-up family". The prospective adopters were assessed very quickly (within three months) because the children had been waiting a long time, and agency staff worked closely with the foster carers to plan the introductions.

What makes a difference when recruiting adopters for siblings?

The five LAs gave varied responses to this question. In particular, they emphasised the importance of having a social worker who really knows the children, providing very good information, and offering an adoption allowance and support package to reassure potential sibling-group adopters that they will be able to manage. Here are comments made by two of our LA respondents:

> The thing that makes a really big difference is if their worker knows [the children], which is very simple, and if their inform-ation is accurate and up to date, and people are confident in the information they have and in the support that follows it. (LA 5)

> I think now that we are able to advertise that an adoption allow-ance will be attached to this placement, I think that enables more people to come forward (. . .). And the availability of having a play specialist, a therapist. If parents are struggling with a child's behaviour (. . .) we can get [our] play specialist in quickly so they don't have to wait, and that's proved to be really useful. That is really a very good resource. (LA 4)

Although agency staff also emphasised the commitment and motivation of social workers, sometimes it was simply a question of getting the basics right, as one manager advised:

Be responsive to them when they say they want to adopt siblings. (LA 1)

In the next chapter, we will consider how our sample of adopters had been recruited, what their motivations were and the factors that led them to consider adopting a sibling group.

Summary

- Adopters for sibling groups are desperately needed and, for this reason, the adoption agencies were willing to recruit, assess and prepare potential sibling-group adopters before any specific children had been identified.
- Most of the adoption agencies used information packs, open evenings or information days, media interviews and various kinds of advertising to recruit adopters. However, their recruitment materials usually contained only a brief mention of the need to keep siblings together. More innovative approaches included in-house exchanges and road shows. Word of mouth was seen as the best recruitment tool.
- Managers said that prospective adopters sometimes spent a long time thinking about adoption before approaching an agency. In their experience, adopters sometimes felt drawn to a large sibling group, when initially they had wanted only one or two children, so it was crucial not to discourage people who might be able to offer more.
- The Adoption Register was much appreciated by all agencies because it enabled LA staff to locate approved adopters quickly for specific children. However, the reluctance of some LAs to pay the inter-agency fee required for a VAA placement limited their use of the Adoption Register. This may also have contributed to the failure of an initiative to find adopters for children who had been waiting longest for adoption in one region.

- To recruit sibling-group adopters, staff emphasised the importance of having a social worker who really knows the children, as well as providing very good information, an adoption allowance and a support package to reassure potential sibling-group adopters that they will be able to manage. The commitment of social workers and the benefits of having a positive approach were also emphasised.

7 Motivations to adopt and choice of agency

It is often assumed that people only adopt when they cannot have their own biological children. In fact, adoption agencies are sometimes reluctant to consider adopters who have not undergone fertility treatment or who want to adopt for other reasons (Selwyn *et al*, 2006). While infertility was indeed the primary motivation for most of our adopters (n = 37), there were other reasons that influenced the choice they had made.

Fertility problems

Being unable to have their own biological children led the vast majority (32) of the parents in our study to choose adoption. Some women spoke of years of tests and fertility treatment, miscarriages and the pain that childlessness had brought. This was expressed poignantly by one adopter:

> *At the end of the day, if you're not doing home life and you work like mad (like we do), if you're not going to be able to pass it onto somebody at the end of the day, what are you working for? (. . .) Yes, we had a huge house that was our home, but it didn't seem like home, because there was only two of us rattling around in it.* (Adopter 7)

The physical, emotional and financial strain associated with IVF treatment often appeared to trigger the decision to adopt, as another adopter explained:

> *We had some infertility treatment, IVF, and at the end of that decided that is absolutely not for us: we couldn't put ourselves through the whole emotional turmoil again. And we walked to the car and by the time we'd reached the car we'd made the decision to start the adoption process . . .* (Adopter 5)

Four couples chose not to have fertility treatment and for them the decision to adopt was perhaps easier, as they had always envisaged having adopted children as well as birth children. One adoptive mother stated:

I'd always said I would adopt, (. . .) and then when we got married and it just didn't happen (. . .) we didn't look into IVF. Let's not make our lives miserable over this – let's adopt! (Adopter 14)

Adoption as a first choice and other motivations

Three couples had decided to adopt instead of having birth children. One stated that adoption was their "first choice" and "just something that we wanted to do". Another adopter, who had experience of working with children, commented:

We presume we can have children. We positively chose adoption rather than try to have our own children (. . .) As I say, we kind of just saw that as an equally valid way of starting a family (. . .) Neither of us are particularly a baby person, which was another factor in it probably – that we knew we wanted children but babies don't particularly appeal to us . . . (Adopter 21)

When this couple talked to their voluntary adoption agency (VAA) about the possibility of having birth children and adopted children, they were told that this kind of arrangement was always a struggle for the adopted child, 'because even though the parents have tried their best to make things fair, there always seems to be an inferiority complex there'. So they decided that they 'would commit to just adopting'. Although they have not promised never to have birth children, they have given their VAA an assurance that any decision will be based on what is right for all of them as a family, not just for them as a couple.

The third couple who chose to adopt instead of having birth children described the suspicious response that they had initially received from their local authority (LA) adoption agency:

. . . because we can biologically have our own children and we've

chosen not to, [the social worker from our LA] said she wouldn't take it forwards because we'd obviously got psychological problems about wanting to take adopted kids rather than actually having our own, and she offered counselling at the Post-Adoption Centre. So we took that and that all went absolutely fine, and at the end of that they said, 'Well why don't you try [another local authority]?' So we tried [this LA]. They were down here within 24 hours of us having made the phone call, and we were on a training course within 48 hours! [. . .] [This LA] said, 'No problem at all – you're ideal.' (Adopter 9)

For the same-sex couple, adoption also seemed to be the best and most practical way to realise their wish to have children, as one partner explained:

We always wanted children and being sort of a same sex couple makes it all the more difficult, but . . . there's no easy way of doing it, so sort of weighing up the pros and cons we came to adoption as one of the more straightforward approaches or things that we could do. It would give us something we wanted [. . .] and, you know, give some children a home. (Adopter 25)

The situation was completely different for a couple whose birth children would soon be leaving home. They decided to adopt because they wanted to 'do something worthwhile'. The adoptive mother commented:

People assume that you desperately want children if you adopt, and it wasn't like that and it isn't like that now. (Adopter 16)

Adopters' reasons for wanting a sibling group

When we asked the adopters whether they felt able to take on a sibling group because they had the support of relatives and friends, a typical initial response was, 'They thought we were mad!' Faced with such incredulity, what enabled these adopters to go ahead undeterred? On a practical level, many stated that they felt able to do it because they had experience of working with children, could provide a loving home and had a large house. However, other themes emerged that helped to explain their decision to adopt three or more siblings.

The adopter's concept of the meaning of "family"

The majority (89%) of the adopters said they wanted to adopt siblings right from the start. The most frequent reason, given by 62 per cent of the adopters, was that they had always wanted two or more children and they felt able to do it because they had a supportive partner and a good support network. Usually they were thinking of two siblings initially, but nearly a third said they had always wanted a large family. One couple insisted, 'We'd always said we wanted three or four', while in another case where the husband wanted two children and the wife wanted four, they compromised at three. However, it was not just a question of numbers but of what they could manage and what would work for their family, as one adopter pointed out:

> I don't think it was so much the number as the actual children that was important, (. . .) so it was more a case of what their individual needs were . . . (Adopter 26)

A third (12) of the adopters made it clear that for them a "family" involved more than one child. These adopters had often grown up in large households, and they wanted to adopt siblings so that their children could play together, look out for each other and have that sense of belonging. Nine adopters stated emphatically that they did not want an only child, because they imagined this would be a miserable experience for the child and possibly also for them as parents. Adopters stated:

> We both definitely did not want an only child. We didn't want a child who would be clingy and who wouldn't have a proper childhood. I wanted a proper family with more than one child. (Adopter 1)

> I couldn't really imagine having an only child. That wasn't – the focus of all your attention just on this one child – that wasn't really my idea of family life. (Adopter 14)

Half of the adopters had grown up in a large sibling group, and many felt it was natural to have three or more children because that was what they were used to. Indeed, several said they did not regard three children as a large family. A few described their extended family and this had clearly inspired one adopter to take a sibling group:

My hero in life is my auntie. (. . .) She had six children and I wanted to be like her. Her house was always so much fun with so much going on, you know. I've always grown up with that, and she's got hundreds of grandchildren! [Adopter 12]

However, it is important to note that 40 per cent of the adopters did not grow up in large families (which, in this study, we defined as families with three or more children). We wondered if adopters' own birth position might have influenced their wish to adopt siblings, but numbers were too small to test for significance (see Table 7.1).

Table 7.1
Respondents' sibling position in their own family

	Number	%
Only child	15	40
Eldest child	10	27
Second child	4	11
Third child	7	19
Fourth child	1	3
Total	37	100

Dislike of the adoption approval process

Another prominent reason given was a wish not to repeat the adoption approval process. Just over half (51%) of the adopters had concluded this was to be avoided at all costs, and they had reached this decision as a direct result of their experiences:

It's a horrific . . . it's a huge process, and it is really draining and time-consuming, and (. . .) we wanted to get it all over and done with in one go . . . (Adopter 18)

. . . it didn't cross our mind at the beginning, but now I've been through it, never again! (Adopter 35)

One of the VAA managers voiced her concern that adopters might choose siblings as a way of avoiding going through the adoption process again, but she also acknowledged that this was a natural response:

If you think about it, this is an incredibly intrusive [process] no matter how kindly or how skillfully it's done. Who else asks you to unpick your whole life and talks to you about the most intimate aspects of your relationship, and then hopefully puts you back together again in some form? But nobody does that to you – not even in IVF, they don't do that. Why would you want to go through with it a second time? (VAA 9)

Some adopters, who were initially thinking of adopting one child and then possibly taking another, changed their minds when they realised the complexity of the adoption process. Time was also an issue, especially for older adopters, as it is seen as good practice to wait about two years before starting the adoption process again. Here are two of the adopters' comments:

I had this little rosy idea about I'd adopt one and I'd love to nurture it and then I'd have another. It was (. . .) very soon made clear to me that actually if you adopt one and you then want to adopt another, you have to wait two years, go through the whole process all over again, and I just thought 'Oh no, I can't do that!' So very early on, we decided that we wanted to adopt two... (Adopter 5)

I'm 50 now, so from a time point of view, you'll be talking, if you adopted a child on its own, you've got to have that child for a couple of years and then you've got to go through the process over probably two or three years again. You're talking five years really, aren't you? (Adopter 15)

Increasing the likelihood of a placement

A quarter (9) of the adopters had listened carefully to their social worker and had concluded that asking for a sibling group would give them a better chance of being considered for younger children and of becoming adopters more quickly. One parent, who had adopted through a London borough, also saw this as the only way of getting white children. Another couple asked for siblings because there were 'very few single healthy children available for adoption'. Sometimes these claims were borne out by their experiences. Their comments provide an interesting insight into the vagaries of adoption procedures:

> *Because we were prepared to take three children, we were in quite a lot of demand (. . .) We had about six enquiries in a week.* (Adopter 15)

> *I felt that I would have a better chance of having a younger child as well as a three- or four-year-old and, of course, that's what happened, because [the youngest child] was only seven months old when they were placed with me.* (Adopter 3)

Although adoption agencies often seek to place children with younger adopters who are healthy and energetic enough to meet the children's needs, the end result can be contradictory in practice. Ironically, the comments of one respondent suggest that older adopters are more likely to be considered for large sibling groups, simply because the children are harder to place:

> *. . . when we realised that we were unlikely to get two children of a youngish age, we started to look at three (. . .) I think when local authorities have got a couple of couples to choose from, age is always a big factor, as we were told that we were too old for [another group of siblings]. While they were considering placing the three of them together, we were looked at quite favourably. As soon as they decided the children's needs were*

too great to place them together and they were going to split the group, they decided that we were too old to take the younger two who were five and three, but we would have been all right for the six-year-old girl. (Adopter 17)

Responding to information about the needs of sibling groups

Eight adopters (22%) had decided to take a sibling group because they believed passionately that it was wrong to separate siblings. They viewed adoption as a way of doing something positive to help children in the care system. Listening to adopters talking about their experiences of taking a sibling group had led some to conclude: 'If other people can do it, then probably we can!' Other adopters had been very moved by presentations given by social workers, as one couple explained:

[The local authority] runs an introduction evening (. . .) and we came away from that and independently had concluded and said to each other that we should offer for a sibling group of three (. . .) That was the moment, coming out of that evening, because they gave you scenarios, and one of the scenarios was this group of three being split up (. . .) and that was it. We have never wavered from that. (Adopter 35)

Sometimes the decision to adopt a sibling group had been inspired by a heart-breaking story in the media. One adopter had phoned an information number given out after a local news feature about siblings being separated. This couple went on to adopt a sibling group and also specifically chose older children, who might otherwise not have been placed at all. The mother commented:

. . . we knew that sibling groups were often split (. . .) and I couldn't be responsible for that, so I said it was a large group or nothing – and that's how it worked out (. . .) We were determined to have older children, because we also knew that older children are often passed over. (Adopter 19)

Sometimes reading and discussing profiles of large sibling groups in adoption magazines had made adopters empathise with the children's need to stay together. One adoptive father explained how this realisation had made him and his wife decide to take three children:

> . . . when you're reading the context and that, saying they could be split, and in my mind, I can't do that, not with children, you know what I mean? I want to keep them together! (. . .) [Seeing a group of five siblings in Be My Parent], that's when I realised then that I couldn't split a big sibling group up. Until then, I was happy with two . . . (Adopter 32)

In a very different case, the adoptive mother was aware that children remaining in the care system often have poor outcomes, and this became a deciding factor. This couple had already taken three young siblings and were "aghast" when the local authority approached them to ask if they would consider taking the two older children. The mother explained:

> I thought these children are going to be part of each other's lives and in ten years time when they come knocking on the door, what will they be like? At that time they would be a huge influence on my children and they could be on drugs, they could be pregnant, they could be back in touch with the birth parents who are very dangerous people – so one of the things that influenced my decision was that it was a way of keeping my children safe. (Adopter 3)

Relishing the challenge or 'doing the right thing'

Six of the adopters not only felt confident but also relished the challenge of taking on a sibling group. In one case, the social worker had mentioned five siblings but then said, 'No, that's impossible. Nobody could do it!' The adopter's immediate response was, 'I could do it! If she hadn't said that, I probably wouldn't have asked. But I thought I want them now!' An adoptive father also confessed to a bit of 'silly male pride' in wanting to take on this challenge – 'the Everest thing'.

There were also a few adopters, including two devout Christians, who saw adopting a sibling group as a "vocation" or a way of doing the right thing or trying to make a difference.

Thinking it would be easier to parent a sibling group

A few adopters chose a sibling group because they believed that siblings would be easier to parent or at least no more difficult than a single child. One couple were adamant that having a sibling group was preferable because 'Children are more contented and happier if they have got someone else with them that they belong to.' Another adoptive mother insisted that 'anyone who takes on one [child] is on a hiding to nothing', and that 'it would be easier to adopt two or three, than it ever is to adopt one.' Other adopters thought that it would be more complicated to adopt again after the family had bonded, or they assumed that contact arrangements would be easier if only one birth family was involved.[6]

Choosing an adoption agency

The adopters gave many reasons for their choice of adoption agency – including location of the agency, the attitude and behaviour of staff, and the publicity and profile of the agency on the internet. Twenty had been approved by a VAA and 17 by an LA. More of those who had chosen a VAA had done so because of their own research or a recommendation from other adopters, or because the staff in the agency had made a good impression. Indeed, all of the VAA approved adopters said that one of the reasons they had chosen their adoption agency was because they liked the staff's attitude or approach. In contrast, less than half (47%) of the LA adopters chose their agency for this reason. Five LA adopters did not even realise that they had a choice of agency. However, not all VAAs had made a good impression. One couple encountered a VAA social worker who was "scathing" about the viability of placing sibling groups, so they went elsewhere.

---

6 It should be noted that contact arrangements with one birth family can also be very complex if the siblings have different birth fathers.

Two-thirds of all the adopters (25) had approached an LA first to enquire about adoption. Five had been rejected initially by their LA, including one family whose placement subsequently disrupted. The five adopters gave the following reasons for their rejection: the LA did not need any more adopters, had no children who could be placed with them, or did not want to place children with a same-sex couple, a member of the armed forces or couples who wanted to adopt rather than having birth children.

In another case it was clear that the LA was only interested in placing their own looked after children and had no wish to participate in recruiting adopters for children in other parts of the country. This approach inevitably reduced the choice for children and adopters in their area, and it could also mean that potential sibling-group adopters were not considered, as the adoptive mother explained:

> They were saying we weren't in the right location for them. We were too close to the city centre, and if they placed children with us, the problem was when we took them into town the chances are we could easily bump into birth family . . . They said they would accept us, but we wouldn't be classed as priority: we would have to go on a waiting list and they weren't sure how long we'd have to wait (. . .) So we felt a bit cast aside really (. . .) so we looked at voluntary agencies. (Adopter 32)

The importance of providing a prompt and positive response is highlighted in the following comment by one adopter who despaired of her LA and turned instead to a VAA:

> We started going with [LA], but they just didn't come back to us. We didn't get a response from them and it was very impersonal, so we looked up on the internet [to find] adoption agencies (. . .) and when we spoke to [VAA], they were just really friendly and helpful and responsive – everything the council hadn't been. (Adopter 21)

A few adopters who had been local authority employees decided not to adopt through their LA because they feared they would receive an inferior service. One explained why they had gone to a VAA instead:

> *[The VAA's] sole job was to find children for families, so they had no other agenda (. . .) They weren't trying to push children – the wrong children – onto us (. . .) They were committed to finding the right children for us, not just ones that had come up on their books.* (Adopter 17)

Three adopters said they had not approached their LA because they had heard that they were likely to be rejected because they were "the wrong colour" or "the wrong age". Another adoptive mother (aged 43) stated she had been told by an IVF counsellor that she was too old to adopt, but despite this inaccurate information she contacted her LA, who accepted her application.

The sibling-group adopters appreciated social workers who responded promptly and who were honest, friendly, professional, realistic and encouraging. These attributes were more often reported in VAA staff. They also appreciated agency staff who were "professional but human" and who allowed them to go at their own pace. In particular, they wanted a social worker who was experienced and knowledgeable, and to whom they could relate easily:

> *I think the adoption social worker was very knowledgeable and clearly knew what she was talking about – and that helped a great deal. When you are trying to place siblings, you really need to know your stuff.* (Adopter 3)

Conversely, they were angered by social workers who made them feel patronised or undervalued, regarded them with pity, or were "pushy" and "interrogating". A key factor that persuaded many adopters to choose a VAA was the promise of life-long support:

> *. . . she said that they were used to placing larger groups and supporting people through that, and continuing the support as a life-long support. It wasn't once you'd done it, that was it and*

you were dumped. It was, 'If you need support, we'll always be there' [. . .] and they were on your side. (Adopter 19)

It is clear that LAs still have a lot to do to improve their practice and reverse the negative perceptions held of their services. In the next chapter, we explore how the adoption agencies assessed prospective adopters and what characteristics they were looking for. We also report the adopters' experiences of the assessment process.

Summary

- Most of the parents (89%) chose to adopt because they could not have their own children. However, four couples (including the same-sex couple) said that adoption was their first choice as the means of having a family, and one couple adopted because they wanted to do something worthwhile.
- The majority (89%) said they wanted to adopt siblings right from the start. Usually they were thinking of two siblings initially, but nearly a third said they had always wanted a large family. The most frequent reason, given by 62 per cent of adopters, was that they had always wanted two or more children and felt able to do it because they had a supportive partner and a good support network.
- The adopters' reasons for wanting a sibling group included: believing that a family should consist of more than one child; not wanting to repeat the adoption process; having grown up in a large family; thinking this would give them a better chance of adopting young children or obtaining children more quickly; wanting to prevent siblings from being separated; relishing the challenge of adopting a sibling group; and thinking it would be easier than adopting a single child.
- Two-thirds (25) of the adopters had approached an LA first, but less than half (17) went on to adopt through the LA. Five adopters did not realise that they had a choice of adoption agencies.
- Five adopters had been rejected initially by their LA before being approved by another agency, and one of these families subsequently had a disruption. The reasons given for rejection were that the LA

did not need any more adopters, had no children who could be placed with them, or did not want to place children with a same-sex couple, a member of the armed forces or those who wanted to adopt rather than having birth children.

- All the VAA adopters said they had chosen their adoption agency because they liked the staff's attitude or approach, but only 47 per cent of LA adopters said this. Adopters appreciated social workers who responded promptly and who were experienced, honest, friendly, professional, realistic and encouraging. The promise of life-long support was a key factor for those who chose a VAA.

8   Assessment

This chapter considers how local authority (LA) and voluntary adoption agency (VAA) staff assessed prospective adopters to see if they were suitable to adopt a sibling group. It then describes the adopter's experiences of being assessed.

Views of adoption agency staff

In the last decade, increased funding has enabled many LAs to employ more adoption social workers (Deloitte, 2006), but a high turnover of children's social workers has also been reported. As this has been a significant change, adoption agency respondents were asked how confident they were in the skills of their staff.

All the VAA and most of the LA managers thought that all or most of their staff were competent in assessing the ability of prospective adopters to parent a sibling group, but one LA manager thought that only some of the team had the necessary skills. Managers made it clear that newly qualified workers would not usually be expected to undertake these complex assessments. Several VAAs and some LAs had a remarkably stable workforce, which suggests perhaps that working in adoption can be very satisfying. Here are two comments by adoption managers:

> *We only employ highly qualified, very experienced staff. We've got social workers who've been with us over 20 years (. . .) so they know what they're doing.* (VAA 3)

> *Our adoption team is very, very experienced. I'm the youngest member of the team, and I have worked for [LA] for 19 years! Everyone has done children and families work, so they have a very longitudinal view of adoption.* (LA 5)

Having years of experience was perhaps a crucial factor in their ability to place large sibling groups, as training on sibling issues did not appear to be widely available.

Training for social workers in assessing potential sibling-group adopters

The confidence of agency staff in dealing with sibling-group adoptions was reported as having very little to do with formal training. None of the staff in VAAs and only one LA worker mentioned the availability of specific training on sibling-group issues in adoption. One VAA manager commented:

> It's more on-the-job training, like learning from each other (. . .) I think there has to be an ethos and a sort of proportion of knowledge vested in an organisation that can help people develop that (. . .) There's got to be people around you who are bouncing ideas off you and learning via that way, and I think we have that sort of environment (. . .) I'm sure we do go on courses about placing siblings, but I don't think that's where the bulk of the learning takes place. (VAA 3)

Training on sibling-group issues, if it was available at all, seemed to be included within courses on attachment and trauma. These courses were usually very expensive and, consequently, agencies could often only fund one place. The trained team member was then expected to cascade the information down to other members of staff.

Invariably, adoption agencies attributed the confidence of their social work staff to experience in placing siblings for adoption. Some also emphasised that working in a team where such placements occurred regularly had led to increased confidence and optimism among all team members.

Undertaking assessments of prospective sibling-group adopters

We asked respondents in the 14 adoption agencies what might encourage them to think that someone might be a suitable adopter for a sibling group. As numerous factors are involved in such a decision, it was perhaps not surprising that there was a wide range of responses and similar requirements were often expressed in different ways. The managers were concerned that the adopters should: be able to understand and empathise with the children's needs; have the desire, motivation and determination to take on a sibling group; and have experience of working with or caring for children. Some emphasised the need for the adopters to be flexible, intuitive, capable of coping with stress, and able to spend time with the children. Others expected them to be practical, healthy and financially secure, and to have a strong relationship, a good support network and suitable accommodation. While many of these requirements would have been similar for other adopters, they took on a heightened significance in the context of a sibling-group placement.

All of the respondents, except for one LA manager, thought there were additional areas to consider when assessing adopters who wanted a large sibling group. In particular, social workers wanted to know whether the adopters understood sibling dynamics and would be able to differentiate and meet the competing needs of individual children. In one VAA, adopters were shown a short video of a family and then asked to talk about the children's interactions. The purpose of this exercise was to see whether they simply viewed the children as a group or if they were aware of the behaviours of individual children. Here are the comments of two LA managers:

I think it would be about their experience of children and their confidence in managing a group of children who may have been treated differently in the family and may have had very different roles, and how they would manage different attachment behaviours within a wide age range. We just need to be sure that people can balance the different needs of children. We would want to ensure they had enough support in their lives, whether that was the community, friends or family. (LA 2)

. . . you want warm and tolerant people. I mean, if you look after a group of children, you're going to have to be tolerant (. . .) child centred and focused, because you're responding to three or more children with very different needs . . . you need to be flexible about being at home perhaps for longer than with other children, to help provide that stability and consistency. (LA 3)

Social workers also wanted to know whether prospective adopters were trying to replicate their own experiences of family life. Did people who came from large or small families realise that this was not going to be the same? Could they reach a realistic compromise about how many siblings they wanted? As one VAA manger explained, it was important to explore the adopters' beliefs about what constitutes a family:

Some of the people doing well with threes and fours could absolutely lose the plot with the one. It's horses for courses really. Unpicking what does family life mean for this couple. (VAA 6)

Two LA managers said that childless couples would have to be observed "interacting with children to see their child-centeredness". Anticipating such concerns, VAA staff were very proactive in encouraging prospective sibling-group adopters to acquire experience of caring for children through voluntary work. They also pointed out factors that LAs were likely to consider essential in any sibling-group adopter, as this respondent explained:

I think [LAs] are looking for a stay-at-home parent, looking at support networks, looking at childcare experience. These are the three things that are crucial – and other strengths, of course. (VAA 2)

In particular, there was a strong emphasis on practical considerations when adopters wanted to take larger sibling groups. A social worker who had placed two groups of five siblings (unfortunately outside the time limits for this study) commented:

I think there are practical things like how much time the adopter can spend at home. With the five [siblings] that I placed, that worked particularly well because the adopters were both home based – they worked at home. With the other group of five, the adopters had professional experience of children and also parenting experience with older children. (VAA 5)

Another social worker spoke about sibling-group adopters having to be prepared to set their own needs aside, 'because the children will come in and leave very little time for them as people or as a couple'. Adoption staff also wanted to be sure that the adopters had the emotional and physical capacity to cope with the challenges of caring for three or more siblings, as one manager explained:

We would have a greater emphasis on resilience, the network of support they have. We do an awful lot of work looking at their own vulnerabilities, because you're going to have a range of characters in a sibling group who are very adept at finding vulnerabilities (. . .) We often say, as much as they can prepare themselves, you still won't be prepared for the shock of your life (. . .) A lot of adopters describe a tiredness that they just did not expect, even though we told them! (VAA 1)

One VAA manager described the scale and complexity of the task that sibling-group adopters were undertaking in the following terms:

Just the sheer impact of taking three kids is like giving birth to triplets then plus, plus, plus, plus, except you don't just feed, burp, change, play with them, put them back to sleep. You have all the other issues of older children struggling with coming to a new family, a new lifestyle, a new place; some being in school, and being terrified out of their tiny minds, and therefore reverting back to a lot of interesting behaviours, that may or may not have come out in the child permanency report. (VAA 9)

Having a strong marital/partner relationship that had been 'tried and tested' was seen as a crucial issue to assess. In particular, agency staff stressed the importance of adopters being united in their determination to adopt a sibling group and able to support each other through any difficulties. Here are the comments of two adoption agency staff:

They have to be in it together (. . .) The determination to do it is the key factor – they are driven to do it. (LA 1)

I'm looking for flexibility – people who don't have rigid ideas of how things should be (. . .) A calm kind of person, a person who has good insight about their strengths and vulnerabilities (. . .) Especially I'm looking for the relationship between the two, if it's a couple. You know, I give them realistic case studies. For example (and this is quite frequent), if a child says, 'I don't love you' and they gravitate towards one person, I'm looking for reactions to those situations: what's their partner going to say? Or if a partner says, 'Adoption isn't right for me. I'm not coping with these children. They're going to have to go back', what's the other partner going to say? I want a partner who can support that other partner but also bring them out of that negativity. (VAA 2)

Interestingly, one VAA manager refused to specify any crucial factors or desirable qualities for sibling-group adopters on the grounds that adoption agencies should be enabling people to fulfil their potential, not looking for reasons to limit eligibility:

I hope we would take the premise that everybody might be suitable for a sibling group, so let's start there (. . .) We want to achieve the best for people rather than be minimalist about it, so let's go on a journey and see what you can achieve rather than what you can't achieve (. . .) Let's help them with their aspirations (. . .) I think there are lots of people who need to be helped to see that – they don't think they've got the skills to achieve certain things, and they have (. . .) It's about encouraging them. (VAA 3)

Financial security

Although there was some concern about 'less people putting themselves forward for siblings' in the current economic climate, LA managers were divided as to whether adopters needed to be financially secure. While they did not want to take on anyone who was struggling with debts, they differed in the extent to which they were willing to offer financial support. Three LA managers thought that providing an adoption allowance might be necessary to enable adopters to take a sibling group, and one of them stated, 'It is our job to help them do it by providing generous allowances.' However, VAA staff were very sceptical about whether financial support would be provided. Their view was that adopters could not always depend on LAs to provide good financial support. One manager commented that LAs which refuse to pay adoption allowances, 'are not going to get adopters for three kids' unless they find someone with substantial financial resources.

Suitable housing

There seemed to be a general assumption that the adopters would have a large enough house to accommodate a sibling group. This could be problematic in London, where the high price of property meant that few adopters had much spare space and often both parents had to work to meet their mortgage payments. As a result, siblings were sometimes placed a long way from their home area. Nor was the situation any easier for prospective adopters living in social housing, as one VAA manager explained:

> . . . local authorities or housing associations will not re-house you until the children are in place. Even if you approve people, they won't move them until the children are placed, so what do you do? Place three children in a two-bedroom flat in the hope that they're going to be re-housed? (. . .) I can understand them not doing it before, but if the panel has agreed the match, why cannot the housing authority then look for a larger property for them? (VAA 8)

However, the size of accommodation did not appear to be a major issue for adopters working in the armed forces. The military were said to be very supportive of adoptive families and, if their accommodation was not large enough, they would be moved (whenever possible) to larger accommodation. A manager in the VAA working with families in the armed forces said they had 'an amazing number of people who want sibling groups'.

What kind of applicants might be ruled out by adoption agencies?

Adoption agency managers gave varied answers to the question: what kind of adopters would you not consider for a sibling group? Applicants who were unlikely to be considered for a sibling group included those who were emotionally vulnerable, socially isolated or single, and anyone who was struggling financially. Age was not a barrier, but several adoption staff said they would be concerned about adopters who were not fit and healthy or who had a serious disability. Most would not consider those with birth children still at home. One social worker said she would rule out any adopter who was not willing to promote contact with siblings. Another expressed reservations about women who seemed to need a lot of time for themselves. Generally, agency staff said they would refuse to consider people who were unrealistic about what adopting a sibling group involved. A VAA manager commented:

> *I think what we try to work out is those individuals who will feel comfortable with the sort of family life that comes with a larger sibling group – a noisy, more chaotic household – and who's going to think, 'That's really great and how family life should be,' and who's going to think, 'I'm out of control here. This is horrendous. Get them out!' (VAA 6)*

One LA manager also indicated that some applicants might be rejected on the basis of their application form without even being seen because social workers would only do an initial visit if they thought the applicants were potential adopters.

Assessing the prospective adopters' birth children

Most of the adoption agency staff said they would not place a sibling group of three or more children into a family where there were birth children living at home. This was because they believed: it would be difficult to match children successfully; the impact on the birth children could be overwhelming; a sibling group would alter the family dynamics; and there would be an increased risk of disruption.

Two LA respondents who were prepared to consider placing a sibling group into a household with birth children emphasised that the birth children had to be fully involved in the assessment so that they could understand what it would mean for them. One manager spoke about discussing things like having to share toys and space, having less time with their parents, and how the birth children would feel if their toys got broken or an adopted child was very demanding of the parents' time and attention. The other manager insisted that birth children must be actively involved in the assessment:

> It must be a family assessment, not just a couple assessment. You can make it fun. We do family projects with children to get them to talk about their family and themselves, what they are like, what it will be like to have more children in the family. (LA 1)

Five respondents from adoption agencies mentioned sibling-group adoptions where *adult* birth children had been supportive and played a crucial role in caring for the children. Indeed, adult birth children sometimes provided the support that made it possible for adopters to take on a large sibling group. One manager commented:

> One of the fivesomes that we placed – they did have children of their own, older children. I think they were adults by then and they played quite a significant part in some of the practical arrangements and some of the support arrangements for the children. So clearly they were involved in some of the discussions about what the needs of the children were, and how collectively they might respond to the children's needs. (VAA 3)

Assessing sibling groups for adoption

With regard to assessing the siblings' relationships and attachments, the role of the social worker seemed to vary considerably. In some LAs, the social worker had the lead role, although a paediatrician or a CAMHS worker might also be involved. One LA had a consultation service run by an educational psychologist, who would consider all the information on the children with the social worker and foster carer and give a written view on their attachments. In another authority, social workers were often advised to have assessments done by someone who was not emotionally involved in the case, although they sometimes had to do assessments without specialist advice because of funding limitations. Two managers mentioned using the BAAF guide *Together or Apart?* (Lord and Borthwick, 2008).

The adopters' experiences of being assessed

Just over a third of the adopters (13) had announced right at the beginning of the assessment process that they wanted to adopt a sibling group. Sometimes this had helped to focus the whole assessment on sibling issues, as one adopter explained:

> *Well, because we'd always said we wanted three or four, I suppose it was just incorporated in the assessment all the way through. It wasn't, you know, tagged on as a last minute thing or one session or anything like that . . . so whenever you looked at any particular issue, it was with regards to having all those children and how you'd manage different sibling needs.* (Adopter 24)

However, many adopters found it difficult to explain how sibling issues had been addressed during their assessment. This was perhaps because they were being assessed, and their social worker was focusing on getting to know them before considering how many children might be placed with them. Some agencies also used a standard assessment process for all adopters, which occasionally gave sibling-group adopters the impression that they were not being listened to. Here are two of their comments:

> *. . . the process of assessment was the general process essentially, that they would use with potential adopters irrespective of how many children they wanted to adopt.* (Adopter 19)

When we talked about the kind of children that we'd be looking for, our social worker actually always said "child" and (. . .) we would say, "No, we want two", and she'd keep saying "child" in the singular (. . .) which I found quite strange. (Adopter 33)

A few adopters spoke about social workers wanting to know whether they had the capacity to deal with more than one child and requiring them to gain childcare experience, perhaps by doing voluntary work in a local nursery. However, five adopters said that sibling issues had hardly been mentioned in their assessment:

During our actual assessment, it wasn't really brought up. It was just this passing comment (. . .) at the beginning. (Adopter 10)

We actually never talked about three [siblings] in assessment – it was after that (. . .) There was never any encouraging towards that. (Adopter 33)

One adopter complained that the social workers 'weren't just assessing whether we had the capacity to adopt – they were assessing whether we thought the same way as them'. He commented:

. . . when they said we had too many books in the house, and that I was too intellectual and so wouldn't be able to deal with the children because they were guaranteed to be failures in life, I took exception to that (. . .) [For] one of the people in charge of adoption to be telling me that my expectations needed to be low and I might be disqualified because they might be high seems to me to be something that should have disqualified her from working in adoption. (Adopter 4)

It was surprising that many of the adopters thought their assessment was not focused on their capacity to parent a sibling group. Perhaps the format of the assessment encouraged social workers to focus on adoption in a general way rather than being more specific. The sibling-group adopters in this sample also tended to be self-assured and confident, and this may have affected the way the assessment was conducted.

Adopters' reasons for thinking they could manage a sibling group

There were many reasons why adopters thought they would be able to manage three or more siblings. Most attributed their confidence to experience of working with children (73%) or caring for children (81%). The vast majority (89%) also thought they would receive support from friends and relatives, as one adopter explained:

It's your family you have to rely on, when you get home. You're not going to ring the social worker at 2am and say, 'This child can't get to sleep. Could you come and help?' (Adopter 7)

Nearly two-thirds of the adopters had grown up with siblings, and some assumed that because their mother had coped with three children they would be able to do the same. However, the key factor, identified by 89 per cent of the adopters, was just the fact that they really wanted children. In the words of one father:

I didn't want to get to the end of my life having not tried to nurture children. (Adopter 35)

Generally, the responses of VAA and LA adopters were very similar, with one notable exception: 85 per cent of the VAA adopters thought that the support provided by their adoption agency would enable them to manage a sibling group, but only 41 per cent of the LA adopters felt confident for this reason.

Almost a third of the adopters (32%) had religious or humanitarian reasons for thinking that they would be able to cope with a sibling group, as one mother explained:

We trusted that God would give us the strength to deal with whatever was going to come. (Adopter 21)

However, almost as many adopters (30%) had confidence in their own abilities and "just assumed" they would be able to cope. Often this confidence was rooted in the strength of their relationship, but one mother was strongly encouraged by her teenage son:

> *He was so positive about his own upbringing and what I've been able to give him. He said if I felt that was something I wanted to do, he felt I should go out and do it because it would be good.* (Adopter 16)

In the next chapter, we examine how the adoption agencies prepared the adopters. The adopters comment on their experiences of being prepared for adoption.

Summary

- Staff in the adoption agencies were usually experienced and the workforce was stable. It appeared that for many workers, adoption practice was satisfying and fulfilling.
- The confidence of agency staff in dealing with sibling-group adoptions was attributed to practical experience. Specialist training on dealing with sibling issues in adoption did not appear to be widely available. Staff who worked in teams that regularly placed siblings were described as being more confident and optimistic that sibling group placements were achievable.
- Adoption staff wanted to assess whether the adopters: would be able to differentiate the needs of individual children; understood sibling dynamics; had practical experience of caring for children; had the support of family and friends; could cope with stress; had realistic expectations; and were united in wanting a sibling group.
- There seemed to be a general assumption that the adopters would have large enough accommodation for a sibling group. This resulted (particularly in London) in some siblings being placed far away from their home area.
- Agency staff stated that applicants were unlikely to be considered for a sibling group if they were emotionally vulnerable, socially isolated, single or struggling financially. Age was not a barrier, but

several adoption staff said they would be concerned about adopters who were not fit and healthy, or who had a serious disability. Most would not consider those with birth children still at home.

- Two LA respondents who were prepared to consider placing a sibling group into a household with birth children emphasised that the birth children had to be fully involved in the assessment.
- Most adopters could not identify how sibling issues had been addressed during their assessment.
- The reasons the adopters gave for thinking they could manage a sibling group included: experience in working with or caring for children; expecting to receive support from their adoption agency or from family and friends; growing up with siblings; and just really wanting to have children.

9 Preparation for adoption

Before children move into adoptive families, it is usually the children's social worker who prepares the children for the move, while adoption agencies prepare the adopters. For adopters, preparation can include training courses, talking to adopters who already have children placed with them, and involving other members of their family in the process. For children, preparation means ensuring that the child understands and is ready to move into an adoptive home, and this will often include life story work. Sibling groups may need extra preparation, especially where they have been living separately in foster care and the plan is to reunite them in an adoptive home.

In this chapter, local authority (LA) and voluntary adoption agency (VAA) staff describe how sibling-group adopters and their families are usually prepared, and adopters comment on their experiences of being prepared. Although VAA staff are rarely involved in preparing children, we also include their views on how well this task is usually done.

The adoption agencies' views on preparation

All the agencies provided initial preparation training but the amount of training varied by agency. Four days' training with intervals in between seemed to be fairly common but, as one agency acknowledged, 'Four days doesn't give you a great deal of time.' None of the adoption agencies provided specific training on adopting siblings. Remarkably, one VAA had designed a course on siblings that had been cancelled due to lack of take-up. However, they were intending to offer it again, this time across the consortium.

None of the LA agencies provided additional training for those who expressed an interest in adopting a sibling group. One LA manager, when asked if sibling group adopters had additional training needs, stated:

*They may do, but we don't provide anything extra for them (. . .)
The preparation training is the same for everybody (. . .) It's the
BAAF training that's rolled out across the country, so we cover
all the essentials in terms of contact and telling and the
backgrounds of children.* (LA 5)

It appeared that additional training was more likely to be provided by
VAAs. For example, one VAA manager stated that their post-approval
training could be expanded to include siblings, while another described
a comprehensive programme of training with additional modules
before approval and after placement. Another VAA provided training
for friends and relatives of adopters. This was seen as a good way of
ensuring that adopters received appropriate and effective support, and
the social worker emphasised the importance of involving key members
of the adopters' support network in the whole adoption process:

*This is for the friends and family who are the main support for
our families, and we feel that for them to understand the
children in the care system, they need to have an understanding
of the reasons behind the behaviour. So we do a one-day
workshop and that is so valuable. Once people come to those
workshops, I follow on and do an interview with them (...) and I
bring them into the assessment. For example, in one of my
cases, the [adopters'] first language was not English (. . .) and I
felt that they would struggle with education because the two
older boys were very behind with their education. But one of
their nieces had trained to be a teacher, so I brought her in early
on during the meeting with the schools, because I thought she
would have a deeper understanding of where these children
were and she could relay that to her aunt and uncle (. . .) So I
would tell the [children's LA], 'This is their main support, and I
think they need to be part of the process as much as possible,'
and some agencies welcome that, some frown.* (VAA 2)

Staff in four agencies indicated that additional training might be
provided later for the adopters if any of the children had a specific

behavioural issue. However, it was far more likely that guidance and support on caring for a sibling group would be provided directly by the social worker after adopters were approved. To help prospective adopters to develop a more realistic view of what parenting a sibling group might be like, all the adoption agencies stated that they used DVDs of siblings, directed prospective adopters to relevant articles and research, and invited adopters who were parenting siblings to come and talk about their experiences. In one LA, a play therapist provided training sessions on attachment and gave examples of the difficulties that might arise and how to manage them.

Providing opportunities for networking

Staff from six adoption agencies said they arranged for prospective sibling-group adopters to meet or link up with others who had already adopted siblings. This was achieved through buddy schemes, organising private meetings, or paying for membership of Adoption UK so that the adopters could use the message board. One VAA manager commented:

We would be trying to get them paired up with someone who has done it before. We have a buddy system. Would maybe encourage them to take out their relatives' children for a day and get them to evaluate people whom they see dealing with children – would they deal with it differently? (VAA 3)

Encouraging adopters to gain childcare experience

When the prospective adopters had very little childcare experience, almost half of the agency respondents (6) said they would encourage adopters to undertake voluntary work in nurseries, schools, Brownies or Beavers. They also spoke about encouraging adopters to 'borrow other people's children' (often nephews and nieces) and have them to stay for a day or a weekend. However, none of the agencies arranged for prospective adopters to experience parenting children for a day (a tactic featured in David Akinsanya's Channel 4's series, *Find Me a Family*[7]).

---

7 Channel 4, 11–13 May 2009, 9 p.m.

Sharing children's profiles

Research in the US (Smith *et al*, 2008) has suggested that it is beneficial for those who are going through assessment and preparation to see the profiles of children who are waiting for an adoptive family. It has been demonstrated that this keeps prospective adopters engaged and provides much-needed information on the characteristics and needs of children waiting for a placement. This perspective was clearly shared by one VAA manager, who described it as a good way of helping adopters 'to see what issues matter to them most, so they become more skilled at deciding what kind of children they want'. However, this was not a universal approach among LAs or VAAs. Some agencies never shared children's profiles with unapproved adopters, and others did so only as a means of checking how flexible the adopters were.

Encouraging adopters to take a sibling group

Most of the adoption agencies emphasised that they would not push any adopter to take more children than they wanted or would be able to manage. Indeed, staff in two LAs said they would never encourage prospective adopters to consider taking siblings. However, seven VAAs and one LA said they often encouraged adopters to consider taking a sibling group and helped them to recognise that they had the ability to do it. A common approach was to explore how many children the adopters wanted, and if they were thinking of adopting one child and maybe another later, they would discuss the pros and cons of doing that and the possibility of taking siblings. Sometimes the reverse occurred, and staff were so concerned that taking three siblings would overwhelm the adopters that they 'talked them down one'. However, if a social worker assessed a prospective adopter as being capable of taking a sibling group, this could be communicated to the prospective adopters in a way that was empowering. One VAA manager described an adoption social worker who was very good at doing this:

We had one social worker who had an uncanny knack of being able to make families aspire to achieve things they thought were impossible, and she always found the right children for them, often sibling groups (. . .) She just kept beavering away in a quiet methodical way, and that has rubbed off on others. It's a bit about inspiration – if you see the best in people, you can do it actually. (VAA 3)

Preparing the children for placement

It is the responsibility of the child's local authority social worker to prepare the child for adoption. All the LA staff acknowledged the importance of doing this well, and one manager admitted that two placements had recently disrupted because children had not been well prepared. Unfortunately, children's social workers were not always experienced in this work and, if this was the case, staff said they would have to rely on guidance from colleagues or BAAF publications such as *Ten Top Tips for Placing Siblings* (Argent, 2008) and *Adopted Children Speaking* (Thomas *et al*, 1999).

Another LA made the preparation for adoption enjoyable by involving the children in writing their profile and 'getting really good photos – they like that'. However, there were concerns about who would have the time to do this work, and whether there was time for each child to be seen individually, as one respondent explained:

. . . if [the children's social worker has] not got the time to do that, which they often haven't, the adoption worker or the play specialist do specific preparation work for the move (. . .) I think sometimes it's presumed, because a sibling group have got each other (. . .) 'Oh, they'll be okay, they've got each other,' but it's different than what they've had. All children need to [have] direct work done with them to identify what their fears are and (. . .) help them process their own thoughts and fears individually. (LA 4)

This LA had provided funding for their play specialist to do specific work on preparing sibling groups for moving to their adoptive homes. She was also able to provide advice and suggest strategies for social workers dealing with complex cases.

Another social worker highlighted how the LA's case management system recorded sibling groups as "one case", which created additional pressures:

If you have a sibling group on your caseload, it still shows up as one case for a children and families worker, so you could have four children to move onto adoption – and the volume of paperwork to get to panel now! (. . .) So I think very early on, children and families workers need somebody to share the work with, particularly if it's at a very critical stage and some of the children may have a different route to permanence. (LA 5)

Preparing siblings for being re-united in an adoptive home

Preparing children and undertaking life story work was more complicated, when children were living in separate foster homes – a situation experienced by almost half of the children in our study. Adoption staff acknowledged that it was difficult to re-unite siblings successfully if they had lived separately for a considerable time. VAA staff were very dubious about this (sometimes as a result of bad experiences), but some LA managers thought these difficulties could be overcome if regular contact was established quickly and increased before the introductions:

. . . you need to have sorted out the contact really at quite an early stage, and I think that helps to demonstrate to the children that you are going to be planning for them together. It also allows you to do the work together with them as a whole sibling group, which (. . .) is absolutely vital. (LA 3)

In these circumstances it could be helpful for children to work through their feelings with a therapist. This was because some siblings might not even be aware that they were related, and being brought together in a new adoptive home would often mean changes to their status and position within the family and to the amount of attention they received. For example, the oldest child in one foster home might become the middle child in the adoptive family.

Sometimes the siblings were brought together in one foster home before introductions began, but this could be fraught and was not generally recommended by the agency staff interviewed. If the foster carers got on well, arranging overnight stays seemed to be a better option, particularly for large sibling groups, as described below:

With the five that I placed, because they hadn't lived together for quite a long time, we organised with one of the foster carers that she would have all of them, so they would wake up together and do all of those normal things together that they hadn't done. They were not moved but they went there for a weekend or overnight, so they could experience all the normal routines of living together, before moving in with the adopters. (VAA 5)

The views of VAA staff on the preparation of siblings

VAA staff were asked how they checked whether the children had been well prepared for adoption by their LA social worker. Most of them asked the LA social worker if life story books had been completed, if the children had specific difficulties, and if they had received any therapeutic support. Three-quarters said they read the children's case files, and some thought this should be done routinely for every placement. However, some LAs were reluctant to grant access to case files, and sometimes VAA staff only viewed the files if problems arose after placement. Two VAA respondents spoke about wanting to meet or talk to the foster carer to find out how much the children understood about the situation, as in the following statement:

We ask how they're going to prepare the children, whether there's a life story and, if so, how it's been done. You'd also be asking the foster parents what the children's perception is of the plan – what do they understand? Have they had goodbye contacts with the birth parents? Has there been any assessment of the sibling relationships? (VAA 5)

Obtaining high-quality child assessments was not easy. One VAA respondent deplored the standard of assessments in sibling placements and emphasised how important it was to know about any issues and demands that the adopters would have to face:

. . . very often these children have not had good assessments about whether they should be placed together. Some authorities are increasingly using CAMHS and psychologists to get some guidance on this, which, you know, is encouraging, but it's not generally available (. . .) Social workers are far too optimistic – because the children make progress when they come into care from chaos and neglect, they are seen as 'catching up' (. . .) I want realistic views of what the demands are going to be and what the issues are likely to be. It is very difficult getting this information from agencies. (VAA 4)

Two VAA respondents questioned whether it is even possible for LA social workers to prepare children well for adoption. As one manager pointed out, preparation can be a painful process not only for the children but also for the social worker:

People can have sat down and talked to children about all sorts of issues, but it doesn't mean that the children have absorbed that information or dealt with the emotions associated with it. It's a very painful job to help children to process all those difficult losses they've already had and, as we know, children sometimes protect adults from the pain. (VAA 6)

Unfortunately, most of the VAA staff had experienced cases where children had not been well prepared for adoption. This included a case where children who were about to be placed with a same-sex couple had been prepared for a "mummy" and "daddy".

Multi-agency preparation for an adoptive placement
When we asked adoption staff what multi-agency work would be required to prepare for the siblings' move to their adoptive home, their responses indicated that most of them were thinking in terms of specific support for individual children after placement rather than support for the siblings as a group. They spoke about liaising with schools and with medical and CAMHS professionals, and arranging specialist services for children with special needs. This was easier to

organise when the adoption agencies themselves employed therapists or educational psychologists and had good working relations with external agencies, as one LA manager explained:

It depends on [the children's] needs. Definitely education. We have an educational psychologist on our team, who is on the panel. She helps out in finding school places. They [educational psychologists] do a lot of post-adoption support with us and provide tips on how to help a child with attachment difficulties. We have good relationships with child development centres, and we can sometimes get therapeutic help paid for by the health authority or funded jointly. (LA 1)

The emphasis was on ensuring that children and their adopters would not have to wait for specialist support services. For example, transitional allowances to provide individual support in school were said to be very beneficial for children who had suffered greater adversity or needed to catch up, but this had to be planned in advance so that it was 'available at the beginning of a placement rather than waiting until it unravels . . .' Similarly, it was important that children moving into a different area did not automatically go to the bottom of the waiting list for mental health services.

Sometimes LAs organised a multi-agency meeting to ensure that the support plan would be implemented. This was described by one manager as follows:

. . . the pre-adoption placement planning meeting with the adopters and their worker and our workers is about actually making sure we've got all aspects of the (. . .) support plan in place. [We do that] always with large sibling groups, and we try and make that, you know, as multi-agency as you can, depending on what you are building into the adoption support plan. (LA 3)

Two managers clearly viewed child appreciation days (sometimes also referred to as life appreciation days) as a very effective form of multi-agency work that should always be undertaken prior to a sibling-group placement. One stressed that it was important for the adopters to be accompanied by their own social worker to these meetings, because they could ask questions that might not occur to the adopters and check in advance if they would be able to meet professionals such as the health visitor.

While LAs were responsible for organising multi-agency support, VAA staff often had strong views about what should be provided. Most of the VAA respondents wanted to ensure that the adopters had a chance to get to know the foster carers before the start of introductions, because this could be helpful in preventing problems. If the children had been looked after for a long time (as often happens with sibling groups) and the foster carers had become very attached to them, establishing some rapport between the adopters and the foster carers was seen as a good way of enabling the carers to feel confident in handing the children over to their new parents.

One VAA manager was particularly proactive in seeking the views of all the different professionals involved in a sibling-group placement, as she explained:

> *It's a complex business. What is needed is a series of meetings – formal or informal – which at some point will include the foster carer and their support agency, the adopters, the children's social worker, the family-finder and anyone who has done work with the children around preparation for moving. You need to have some discussions with whoever is responsible for agency finances – they're key. You need to ensure that all these voices are heard. You need dialogue between all these people, preferably together in the room. (VAA 6)*

When children were placed abroad, multi-agency work was even more complicated as the adoption agencies had to comply with the various requirements of service providers in different countries. This was a common occurrence for the VAA working with families in the armed forces. Their manager commented:

[Local authorities] have to get their head round the fact they've got to notify us if it's an overseas command, and liaise with a very specific educational system of service education (. . .) We are the support in an overseas command through our social work service, not through the adoption service, but we have specifics which throw local authorities. For example, if there's a statement of special educational need, that child cannot be placed in Germany or wherever, until the education service has considered whether they can meet that child's needs. Can't just go and turn up (. . .) We will also ask our social workers to do statutory visits for the local authority, if local authorities don't want to do it themselves. (VAA 7)

Having considered the views of agency staff, we now consider how our sample of 37 adopters experienced their preparation for adopting a large sibling group.

Adopters' views on preparation for adoption

Less than half (41%) of the adopters said they had found their preparation training helpful. This was perhaps not surprising, as short preparation courses can only cover the basics. There were several complaints about courses being too superficial. For example, one adopter was disappointed because the training never 'stirred emotions' or enabled them to consider how things 'would feel in real life': it never made you 'look deep inside yourself and see what your reactions were, and why they were the way they were and, therefore, how you would deal with [it].'

Nevertheless, many adopters (including some of the 59% who said the preparation courses were not helpful) identified some aspects of the training that they had really appreciated. Some (9) particularly valued listening to adopters talking about their experiences. These real life situations had made them feel more confident that they could do it too, and some regarded this as the highlight of their training. One adopter commented:

A guy came in [. . .] and talked about adopting his little girl, and he was there for about an hour and a half, and we learned more in that hour and a half than we did in the whole four days. He was open and honest, and he was just great. (Adopter 29)

Involving birth parents and foster carers in the preparation courses also helped to give the adopters an understanding of different perspectives on adoption and perhaps an insight into children's needs and ways of meeting them.

Crucially, explanations from social workers about the backgrounds of children in care and the impact of abuse and neglect on child development had helped some adopters to think about what had happened to the children, the losses they had endured and the challenges they faced in coming to terms with their past. For five couples this has been a "real eye opener". Being able to work on scenarios and discuss particular issues could also be very helpful. One couple appreciated having to think about uncertainty with regard to children's medical conditions, because it made them feel prepared for whatever might happen. Exploring their own emotional responses could be enlightening, and two adopters thought that *every* parent would benefit from this kind of training:

I personally feel that all parents should go through this [. . .] I mean you need to deal with the issues in your past so you don't dump them on your children, and especially if you've got children who have had an unstable background, the last thing they need is all your problems. (Adopter 11)

For seven adopters (19%) just having the opportunity to meet other prospective adopters and start building a support network was the most important thing. They had found this a valuable source of support after the children were placed with them.

One issue mentioned by a few adopters was the need for the "worst case scenario" approach to be balanced by 'a bit more positivity'. Two adopters had been shown a video titled *Adoption Hell*, which apparently reduced some prospective adopters to tears and made everyone wonder, 'Why are we doing this?' Interestingly, one of them thought this was a good approach, because there were 'times when it's going to be tough' and 'you need to be fully committed', while the other commented:

> I'd say what was missing was any form of positivity. The message was this will destroy your life and you will be miserable forever, and the only thing (...) that kept me hanging on was when we got people who'd actually already adopted come in (...) I can still remember one bloke saying, you know, 'These are my kids and I love them, and I feel every bit a father.' And when he said that, and when he talked about, you know, the joy of just (...) being with his family, at that point it was like okay ... (Adopter 4)

In addition, some adopters thought that other issues might usefully have been covered during preparation, for example: fears of making the wrong choice and not liking the children; helping the extended family to get ready for adoption; and enabling adopters to interact effectively with schools. There were also comments about whether training was provided at an appropriate stage in the adoption process. While one adopter said that she would have liked to attend a trauma and recovery course *before* the siblings were placed, another two emphasised the benefits of post-adoption training:

> Sometimes you feel you really want the kids to be taken away for two weeks and for you to go on another course! (...) A different sort of course (...) where you can just concentrate on trying to air and explain to yourself all these situations that you didn't know were going to arise and were therefore not prepared for. I mean things like guilt – constant guilt that you got it wrong. That wasn't mentioned, and every adopter I've spoken to has that on a daily basis, and just the emotional impact it has on you as a person. That wasn't given any time at all, and that's significant in our ability to cope. (Adopter 17)

Preparation for taking a sibling group

Very few adopters said their preparation training had specifically addressed sibling issues. One couple stated that their VAA had provided 'half a day all about siblings', while another adopter described how her LA had approached this issue:

> I think they did talk about the interaction between siblings, and also the fact that it could be difficult to meet the needs of siblings (. . .) They got some profiles out of Children Who Wait and got us to read through them and identify what the issues could be with the siblings and things like that . . . (Adopter 27)

There were frequent complaints about a lack of practical information or strategies for coping with a sibling group. Here are two of the adopters' comments:

> I think there probably wasn't enough on how to deal with those specific needs or behaviours of children once you've got them (. . .) It was all very theory and knowledge as opposed to (. . .) what you do on a day-to-day basis. (Adopter 6)

> [What was missing was] what do you do when you get home with three children? (. . .) I remember us getting home, and I said to [wife], 'What do we do now?' (Adopter 15)

In particular, some adopters had wanted more preparation to help them understand attachment issues. In some cases, the lack of information on attachment difficulties had been compounded by a lack of appropriate support after placement. As a result of this, one child had returned to foster care, as this adoptive mother explained:

> I think the biggest thing is a complete lack of reference to attachment difficulties and a complete failure to get us to comprehend that when these kids came to live with us, they would present as very much younger children and would need to be parented as very much younger children. I also think they make no acknowledgement of the need for extremely high

levels of self-care (. . .) [when] taking on three children that have had a really traumatic background. (Adopter 13)

Six adopters, however, believed that nothing could ever have prepared them for the reality of adopting a sibling group, as in the following statement:

I don't think that anyone can prepare you for the onslaught of caring for three children (. . .) No one can tell you how tired you will be! (Adopter 1)

Did adopters think that any of their agency's concerns were unreasonable?

About a third (12) of the adopters had thought during assessment or preparation that their adoption agency's concerns or requests were unreasonable. Four had since changed their mind and could now understand why social workers had been concerned. Examples of requests viewed as unreasonable included: being asked to get another sofa because the children should not sit on the adoptive father's lap; having to give their 'views on coloured people'; and being asked to use contraception for a year after the children were placed despite being infertile. A few adopters had been irritated by questions put to them by the adoption panel. One adopter described the intensive probing as 'a bit like being before the Gestapo'. A husband who was intending to be the main carer was outraged when he was asked at panel 'How on earth did I, as a white man, think that I could possibly look after children on my own?' Generally, however, the adopters accepted questioning as a necessary part of the process and understood that social workers had to check that they really wanted a sibling group.

Being encouraged or pressured to take a large sibling group

Adopters responded very differently to suggestions about increasing the number of children they were willing to adopt, and this depended very much on their adoption agency's approach. One couple who had been encouraged to take more children than they originally intended said they felt "really proud" when their social worker told them that she thought they could easily parent three children. They emphasised that there was no pressure, and they felt able to consider this because, crucially, there was a promise of life-long support. Another adopter smiled as she recalled exactly what their social worker had said to them:

> I remember her words vividly saying, 'I think you would be perfectly suited to having two or three children, because of the loving, caring family that you are.' (Adopter 18)

However, statements by other adopters indicate that there is a fine dividing line between encouragement, persuasion and pressure. One adoptive mother, who had been totally overwhelmed by the demands of her three siblings, described her social worker's approach as follows:

> [The social worker] said, 'Okay, what are we looking for then?' And we said, 'Well, a boy and a girl under five,' and she said, 'Everybody wants that, you'll never get that (...) and they're few and far between (...) Okay, let's broaden your horizons a bit. Older? More?' We said, 'Well, we had wondered about three.' She said, 'Three, good! They'll snap your hands off with three. Jolly good! (...) Okay, now you're not going to get three under five (...) because of the age differences', and then we moved up to about [age] seven. So we said, 'Three under seven.' 'Lovely, sorted!' (laughter) (...) It wasn't done in an undue way (...) but yeah, possibly a bit over persuaded. (Adopter 31)

Five adopters said they had been pressurised or persuaded to take more siblings than they had intended, and in three cases this apparently happened just before the panel met to discuss their application. Most of these cases (4) involved VAAs, and some adopters expressed cynicism about the motivation of VAA staff, as in the following statement:

> ... she came out and she looked around the house, and her comment was, 'Oh, it's a beautiful house for three!' (...) They do the same amount of work for one, two or three children, but

they get three times the amount of money (. . .) and yes, for that reason we were pressurised into doing it. When we went to panel, we were still saying, you know, 'Really two is where we want to be', but they put us forward for three, and of course, once we're approved for three, then that's it (. . .) She completely, you know, discounted looking at two, completely. It was always three, so we were heavily pressurised by that stage. (Adopter 10)

It is worth noting that in two cases where adopters wanted two siblings but were talked into taking three, the placement had partially disrupted. In a third case, where the adopters had felt pressurised to take a sibling group, they had come very close to ending the placement a few times. A fourth adopter, who had been persuaded to take three children, showed very little warmth when talking about them.

Attempts at persuasion had sometimes been rebuffed. In one case, an LA social worker was said to have mentioned a payment of £10,000 if the couple agreed to take a specific sibling group, but they had rejected this as "bribery".

After the adopters were approved by the panel, the search for the right children began in earnest. In the next chapter, we look at how the adopters were matched with a sibling group or found suitable children themselves, and what sort of information was provided to help them decide that these were the right children for them.

Summary

- Agencies generally provided four days' training for prospective adopters. None of the LA adoption agencies in this sample provided additional training for those who expressed an interest in adopting a sibling group. Some VAAs provided more modules and one offered a workshop to educate close family and friends about the experiences and needs of looked after children.
- Agency practice differed in whether they facilitated meetings between prospective and actual adopters or involved family members and friends; in whether they were willing to share profiles

of waiting children with prospective adopters; and in how they prepared children for placement.

- Preparing children for adoption could be painful emotionally for the child and the worker, and this work was more complex when siblings had been living in separate foster homes for a considerable time. Children's social workers were not always experienced in preparing children for adoption.
- Completing all the adoption forms for each child in a sibling group was time consuming. In some agencies, the social worker took the lead in assessing the siblings' relationships and attachments, although a paediatrician or a CAMHS worker might also be involved. Sometimes these assessments were done by specialists. VAA staff needed to understand the children's background so they could help adopters to make sense of their behaviour, but LAs were sometimes reluctant to grant access to the files.
- Less than half of the adopters thought that the preparation and training had been helpful. Adopters wanted preparation to be more focused on adopting a sibling group and helping children with behavioural and attachment difficulties. Some complained that always presenting the "worst case scenario" was a very negative approach. Sometimes they found it more helpful to listen to adopters who had already taken children.
- Most of the VAAs said they often encouraged adopters to consider taking a sibling group. This could be empowering for adopters, but there was a fine line between encouragement, persuasion and pressure. Five adopters had felt some pressure or persuasion to take more siblings than they had intended, and two of these placements had disrupted.

10 Matching and providing information

This chapter looks at how social workers matched children and adopters, how the adopters made their decision, and what information was provided about the children. LA adopters are usually matched with children from the same local authority (LA) or from an authority within their region. In contrast, voluntary adoption agency (VAA) adopters are matched with children from all over the UK and these placements incur an inter-agency fee (Selwyn and Sempik, 2010), so VAAs have to be more active in promoting their adopters.

The views of VAA staff on promoting sibling group adopters

In order to find suitable matches for their prospective adopters, VAA staff checked LA flyers on children needing placement and regularly scanned adoption magazines. One VAA manager commented that in the previous year they had 'followed up on 249 children to achieve 49 children placed'. VAA staff sought to ensure that LA family-finders were aware of their approved adopters by compiling profiles with photographs, outlining adopters' strengths and abilities and highlighting their willingness to consider taking a sibling group. They were very aware that they were competing with each other to persuade LAs to choose their adopters, so they emphasised any factors that might give their adopters an advantage. For example, the island VAA highlighted the "safety and freedom", which children could enjoy on the island. Others did everything possible to provide an excellent service and believed that this would enable their adopters to excel in the selection process, as one manager explained:

> I think our adopters are better prepared. We've done things like ASIs.[8] We've done specialist groups. We've got therapeutic

8   Interviews to assess adults' attachment style (Bifulco, 2006)

services (. . .) and we can say that our disruption rate is 5 per cent compared to the national average of 20 per cent (. . .) But at the end of the day, it's still down to the local authorities as to whether they are willing to pay for this (. . .) In one case, there were 43 families interested in a sibling group of three, and our family was chosen. (VAA 3)

Sometimes VAAs encouraged adopters to take a more active role in promoting themselves. One advised adopters to ring social workers if they were interested in specific children, because 'if adopters are making that chemical reaction to the children, that means more to the social worker'. Another occasionally suggested that prospective adopters should write their own flyer, explaining their situation and expressing their wishes in very personal terms. (One adoptive couple, who were beginning to despair of being linked with the right children, took matters into their own hands and wrote their own flyer, which they proudly produced during their interview for this study.)

The shortage of adopters willing to take a sibling group meant that those approved for sibling groups tended to have more choice and less competition. However, discussing potential sibling groups with the prospective adopters was still regarded as crucial. One manager stated that social workers needed to be 'working away at that fantasy – "this is the child I was going to have and this is the child I might end up with".'

Two VAA managers stressed the importance of considering the age range within any sibling group. They were particularly concerned about adopters being overwhelmed if none of the children were at school, as one explained:

I have recently had a referral, for example, of baby twins who are in one foster home and they are looking for a family to place them together with their 18-month-old sister [who is] in another foster home – and that is three children under two. How many pairs of hands does an adopter have? I would want to know how that is going to be manageable, and it wouldn't be my first choice to join together those children (. . .) If there is more of an age gap, then each child can have their individual needs considered and met. (VAA 4)

LA views on providing information about specific children

LA managers were asked about the information they provided to adopters who had been matched with a sibling group from their authority. All said that they gave adopters copies of the child permanence report, medical reports and court reports and arranged meetings with the children's social worker and the foster carer(s). Sometimes they also arranged meetings with teachers and birth parents and gave the adopters copies of CAMHS reports, if available. (Occasionally, reports were not shared due to confidentiality issues.) Practice differed in relation to whether they provided child appreciation days or allowed adoptive parents to have access to the children's case files.

The adopters' views on matching

The adopters found out about the sibling group they later went on to adopt from a range of sources (see Table 10.1). More VAA adopters than LA adopters were told about the children by their social worker, but over a third of the adopters had been proactive in finding and choosing children featured in adoption magazines or websites. Three adopters first heard about the children at an adoption exchange day.

As sibling groups are generally thought to be "hard to place", it was surprising that only one adopter said that they had been linked through the Adoption Register. However, it is likely that social workers obtained information about the children from the Adoption Register before sharing it with the adopters. Another possible explanation for the low use of the Adoption Register could be the reluctance or inability of LAs to pay the inter-agency fee that would be required if a sibling group was placed with a VAA adopter.

Photographs

Agencies had different practices with regard to showing adopters photographs of children. Some of the adopters in our sample saw photos at a very early stage, while others had to wait until much later.

Table 10.1

How adopters first heard about the siblings they later adopted

Agency	Source	Number	%
LA-approved adopters	from the social worker	635	
	at an adoption exchange day	318	
	saw profile in *Be my Parent* or *Children who Wait*	529	
	through the Adoption Register	16	
	saw profile on website	16	
	other source	16	
	Total	17100	
VAA-approved adopters	from the social worker	1260	
	saw profile in *Be my Parent* or *Children who Wait*	735	
	other source	15	
	Total	20	100

All the adoption agencies were understandably cautious about how they featured sibling groups in their promotional material. This was especially the case if one of the siblings was a baby, as staff were fearful that the siblings might be chosen simply because a baby was part of the group. One adoptive mother described how her VAA social worker dealt with this situation:

She showed us a picture of the two girls (. . .) and both [husband] and I just went, 'Those are the children for us! . . . we want these two children.' She said, 'Are you absolutely sure?' I said, 'No, you know we've asked for three children.' (. . .) Then she said, 'Well actually there is a third child, but he's a boy and he's only ten months.' (. . .) And, of course, the thing was that they didn't want people to go for this sibling group just because there was a baby, and then neglect the girls . . . (Adopter 11)

In another case, where a baby was the subject of further legal proceedings, the profile contained a photograph of the two older boys but just a drawing of a baby. The LA stated that they were looking for adopters for the two boys and that the legal position with regard to the baby was uncertain, but that any family taking the two boys would also be expected to take the baby. In a third case involving a baby, the adopters said it was difficult because their VAA would not show them a photograph of any of the children until they had made their decision. They accepted this, because they felt that the agency had told them everything they needed to know.

Although adopters had already stated what kind of children they wanted, they were usually attracted by how the children looked in their profile photograph. Adopters commented that it was a 'lovely photograph', they were 'beautiful children', or they 'looked very together, very happy'. Sometimes this was what persuaded adopters to take a larger number of siblings. One proud adoptive father produced the actual photograph, now enlarged and framed, which had persuaded him and his wife to take four siblings. He commented:

Look at that picture! That picture just glowed (. . .) Once you've seen that picture, could you seriously consider splitting that group up? (Adopter 34)

Being involved in preparing their profile could also be very reassuring for the children. One adopter described how the children's social worker had used this as a way of preparing the older children for adoption:

She understood what they needed and she involved them in everything – like writing the advert for Be My Parent. They chose what was said about them, they chose the picture. She tried to give them as much control as possible (. . .) They needed a lot of information to feel safe. (Adopter 2)

Resemblance to the adopters

Almost a third (12) of the adopters were pleased that one or all of the children resembled them physically – i.e. they looked as though they could have been their biological children. Usually they commented on the colour of the children's hair and eyes, but sometimes similarities were so marked that the adopters described this as "uncanny" or "terrifying". Resemblance was often a key factor when adopters looked at a photograph and immediately knew that these children were right for them, as one explained:

> We both were equally drawn to their picture. We could not stop looking at their picture (. . .) I think it was like love at first sight (. . .) They stood out, if that makes sense. We were drawn to them; we felt they looked like us. (Adopter 37)

According to one adopter it was like looking at 'a member of your family', and others speculated that because of this resemblance (which was often apparent to other people) they had been drawn subconsciously to the children:

> I do think psychologically you are drawn to children that are very similar to you because, you know, you could say that these could be our children. They come and say, 'Oh, you can see she's your daughter, she's got your eyes.' (. . .) It was just this, sort of like, inner feeling that these are your children. Yeah, it's a gut reaction. (Adopter 11)

Social workers may have taken account of this resemblance when looking for suitable profiles. Two adopters stated that the children were in the first profile that their social worker had shown them. In both cases the children had a strong physical resemblance to the adopters but other factors also made this a good match.

Feeling a connection with the children

Fourteen adopters (38%) knew straight away that these were the right children for them, but this was not always due to a physical resemblance. The written information in the profile and the child permanence reports could be crucial in enabling adopters to feel some connection or empathy with the children. The following comments were made by two adopters, who were not shown a photograph of the children initially:

> We just felt such a great connection with them, that we just wanted them, didn't we? We just knew it was something about the information, what we'd heard about, what we'd read about the girls . . . (Adopter 32)

> [Child] just sounded like a carbon copy of me at that age. (Adopter 27)

Usually, it was information about what the children liked and the activities they enjoyed that stimulated this reaction:

> . . . when we had their forms, there were so many things in there which almost made us laugh, because there were lots of things the girls particularly like doing that were very 'me', because I used to be a very girly girl, and they both love singing and I love singing (. . .) and I'm mad about shoes and bags, just so many funny little things . . . (Adopter 26)

The age and mix of children

In cases where the adopters were not irresistibly drawn to one sibling group, choosing suitable children generally became a process of elimination, which several adopters described as awful. One couple had a possible link to 22 sibling groups, so their social worker halved that list and then got them to draw up a final shortlist of three whose social workers they wanted to meet. They hated having to choose, but finally decided that it would be better to have a mixed group rather than a single-sex group.

Ten adopters said that the age and gender of the children had been critical factors in reaching a decision. Some specifically wanted young children because they thought they would be healthier and it would be easier to bond. However, others chose older children because they wanted children who could talk or they thought that caring for a baby would not be practical for them. A couple in their fifties liked the idea that an older sibling group 'were roughly the right age for them to be our birth children'. These adopters also recalled 'a very telling comment' by their social worker that 'if you have a baby you don't know what the outcome will be [medically], but if you have older children you have a baseline on which to work.'

Being chosen for specific children
Interestingly, six adopters thought they had been recruited for a specific sibling group, although this was not always clearly stated by the adoption agency. For example, one adopter, who had initially wanted two children, felt that she and her husband had been "ear-marked" for a sibling group of three. She explained what she considered to be the LA's "marketing strategy". Apparently the social worker asked them to consider a scenario: what if you adopt two and the birth mum then has a baby? They responded positively to this question, and the following week they were asked if they could take the three siblings, whom they subsequently adopted. Another couple described how keen their LA social worker was to match them with a specific sibling group:

> . . . as soon as we said that we had three bedrooms and we would take up to three, [local authority] said, 'Right, we've got these three children,' and then explained who they were, what they were, what their names were, before we'd even been approved! (. . .) So we never had any choice of any children, which ones to adopt. It was always, 'We're taking you through to adopt [these children].' (Adopter 9)

The adopters were generally happy to go along with these proposals because they really wanted children. However, some of them had faced major difficulties, which may have been avoided if they and their social worker had given more consideration to whether these were the right children for them.

Interestingly, the lesbian couple were warned by their VAA social worker that they were likely to face prejudice. However, their sexuality was apparently viewed as an advantage by an LA social worker, who linked them with three children whose birth mother 'had too many boyfriends coming to the house'.

What information did the adopters receive, and was it helpful?

Adopters were asked what information they had been given about the children, their histories and their family background before placement. Table 10.2 shows the source of the information and how adopters rated the helpfulness of the information. The age of the children influenced where information came from. Children placed with LA-approved adopters were younger and many were not at school, so teachers' reports were not available but, surprisingly, only four adopters said they had received information from a health visitor. Social workers provided a lot of information, for example, by giving the adopters copies of the child permanence report, photograph albums and life story books, or by allowing access to case files. Some adopters were given access to psychiatric reports on the birth parents as well as mental health assessments of the children. Information was also provided verbally by social workers and foster carers.

It is worth noting that an American study involving 873 adopters (Brooks *et al*, 2002) found that the adoption service which they considered most important was the provision of 'information on child's social, medical and/or genetic history'. This need for accurate comprehensive information was felt very keenly by the sibling-group adopters in our study: they wanted to know exactly what difficulties they might face before taking on such a huge commitment. For example, a couple who were matched with three siblings needed reassurance from a medical adviser that one of the children did not have learning difficulties, because 'that would seem like an even bigger task'.

Child permanence reports

Child permanence reports were made available to all adopters, and nearly all of them found this information helpful. Several VAA

Table 10.2
Information about the children given to the adopters by source and helpfulness

Source	LA adopters (n = 17) %		VAA adopters (n = 20) %	
	Received	Helpfulness	Received	Helpfulness
Child permanence report	100	94	100	95
Foster carers	94	88	100	100
Social workers	94	82	95	90
Medical reports	88	65	90	75
Teachers	53	41	85	75
CAMHS reports	35	17	30	20
Birth parents	29	18	40	25
Child appreciation day	23	23	50	50
Access to case files	12	6	25	25
Other	12	12	10	10

adopters were impressed by the efforts their social workers had made to obtain information about the children's family, the children's history, and their education and health. Unfortunately, one LA adopter had no opportunity to mull over this information because she was only allowed to read the reports in the children's services office. Another adopter claimed that the reports 'created a fictitious idea of the children'. Having an adoption social worker who could decode the professional jargon was sometimes very helpful, and one adopter was grateful that her social worker 'put it in speak that we can understand'.

Medical information
The majority of the adopters had received medical reports on the children, and one couple 'had a three-hour meeting with the medical officer, which was excellent'. However, there were also nine complaints: that medical reports had not been provided until after the

children were placed; that adopters were given only verbal information; that medical reports were too basic or out of date; that adopters had to "push" for this information; or that children's red health books charting medical care were missing. Two adopters expressed concern that serious eyesight problems had not been detected in foster care, and both stated that if there had been any further delay in obtaining treatment, the damage could have been permanent. Again, there was concern that professionals were unduly pessimistic about the children, and one adopter thought this approach could reduce children's chances of being adopted:

. . . if you read all their medical reports, you would think that things are so dire (. . .) so negative, and it was an issue we actually brought up at the time and subsequently. The response to that was that the paediatrician always paints the worst case scenario and the most negative picture, because anything else would be a bonus (. . .) I think it would put many adopters off. I think many children might not be adopted. (Adopter 26)

Reports on the children's mental health had been completed in about a third of cases. The adopters appreciated specialist reports, which gave them some understanding of the relationships between the siblings and prepared them for what to expect, as in the following statement:

They [the VAA] hired a psychologist to do some sort of risk assessment profiles on the children and, you know, we went through them to see whether or not the children were going to be good matches with us and how difficult or easy they were going to be, and the differences in the children (. . .) That was really, really helpful. (Adopter 1)

However, it was striking that many of the CAMHS reports were poorly received by the adopters. Sometimes this was because the views expressed were considered unhelpful or the adopters had the impression that the report had been written by someone who did not know the children, as in the following statement:

We met the psychologist, which was a waste of time. She didn't have a clue . . . she didn't appear to know [the children]. Her reports had delayed the process, because she had originally suggested they should be separated. (Adopter 31)

Information from social workers

The children's social worker usually discussed at length the sibling group and each individual child with the adopters, and this inform-ation was described as invaluable when the social worker knew the children well. However, one couple said they had never met the children's social worker, and a few other adopters got the impression that the social worker hardly knew the children at all. In a case where the social worker apparently visited the children only twice a year, the adopter commented:

. . . it would have been helpful to know more about how they were taken into care. In the end, myself and a CAMHS worker sat down and went through all the information ourselves and pieced together what actually happened. When I asked the social workers why they were taken into care, what was the trigger, they gave me a different answer to what the information looked like when we mapped it out (. . .) a totally different picture. (Adopter 33)

Other adopters complained about the quality of information, part-icularly when there had been changes of social worker. As with the health professionals, some social workers were reported as being very pessimistic about the children's potential. This put the onus back on the adopters (should they choose these children or not?) and left them feeling unsupported and unsure. Adopters sometimes concluded that it was safe to go ahead, because they believed that neglect was less harmful than abuse or thought that there was no evidence of any special needs. Unfortunately, these assumptions were not always correct.

Information from foster carers

Nearly all of the adopters appreciated the information that foster carers were able to provide about the sort of food the children liked, bedtime routines, the things they enjoyed doing, and their other likes and dislikes. Indeed, some adopters said they had based their entire understanding of the children's needs on what the foster carer had told them. This was important in helping them to prepare for the children's arrival. However, there could be problems when foster carers wanted to keep the children – and in these circumstances the adopters were not always confident they were receiving accurate information.

Information from the birth family

About a third of the adopters had met the birth mother or some other member of the birth family. Often they did not find this very helpful, and one adoptive father said he had some difficulty in bonding with a child who strongly resembled her birth mother. However, other adopters thought this was an important thing to do for their children, because it gave them 'an insight' into their past experiences, enabled them to 'empathise more with the children', and made it easier to defuse situations when one of the children wanted to 'put [the birth mother] on a pedestal'.

Child appreciation days

A child appreciation day provides an opportunity for the adopters to meet the team responsible for the children's care and the key people involved with the children. All the adopters who had attended a child appreciation day (14) had found it helpful, and some said it was "brilliant" or "fantastic". To hear what the children had endured from people who knew them well had quite an impact. It also enabled adopters to ask questions, to discuss issues and to have information verified. One adopter said that this had dispelled 'a doubt in [her] mind as to whether or not these children should have been removed from the birth parents'. Social workers in one LA put up large photographs of the children, which made it easier to discuss them as individuals. Here is a description of a very successful child appreciation day:

> *. . . they organised especially for [us] a whole day where we met everyone, everyone who had been involved in their care (. . .) people who had known them and could tell us in person something about their history, and about their character, and about their nature (. . .) The really big thing about that was just how warm everyone felt towards them, and how much potential they felt that the children had, and how much they felt that investing in these children would really bring them on and make them wonderful adjusted adults.* (Adopter 19)

It is worth noting, however, that two child appreciation days were less well organised. One adopter said that 'every single person involved with the children was wheeled into the room at some point', so it was 'a whole day literally of people in and out'. Another couple were frustrated that 'everybody was talking about the birth mother (. . .) and we just wanted to know about the children. The last person that spoke was the foster mother.'

Being allowed to view the children's files

Only five VAA approved adopters and two LA approved adopters had been given access to the children's files, and while six found this helpful, one did not. The latter adopter was suspicious about what had been removed before she had been allowed to read the files. Other adopters had been told that viewing the files was prohibited, although their social worker had sometimes read the files and fed back information.

Did the adopters think any information was missing?

Most adopters, 76 per cent of LA adopters and 60 per cent of VAA adopters, stated that they had not been given all the information that they should have received. Only 11 (29%) were satisfied that they had received all the necessary information. While these are alarming findings, it is possible that in some cases social workers did not possess all the relevant information. Research has also shown that adopters do not always absorb information when emotions are running high (Selwyn *et al*, 2006]. One VAA manager commented:

It is unbelievable how big the gaps are in the children's recorded history, and often we learn about things later – and you think where did that come from! And, of course, that gives the adopters the impression that things have been withheld, whether they have or not. (VAA 6)

Many adopters complained that vital information was missing or was provided very late in the adoption process. For example, one couple were only told after being matched with the children that the three siblings were living in separate foster homes and had not really met each other. Two other adopters were not told about sexual abuse or a serious medical condition until they were being introduced to the children. Failure to provide essential information about the children's circumstances, or about medical or behavioural problems, could give the adopters a false impression, and make it harder for them to know how to respond to the children's needs. This could have serious consequences, as in the following case:

We did not know that [child] had cocaine in his urine (. . .) We did not know the birth mother had taken drugs whilst pregnant (. . .) We didn't know that all three children had witnessed domestic violence. We found that out at the disruption meeting last month. I remember asking, specifically asking, if the birth mother had been taking heroin when she was pregnant, and being told quite categorically that no she hadn't, so it was quite a surprise that this has all come out of the files. (Adopter 13)

Six adopters said they had not been given sufficient information about why the children had been removed from their birth parents, and they were concerned that this would cause problems later. One adopter, who claimed that the child permanence report 'didn't suggest that anything was wrong at all', offered a possible explanation:

It's almost like, because the dogma is one should never criticise the birth family, social workers take this to the extreme and have sort of written out any potential criticism of the birth family from the paperwork which we've got. Well, unfortunately, that's going to leave us with quite a challenge when it comes to explaining to the children why they were taken away. (Adopter 4)

This failure to explain clearly why children had to be removed from their birth parents can indeed lead to significant problems later, as the children may conclude that they were mistakenly removed from a loving family. In these circumstances, continuing contact with the birth family may reinforce such beliefs and trigger difficult behaviour, which eventually undermines the adoption (Loxterkampe, 2009). Delays in providing information also created potential problems for the adopters. One couple were concerned that the birth parents might turn up on their doorstep, because they had given their telephone number and address to the older (unadopted) siblings, before being told that these children had direct contact with their parents.

How were the adopters' concerns addressed by social workers?

Over half of the adopters (57%) felt unsure or hesitant about proceeding at some point. Mostly they were concerned about medical issues, the extent of learning difficulties, and the possible long-term effects on the children of exposure to drugs or domestic violence. The way in which VAAs and LAs responded to these concerns varied considerably. The adopters really appreciated social workers who were willing to talk things through, treated their concerns as valid, and could advise them on what sort of behaviour to expect from the children. Having a good relationship with their social worker was crucial in enabling adopters to feel confident about taking on a sibling group, as an LA adopter explained:

... she's our friend and social worker, and we are her equal, and it's been a fine relationship, and it's been because of that rela-tionship that we've been able to sail through this. (Adopter 8)

Ten adopters were satisfied that they had been given the necessary reassurance. However, 11 adopters (30%) said they had not received a satisfactory response. They reported that their concerns had been "brushed under the carpet", that social workers had responded with "platitudes", that they had failed to provide any answers or that they had offered false assurances.

Preparation to meet the needs of specific children

We did not ask the adopters whether they had received preparation to enable them to meet the needs of the specific children whom they were going to adopt. However, the need for targeted and specific preparation emerged as a theme from the interviews. This included the importance of being assessed and prepared for a sibling group and then, after approval, having specific preparation for the particular children who were going to be placed. Adopters who were prepared in this way gave examples of good practice, as in the following statement:

> *Our worker (. . .) produced three packs and in each of them was an A4 sheet of things that may or may not happen. For example, we knew [child] had a food issue. [Our worker] gave a lot of thought to how the girls might be, and individually how they might be when they were first placed. She also gave us information on games and theraplay to try with them and strategies (. . .) She was a huge support as well. (Adopter 30)*

Another couple commented that a psychologist's report was very helpful, 'because she went into the whole dynamics of the family – the fact that one child wanted the attention that another child was getting and their food issues'. They appreciated the information and advice contained in this report, and said that it 'was practical and it prepared us for what to expect'.

However, it is not always necessary to involve a psychologist if adoption social workers have the necessary specialist training. One adopter described how the LA adoption team emphasised the need to establish routines, particularly for children with attachment difficulties. She and her husband had a meeting with the post-adoption support team a week before the children were placed, and a social worker ("an attachment specialist") went through the information about the children, pointing out behaviours they should expect. He then gave them 'the visual timetables, the routines, the kind of things that help the managing of behaviour problems'. Visual timetables substitute pictures for words, so this family had different pictures for things such as breakfast, school, going to the park, playing with play dough or meeting grandparents. Crucially, the children helped to put the timetable together by drawing the pictures, and it was then hung on the fridge so everyone could see what was going to happen each day. This approach was particularly effective with the child who had borne the brunt of adverse experiences in the birth family, as the mother explained:

> . . . actually during our first meeting with the children, we sat down and (. . .) made a visual timetable with the children, so they put in pictures of the things that we were going to be doing during the introductions (. . .) So when we came to doing it at home, about what our family life was going to be like, they knew exactly what it was all about, and they knew that they had that security (. . .) I mean [child] would just sit there on the floor sometimes and just study it, and so he knew exactly what was going to happen and that gave him security. [Social worker] was saying that quite a lot of children, especially when there have been issues with food, like to know exactly (. . .) what they're going to have for pudding or for tea tomorrow. So that then got me into the mindset of thinking, 'Okay, I'm going to plan our meals, so that when I get that question (. . .) I've got an answer.' And it's something that we still do, and (. . .) if ever [child] is having a wobble, he'll just go right back to doing the visual timetables, and after about a week he's happy, he's fine (. . .) Case-specific attachment support before meeting the children I think is a huge bonus. (Adopter 18)

Having decided which children they would like to adopt, the sibling-group adopters could not wait to meet them. In the next chapter we look at how LAs planned the introductions and adopters' experiences of meeting the children and getting to know them.

Summary

- The VAAs sent profiles of their approved adopters to LA family-finders, outlining the adopters' strengths and abilities, what they wanted and what they could offer, and highlighting their willingness to consider taking a sibling group.
- The shortage of adopters willing to take a sibling group meant that those approved for three or more siblings tended to have more choice and less competition.
- Adoption staff were wary of showing photographs of babies to potential sibling group adopters, in case they wanted the baby but were not really interested in the older siblings.
- A third of the adopters were proactive in finding the children they wanted through adoption magazines, but six adopters thought they had been recruited for specific children.
- The adopters were usually attracted by how the children looked in their profile photograph, and sometimes this persuaded them to take a larger sibling group. A third chose children who resembled them. Information about the children's characters and activities also helped adopters to feel a connection with them.
- Adopters said that the most helpful sources of information were foster carers, social workers and the child permanence and medical reports. The 14 adopters (38%) who attended child appreciation days all said this was helpful.
- Only 11 adopters (29%) were satisfied that they had received all the necessary information and many complained that information was missing or provided late in the adoption process. A few thought that they had been given a false impression of the children, which made it harder to meet their needs.
- The adopters really appreciated social workers who were willing to talk things through, treated their concerns as valid, and could advise them on what sort of behaviour to expect from the children. Having a good relationship with their social worker was crucial in

enabling adopters to feel confident about taking on a sibling group. However, 11 adopters (30%) said they did not receive a satisfactory response when they raised issues with their social worker.

- It was very helpful when social workers attended child appreciation days with the adopters and advised them on ways of helping children with attachment difficulties, for example, by establishing routines and using visual timetables.

11 Introductions

In this chapter, adoption agency staff offer their views on how sibling groups should usually be introduced to their adoptive parents and what can help to make this process easier for adopters and children. We then discuss the way adopters were introduced to the children, got to know them, and gradually (in most cases) assumed responsibility for their care. They also comment on whether the plans made by their social workers worked well.

Agency views on the "introductions" plan

Numerous factors will affect how and when introductions take place (e.g. school term times, work commitments and holiday plans), but agency staff stated that the needs of the children should always determine the components of the plan. All the adoption staff stated that they held a planning meeting to discuss the proposed introductions plan, to agree the arrangements, and to ensure that adopters, social workers and foster carers all knew what was expected of them. Respondents thought it was important for the children's social worker and the adopters' social worker to agree a proposed outline before the planning meeting, so that arguments between workers did not take place in front of adopters. Agency staff described a common introductions procedure that can be outlined as follows:

- The children's authority holds a planning meeting where social work staff, foster carers and adopters agree a detailed timetable for the adopters to meet the children and spend time with them.
- Introductions take place over an average 10–14-day period, but the length of time varies according to the needs of the children – it could be shorter for younger children or longer for older children.
- Adopters are nearly always introduced to all the siblings together at the first meeting, which in most cases takes place in the foster

carer's home and lasts for one or two hours. If the children are living in separate foster homes, they are usually brought together for the first meeting.

- The amount of time that the adopters spend with the children each day gradually increases, until they are taking the children out unsupervised for the whole day.
- The timetable specifies times when the adopters get the children up and dressed, make meals for them, bath them and put them to bed, and also times for them to get to know each child individually.
- A review meeting takes place halfway through the introductions, so that any issues can be addressed and arrangements changed if necessary.
- A break is usually planned halfway through, so that the adopters have time for reflection and the children have time to say goodbye to their friends.
- During the second week, if the adopters do not live too far away, the foster carer brings the children to the adopters' home so they can see where they will be living and explore their new surroundings before moving in.
- At the end of introductions, the foster carer often drives the children to the area where they will be living, stays overnight in a hotel and then brings them to the adopters' home. Sometimes the foster carer and the children all spend another night in the hotel before the final handover, or the carer remains in the area for a few days afterwards.

Managers, particularly those from voluntary adoption agencies (VAAs), emphasised the need to be flexible during the planning and throughout the introductions in order to respond appropriately to the children's emotional needs. Here are two of their comments:

It depends on the ages of the children, how much contact they have had with each other. Every situation will be unique and you will have to plan how to meet their individual needs. I don't think there is a formula. It's all about being flexible. (VAA 3)

[In one case] the introductions became very fraught because the oldest child was very anxious. He desperately wanted to see where he was going. Although he had photographs of the adopters' house, he needed to go there. So we had to listen to that and shorten the introductions, because things were going pear-shaped (. . .) Once the child saw where he was going, saw the environment, saw the school he would be attending, a lot of his anxiety was gone. But ideally for young children I don't think it should be too drawn out, and for the older child you need to ask what's going on in their mind. (VAA 2)

Adopters' comments on the introductions plan

In real life, children and adults have particular needs, and events do not always go to plan. We asked the adopters about their experiences of being introduced to the children. Most (89%) adopters had attended planning meetings, and usually they stated that the arrangements had helped to ensure that the introductions went smoothly. Satisfied adopters often commented on the careful planning and the ways in which the children's needs were addressed by social workers, as in the following extract:

You had a real sense that all parties were concerned with what would work best for the children (. . .) It was very child focused and as a result it worked really well. (Adopter 4)

The adopters appreciated receiving a copy of the introductions plan in advance. A carefully planned and detailed timetable could be very reassuring for adopters who were feeling overwhelmed, as one adopter explained:

. . . when you're faced with it right at the beginning, when you've only just met [the children], to look at the plan and see 'Oh my God! We're going to be taking them to a rare breeds farm for like a whole day!' You just don't want to look ahead! But then you see the bit where it says, 'And you will make some lunch for

them, while the foster carer goes out in the garden.' So it was all right really. (Adopter 2)

Unfortunately for one couple, the plan was not finalised until 5pm on the last working day before the start of introductions. Two of the children's authorities also decided to renege on financial agreements just before the introductions – one refusing to provide a hire car and the other urging the adopters 'to take no financial support'. The adopters were able to deal with these situations assertively, but one couple said they had come close to pulling out.

The adopters tended to be scathing about local authorities (LAs) that stuck rigidly to the agreed plan when it was not working well, and sometimes they took action themselves to resolve the problem. In one case, where a baby was very attached to her foster carer, the social worker recommended that the adopters should be allowed to stay overnight at the foster carer's home and start taking the baby out for a short time on their own after gaining her trust. However, the manager would not agree to any change in the plan. In the end, the foster carer and the adopters decided to implement the social worker's suggestion anyway, and the adopter said that the change of plan "worked beautifully".

Accommodation and transport – agencies' and adopters' views

Four of the five LA respondents said they would book self-catering accommodation for the adopters in preference to booking a hotel. This was because 'hotels don't really work for sibling groups', while providing self-catering accommodation, such as a large mobile home, would give the adopters "some freedom" to spend time alone with the children. One LA manager expected the adopters to make their own booking but offered to pay for some overnight stays in a hotel near the foster home, even if the adopters did not live far away, because they would be 'exhausted and emotionally drained' by the introductions.

VAA adopters were significantly more likely to live many miles away from the local authority that was placing the children, in comparison with LA adopters who were more likely to adopt children from the same area.[9] This had implications for the planning of introductions. The adopters really appreciated authorities that made all the necessary arrangements, because this meant they could concentrate on getting to know the children. Most of them also liked having self-catering accommodation, especially when the weather prevented them from spending much time outside with the children. One adopter commented:

> The girls' local authority arranged for us to have a cottage (. . .) because it was January, cold weather, and it was wet and windy (. . .) and so we'd have a place to go back to that was comfortable for us all to relax and start to get to know the girls (. . .) That worked really well. (Adopter 32)

Many adopters, however, were offered hotel accommodation by their children's LA, and sometimes they found this very restrictive, as the following statements indicate:

> . . . introductions are hell (. . .) How can you meet a child, when you're staying in a hotel? (Adopter 8)

> . . . thank goodness the weather was good enough to be out and about, because I think we would have really struggled if it was wet (. . .) because we only had a hotel room as a base, which we couldn't take children to. (Adopter 5)

Most of the adoption staff did not think it was a good idea for the children to stay overnight with the adopters in short-term accommodation, because they might think it was their new home. This was borne out by the experience of two adopters who had the children for overnight stays in their rented accommodation. In one case, the adopters thought that the younger children were a little bit unsure whether this was where they were going to live, and the other adopters

---

9 χ^2 (1) = 4.852, p<0.05

said their holiday let was cold and dirty, and the children could not sleep because they were frightened.

Sometimes staff at the children's local authority did not seem to give much thought to booking accommodation for the adopters and making sure that it was conveniently located. One couple said they had driven 2,500 miles in three weeks, partly because their rented cottage was 'miles from anywhere'. Another couple had to search at night for alternative accommodation because the hotel booking had not been made, and two adopters said *they* had arranged the booking because their social worker was so indecisive. Arrangements were always more difficult when siblings were living in different foster homes, as the adopters could spend most of their time driving from one foster home to the next. This was a contributory factor in the following case, which is an example of how *not* to do introductions:

Case example
The three children were placed separately with three foster carers who did not live close together. The social worker did not know the children well and initially took the adopters to the wrong house. The adopters found a hotel but the LA said it was too expensive. As a result, they had to stay in Travelodges, which were booked up so they had to change hotels about four times during the two weeks of introductions. The adopters were expected to drive from one house to the next, doing bedtime and breakfast routines with each child individually. On the last day they had to drive to the three different foster homes to pick up the children, and they had to wait for the social worker, who was an hour late. Then they had to drive home (a five-hour journey). Their adoption social worker turned up to check how things were going within half an hour of their arriving home, and the adoptive mother commented, 'I could have happily bit her head off.' (Adopter 14)

Transport
Three LA managers said they would arrange transport for the adopters if necessary, but it was clear that the other two expected the adopters

'to have their car sorted by the time introductions start'. If this was not the case, the adopters' social worker would negotiate with the children's local authority about payments for a hire car and/or child car seats.

Many of the adopters interviewed in this study confirmed that they already had a car that was large enough to take the children. However, they wanted to be told in advance what expenses would be covered and to be reimbursed within a reasonable time. Unfortunately, one couple were still waiting a year later for their travel expenses to be paid.

The first meeting between the adopters and the children – agencies' and adopters' views

For a third of adopters (33%), the "first" meeting was a private event with just the foster carer present; 43 per cent had the children's social worker and the foster carer present; and in a few cases (7) the first meeting involved several people. One adopter described this as the "world and his wife" looking on. Generally, the first meeting with the children took place in the foster carers' home, as this was the place where the children were most likely to feel comfortable. Agency workers thought it was important for the children to see the foster carers welcoming the adopters into their home, so that they in turn felt able to accept the adopters. However, in two cases, the foster carer was not present at the first meeting, and instead the first meeting took place in the agency office.

The introduction process was often described as "unreal" by both adopters and adoption agency staff because of the tensions and anxieties ('like the morning before a wedding') and the adopters' sense of having to perform in front of other people. Adopters described their experiences in the following ways:

> To be honest, it was not a very pleasant experience, very awkward, like being in a goldfish bowl (. . .) It's very strange, walking into a house to meet three children that we knew a lot about and they knew about us, but we'd never actually seen them, and we were supposed to have a very perfectly natural

meeting with them under the scrutiny of four other adults, all watching (. . .) I think from the others' point of view, they were watching a very touching moment – 'Oh, isn't it cute that the children have got a family now!' – but it was very embarrassing. (Adopter 1)

I mean, when you first hear about it, they say, 'Do an hour, an hour and a half the first time.' You think, 'An hour and a half! For goodness sake!' But I can tell you, after an hour and a half I needed to lie down in a darkened room, because of emotional fatigue on both sides! (Adopter 35)

Some of the adopters' social workers chose not to attend the first meeting, perhaps because they were aware of the pressure on the adopters or were confident of the foster carer's ability to handle the situation. However, the children's social worker was usually there to see how the children reacted to the adopters. If the adopters' social worker was not present, they would phone the adopters later in the day to ask how everything was going. Some adoption staff emphasised the importance of allowing adopters to express any feelings of uncertainty at this point, as one social worker explained:

Sometimes adopters feel that they are on a conveyor belt and they cannot get off, and I think that first meeting when they meet the child, they have a gut instinct whether the chemistry is there or they just feel ambivalent towards the child. You know, these feelings need to be explored. (VAA 2)

It is perhaps worth noting that in one of the two placements that disrupted later, the adopters had serious concerns about a child's behaviour right from the first meeting, but said that they were told by social workers, 'That's just the way she is'.

Most of the adoption agency staff and the adopters emphasised the importance of all the siblings being introduced together at the first meeting, even when the siblings were living apart. This was thought to be necessary to prevent resentment, jealousy, any suspicion of favouritism, or the establishment of a "pecking order". One manager explained the reasoning for this policy as follows:

Where siblings have been fostered separately, they are always brought together for the first meeting [. . .] It's something about power and importance between the siblings, and you don't want to create a huge imbalance there. You want them all to be equally important in that first meeting. (VAA 6)

However, two LA managers said that children might be introduced separately if they had been fostered separately.

The length of introductions

While introductions lasted on average 10–14 days, three weeks was not unusual for older children and a shorter time was sometimes considered appropriate for younger children or where great distances were involved. Introductions could be more relaxed when the children were not living too far away from the adopters. For a couple who adopted a sibling group (aged 5–8 years), the process seemed very natural, and they described getting to know the children gradually over a three-week period as being 'like the tide coming in'. Another couple who adopted four children (aged 6–12 years) refused to have a solid block of introductions but met the children at weekends, while building work was done to their house. They thought this had worked very well, and having two siblings to stay at alternate weekends also gave them a good opportunity to get to know the children as individuals.

In two cases, the time allowed for introductions was less than a week, which was too short and overwhelming. In one case where the introductions took only five days, the adopter said that the oldest child later admitted she had not wanted to come to their house because she did not really know them. After only three days of introductions, the other adopter commented:

It couldn't have been worse. Literally, they met us for a very short period of time, then they were deposited with us and basically told, 'That's that!' I do feel for them. It must have been absolutely horrendous for them. (Adopter 17)

The role of the foster carer – agencies' and adopters' views

All the LA staff spoke about the need for foster carers to be fully involved in planning the introductions, and some thought that foster carers might need to have a "buddy" or a more experienced foster carer to help them through the transition, as the children moved to being cared for by the adopters. One LA manager emphasised foster carers' crucial role:

[Foster carers] really are the centre of the care team, you know, so they need to know what's going on (. . .) They need to be supported to do their bit of work around keeping the memory box for the children, keeping photos for the children and working with the child's social worker around life history and life story books. I think there's absolutely no doubt about it – the foster carers are really key people for the adopters . . . (LA 3)

However, social workers were also very aware that some foster carers struggled to manage their own feelings of loss and, as the introductions usually took place in their home, the foster carers were 'in a very strong position to make things easier or harder'.

Most adopters (86%) described the foster carer as supportive and helpful, and only five disagreed with this. Adopters particularly appreciated foster carers who welcomed them into their home, who were enthusiastic about the adoption and had prepared the children well, who stepped back so that they could have time alone with the children, who made it clear to the children that the adopters were mum and dad but also quietly offered support, and who concealed their emotions when they finally handed the children over. One adopter commented:

The foster mum, she's very experienced (. . .) and she makes sure that when they come, you know, she's foster mum and she's helping them to find a new family, and she's looking after them and finding them someone nice, which is lovely. She said to the children, when [. . .] we were taking them, you know, 'I told you I'd find you someone nice. Aren't they lovely?' (Adopter 20)

One couple, who adopted three children under the age of three, really valued the experience of the foster carer, who spent a lot of time telling them about the children's routine and their likes and dislikes. The adopters kept to exactly the same routine, and used the same bowls, cutlery, clothing, bedding and even the same washing powder to promote the children's sense of stability and continuity. In this and other cases involving babies, the foster carers sometimes invited the adopters to stay overnight so that the baby could get used to being cared for by the adopters at night.

It is a testament to the positive relationships that eight foster carers (22%) had established with the children and the adopters that their families had remained in contact, sometimes for years. In one case, where the placement had disrupted and the oldest child had returned to live with his original foster carer, the adoptive mother commented:

That's been one of our saving graces – being close to the foster carer. She's always been that point of support for me [. . .] and she's always giving that message to the kids that you can love somebody and they can love you back, and when you move out of their house, it doesn't mean to say that that's the end of the relationship. And I think that is what's helping our eldest son at the moment. We are maintaining those strong, strong links with him. (Adopter 13)

Encountering difficulties with foster carers during introductions

Despite describing foster carers as supportive in many ways, a third of the adopters (12) had experienced some problems with the foster carer, and this included five who did not think the foster carer had been helpful at all. Some of the adopters felt uneasy in the foster home. They were very aware that the children looked to the foster carer to meet their needs and make decisions, while they felt like visitors and were worried about being intrusive, as one adopter explained:

... you never feel like you're actually relaxing because everything is taking place at the foster carer's home, and although she stepped back a lot, there was very much a case of how much are we taking over? (Adopter 18)

Tensions were almost inevitable when the foster carers had wanted to keep the children or the children were securely attached to them. Children who had been allowed or encouraged to call their foster carer "mummy", found it confusing to be introduced to a new "mummy". Some foster carers were so reluctant to hand over the children that the adopters were unable to bath the children, put them to bed, or even hold them during introductions. One foster carer brought the children to the adopters' house for the final handover, but was then 'completely adamant that she was not going to leave the children' so she took them back home again! Another foster carer made it clear that she did not consider the adopters to be suitable candidates and she interrogated them in front of the social worker about their motivation. In another case, the social worker warned the adopters that the foster carer had sabotaged a previous placement, so they were at least prepared for what was 'a very difficult goodbye'. A similar warning might have been appropriate in the following case:

I expected [the foster carers] to act professionally and they didn't. I didn't expect to have to deal with weeping, wailing, unreasonable adults, who were more interested in their own feelings than the feelings of the children. (Adopter 28)

Four adopters described situations in which foster carers appeared to be "working the system" or offering a very poor standard of care. They spoke about children being given poor-quality food while the foster family had better meals; 'three children sleeping in a room no bigger than an airing cupboard', children being 'locked in their room at night' or having 'dreadful nits and no clothes'. Sometimes adopters were annoyed that social workers seemed incapable of dealing with hostile or uncaring foster carers, but one couple observed:

Unfortunately, when there's a large sibling group placed with foster carers, the local authority is basically helpless (. . .) They have no choice. There was nowhere else to put these children. (Adopter 8)

Preparation of the children – agencies' and adopters' views

While the children's social worker has a crucial role in preparing the children for adoption, how the children view this prospect is also likely to depend on the efforts of the adopters and the foster carer. As one LA worker explained:

Adopters now make books for the children and DVDs of themselves, their house and their dog, whatever's important (. . .) Children like getting a book of their own, and adopters are very careful about how they pitch it really, you know, giving a little more information for older children and more pictures depending on the age of the child and what they're into. So they take guidance from the foster carer and from us – whether to have it in a ring-binder or a tiny little book or something soft or hard (. . .) Some children need to see every room, bathroom and loo, and other children they need to see maybe cooked dinner or whatever. (LA 5)

Some adopters in this study took this further by having photographs of themselves enlarged and made into jigsaws or place mats, so that the children would be able to recognise them easily. Another couple had a photograph taken of themselves with the children during the introductions, and this was on the kitchen mantelpiece when the children arrived at their new home – much to their astonishment and delight.

Adopters who were pleased that introductions had gone well often commented that the foster carer had been very positive and had enabled the children to watch their DVD "again and again". Some foster carers also used other activities to prepare the children for adoption, such as building a model of their new house and devising a timetable of what everyone was doing pictorially each day and the countdown to moving in with the adopters.

However, two families faced major problems because the children's social worker and the foster carers had failed to tell the children why they were being adopted and what was going to happen to them. In one case, the adopters discovered that the oldest child 'thought she was adopted because her parents were poor'. This seven-year-old had been the main carer for her siblings, but apparently the social worker did not think it was "age appropriate" for her to know the truth. In another case the adopter said:

These children were not prepared for adoption. No life story work has ever been done with these children [. . .] So the poor kids had no idea why they were [brought here] other than they'd been told that the foster carers were too old [to look after them], and [the oldest child] thought the foster carers had died, so we had to ring them fairly quickly once the children were here to allay their fears [. . .] They didn't know what foster care was and they had no idea what a mummy and daddy were. (Adopter 17)

Being "claimed" by the children

When the children were delighted to see their new parents for the first time, it was very clear to the adopters that the foster carer had prepared them well:

. . . your immediate thing is will these children like us? [. . .] and these children, these two girls came, just came and grabbed us and pulled us into the house and we were off, you know, and that's got to be down to the foster carers and how the foster carers work it, and that was just fantastic. (Adopter 11)

In particular, the adopters were thrilled when the children spontaneously called them "mummy" and "daddy", and in these cases the adoption seemed to get off to a flying start. One adopter described with tears in her eyes how a very young child, who could only say two words, had pointed at her when she came into the room and said "Mummy!" Another adoptive mother said that one boy had bonded with her 'from the moment he set eyes on me', and she commented that nothing would ever outstrip the way she felt about this child. Adopters who were able to "claim" the children without any difficulty could not explain why: they just appeared to "click". This replicates a finding in a study of foster care (Sinclair *et al*, 2005) that some children "clicked" or "fitted" with their foster families.

The adopters had been trained well enough to know that they could not expect the children to accept them as "mummy" and "daddy" immediately, so they often introduced themselves by their first names but said that they would like to be the children's new mum and dad. Older children sometimes refused to call them mum and dad – but oh the joy when they did!

> *[Eldest daughter] said she would never be able to call us mum and dad – and the first person to call me mum was my eldest daughter! Because it's what she really wanted, and once she did it, the others followed suit.* (Adopter 19)

While it was harder for the adopters to establish an emotional connection with a child who was wary and withdrawn, a VAA manager pointed out that it is normal for children to be wary of strangers 'compared to this almost indiscriminate delight of meeting new mummy and daddy that you get, if children are well prepared'. She stressed the importance of exploring this issue with the adopters, acknowledging their need to be claimed by the children, but also helping them to appreciate the children's feelings.

Reviewing the plan for introductions and placement

The adopters appreciated a review of the plan, where the children's authority was willing to make changes in order to meet the needs of the children or to address issues. However, 20 per cent of the VAA adopters and 35 per cent of the LA adopters said they were given no opportunity to discuss their concerns. Several adopters expressed frustration with LA managers who would not change the plan, even when the adopters thought there was a good reason to do so. Adopters who had experienced problems with foster carers sometimes felt unable to raise this issue with the children's authority because they did not have the social worker's phone number and the foster carer was present at the review. In one case, the review was held at the end of the introductions, so there was no opportunity for any problems to be addressed.

Having been introduced to the children, the adopters wanted to take them home. In the next chapter we look at how the adoption agencies planned the transition and placement of the sibling groups, and the adopters will provide their views on whether this was handled well.

Summary

- The introductions lasted on average 10–14 days, and usually took place in the foster home. The amount of time that the adopters spent with the children gradually increased, as they took over responsibility for their care, e.g. making meals, bathing them and putting them to bed. Arrangements were always more difficult when the children were living in separate foster homes, as the adopters had to drive from one home to the next.
- Two sibling-group adopters, whose introductions took a week or less, said this was too short and overwhelming.
- The adopters were introduced to all the siblings together at the first meeting, but the plan usually specified times for them to get to know each child individually.
- VAA adopters were statistically significantly more likely to live many miles away from the children's authority, and some had to travel great distances, especially when siblings were living in separate foster homes.
- The adopters appreciated LAs who booked conveniently located self-catering accommodation for them, as this meant they had somewhere to relax with the children if it rained.
- The adopters appreciated foster carers who welcomed them into their home, who were enthusiastic about the adoption and had

prepared the children well, who stepped back so that they could have time alone with the children, who made it clear to the children that the adopters were mum and dad but also quietly offered support, and who concealed their emotions at the final handover.

- Although 86 per cent of the adopters described the foster carers as helpful, a third (12) had encountered some difficulties during the introductions, especially when the foster carers could not bear to part with the children.
- Two families faced major problems during the introductions because the children had not been prepared and did not understand why they were being adopted or what was happening.

12 Transition and placement

The transition between the foster home and the adoptive home is stressful for everyone. Adopters are anxious and concerned to do the "right thing", foster carers can be struggling with feelings of loss, and the children themselves can be fearful of change and of the heightened expectations of the adults involved. Therefore, it is important for everyone involved that the transition is managed well.

The agencies' views on planning the move to the adopters' home

Most of the managers in adoption agencies agreed that children needed time to settle in with their new adoptive parents before starting school. Some managers spoke about starting introductions midway through the summer holidays or extending half-term by a further week, as described below:

You have to balance delay for children with obviously the least disruption to their lives, and so I think for sibling groups you'd always want to use part of a holiday for introductions . . . what we like to do here is (. . .) start, if we can, the introductions mid-way through the summer holidays, so yes they get a bit of time before they go back to school (. . .) Schools are very important for children, friendships are very important for children, so those are the sort of things we'd think about. (LA 3)

However, there also appeared to be a general consensus that if there was too much unstructured time during the school holidays, adopters might struggle to find ways of keeping the children entertained. Having some children at school would give the adopters a breathing space or enable them to spend individual time with a younger child. One manager commented:

People tend to get hooked up with school terms, but in the end I think you have to ditch that and just do what is best for the children and the adopters. For a lot of children, school is their security and school routines can give them a bit of security, while also giving the adopters a break. You have to put in more support, if you are doing this in the school holidays. The children can always have time off school, but not the other way round. (LA 1)

Older children needed time to say goodbye to their friends, and schools could help to make this less stressful or even enjoyable. For example, one teacher invited the adopters into the school and arranged a little farewell party for the children. Whatever the situation, managers said that ideally children should start their new school at the beginning of term. One local authority (LA) manager admitted that, unfortunately, this had not happened in a recent case:

I've got a child now that, if things had been planned a little bit better (. . .) when he started his new school, he would have been in his adoptive placement for at least a couple of weeks. Whereas now, because the planning wasn't that brilliant (. . .) he's got to go back to his old school for a week or two and then when he goes to the new school, all the children have all settled in (. . .) and then he's got to be a newcomer coming in two weeks later, which is always difficult . . . (LA 4)

Another key factor to consider when planning the start of a placement is the availability of support services. Several managers ruled out placements starting on a Friday because services were difficult to access at the weekend. Some also emphasised that they would avoid Christmas or anniversaries that might be difficult for the children.

It was thought important for both adopters to be available to welcome the children to their new home, so managers also had to consider whether adopters would be able to take two weeks off work. This could be complicated, especially when placing children with adopters working in the armed forces, as one manager commented:

For us, if someone was going on deployment, we would make sure that they were back and had a clear run of no deployments before we'd even contemplate a placement (. . .) Or incipient postings, I mean if they were about to move we'd make sure that they'd moved . . . it's not only school holidays we have to contemplate, so I think timing is crucial . . . (VAA 7)

The transition to the adopters' home

Staff in adoption agencies said it was important for children to have an opportunity to explore their new home before the start of the placement – to know what their new bedroom was going to be like, to play in the garden, to meet the family pets and perhaps to see the school they would be attending. They generally agreed that having the foster carer bring the children to the adopters' home and then slowly withdraw could help to reduce anxiety and make it easier for the children to accept the transition to their new family. One manager said:

If adopters collect the children and take them – and usually that's what happens – the children may feel they are being abducted from someone they love. And if the foster carer takes the children to the adopters' house, they may feel they are being abandoned (. . .) You have to get the introductions to the point where the children want to go. For older children, it needs to happen early in the day so they are not going to bed immediately they get there, because that's when they do lots of thinking. (LA 1)

Sometimes there would be only one visit before placement, but one LA clearly favoured having several home visits before the children were placed, as a social worker explained:

. . . the foster carer will bring the child for the first visit to the adoptive home and stay, and then the next day (it's usually very concentrated) come back and just maybe have a coffee and leave the child for a longer period – and then it's down to the adopters ferrying back and forth, which becomes hugely

*exhausting for everybody really over any distance. And depend-
ing on the age of the children, we work out whether they have
overnight stays or not.* (LA 5)

However, in some cases social workers had to compromise because
logistics such as travel arrangements made it difficult for the foster
carer to bring the children to the adopters' home. In these cases, it was
particularly important that the albums and DVDs prepared by the
adopters contained lots of photos of the adopters and their home. The
use of a webcam was also recommended by one social worker:

*I think a webcam is also ideal. I had a situation where the
adopters had a webcam and the foster carers had a webcam,
and the child could talk to his new mummy and daddy through
that, and that helped the transition because he was so familiar
with the house, the room, the voices and everything else. I think
that transition went very well.* (VAA 2)

The adopters' views on transition arrangements

The interview did not include a specific question about foster carers
bringing the children to the adopters' home, but several adopters
stated that this had been very helpful. Some adopters were very
relieved that they had not driven the children to their home, especially
if the children were upset to be leaving their foster carer:

*They all cried nearly all the way down for, you know, eight hours,
whatever it was. I just think it would have been too traumatic for
the children to have said goodbye to their foster carers where
they were, as they were bundled into the car with two strangers
and, sort of, driven off. So I think for the foster carers to bring
them down for us, you know, we didn't question it, and it worked
very well.* (Adopter 5)

In four cases, however, there were problems when children visited the
adopters' home before placement and wanted to stay, rather than
returning to the foster carers' home. In most of these cases the

difficulties arose after a sleepover, and sometimes only one child within the sibling group became distressed, as an adopter explained:

> ... from the moment he set eyes on us, from the first intro-
> duction, [child], as far as he was concerned, we were his parents
> and we were leaving him, and it broke [his] heart when we left
> him each time, and it broke our heart (. . .) He kept on saying to
> me, 'Mum, why didn't you come and get me before?' (Adopter 8)

Sometimes the children had quite a lot of possessions that needed to be transported to the adopters' home. It was important that none of their things were left behind, as one adopter emphasised:

> When we came down half-way through introductions, we brought
> all their clobber (. . .) We were very conscious that whatever they
> had that was theirs had to come with them. (Adopter 7)

Adopters also needed time to adapt their accommodation so that it was suitable for the children. As they were all taking a minimum of three children, this could be a major undertaking that needed to be taken into account when planning the placement. Unfortunately, insufficient time was allowed in the following case:

> Our turnaround time to get a non-child-friendly house ready for
> three children coming was two weeks! We had friends painting
> and parents buying furniture (. . .) I mean we were dead on our
> feet before the children arrived, because we'd been up to
> God knows what hour every night, painting and sorting (. . .)
> and trying to work as well (. . .) It was really a rollercoaster.
> (Adopter 17)

Placement

In this section, we explore the adoption managers' views about how siblings should be placed, the adopters' views on whether the placement arrangements had worked well, and the views of three adopters whose children were placed at different times. The decision about how the children should be moved into the adopters' home was made almost exclusively by social workers: only six adopters were asked for their views on this. However, most of the sibling-group adopters (82%) thought that the way the children had been placed had worked well.

The adoption agencies' views on how siblings should be placed

The five LA managers thought that siblings should generally be placed together, but they all stated that individual circumstances would influence the decision. One stressed that if the children were relying on each other for support, it would not be right to place them consecutively. Managers identified the following factors that might lead to consecutive placements: children being re-united after living in separate foster homes; one child having particularly difficult behaviour; a big disparity in the children's ages, or practicalities such as travel arrangements. If one child was an infant and the other siblings were much older, some LA managers thought that the baby should be placed last. Whatever the situation, LA managers stated that everything should be planned well, with nothing left to the last minute or rushed.

The VAA managers expressed similar views, but tended to be more in favour of simultaneous placements, as in the following statements:

We have never chosen not to move children together. That is our model and it's tough, but we think the risk of having a pecking order is greater. We would put more attention into thinking about how you allow each child to develop a relationship with the parents afterwards, but they all come together. (VAA 6)

We would expect that assessment of attachments would already have been done. At the point of placement, children need to come together, because this is for the rest of their lives (...) There may be a situation where for some properly assessed reason children need to be placed separately, but our experience is that almost always siblings are placed together. (VAA 1)

The adopter's views on the transition and placement

Most (92%) of the siblings had joined their adoptive family all at the same time, but children in three sibling groups had been placed at different times. It is worth remembering that almost half of the children (in 17 of the 37 sibling groups) had not been living together in foster care prior to their adoptive placement.

Children placed simultaneously

In 34 families (92%) all the children in the sibling group were placed simultaneously and most adopters believed that this had been a good decision. Indeed, ten insisted that it would not have worked if the children had been placed consecutively. Some adopters thought that separating the children, even for a short time, would have been harmful, as this adopter stated:

> There was no other option, because (. . .) that's their security, that's all they've ever known (. . .) the three of them together, and what we have always tried to instil in them is that each one of them is important as an individual but all three are important as a group. And to take a child one before another or two before one, there's no way that you could split them up, so that they actually all felt as much worth as the other. (Adopter 18)

Three adopters had refused to consider consecutive placements, two on principle ('. . . we just immediately said no!') and the third because the distance involved would have made it impossible to maintain contact with the child left behind. One adopter insisted that the children needed 'to start life with us together as one family', because otherwise it would have introduced an element of competition or uncertainty – 'Why is he going first and not me?' – which could have undermined their trust in each other.

Adopters had particular concerns about the possible consequences of sequential placement when one child had been acting as a parent to the others. One adoptive mother believed that if the oldest child (always 'the one in control') had been placed first, that would have made the position of the insecure middle child 'a little bit weaker'.

Others thought that placing a "parentified" child first would cause distress and anxiety for all the children. Here are two of their comments:

[The two younger children] looked to [their older brother] for everything, and so he was their security – if [he] says it's all right, then it's all right! So to be together meant that they were safe together, they were in the same boat (. . .) I think being separated would have destabilised them more. (Adopter 16)

[The oldest child] was very protective of the two younger ones (. . .) She was only five and she'd been a mother (. . .) probably since three she was looking after them, she was feeding them and everything. [If she had been placed first] I think she would have been too worried (. . .) She would have wanted to know what the other two were doing, and would she ever see them again? (Adopter 23)

However, this view was not shared by a couple who had experienced a successful sequential placement. Moreover, two adopters who had found it very difficult to bond with a particular child thought this problem might have been alleviated if the siblings had been placed one after the other. An adopter whose oldest son had recently returned to foster care commented:

I think we should have had [the oldest child] initially and spent some time and got him settled with a bit of a bond – then bring in the twins. I think it should have been done much more slowly and systematically, adding one child at a time. We were just living in Numbsville, because they present as very, very much younger. The nightmare of trying to dress three children under the age of four! (Adopter 13)

Placing siblings consecutively

Although it was sometimes suggested by LA managers that there should be gaps between the placements of siblings, consecutive placements were only made in three of the 37 families. Interestingly, in one case the delayed placement of a "parentified" child had apparently worked well, although this was not part of the initial plan. This case involved a sibling group of five, and at first the LA workers decided to separate the sibling group and place only the three youngest children with the adopters, whom they feared might be overwhelmed by the children's needs. Eighteen months later, having failed to find adopters for the two oldest children, the LA social worker asked the couple if they would consider taking them too – and they did. The adoptive mother commented:

All research would say you do not put the younger three in and then the older two, but you know what? It was definitely the right [thing]. I know it was an accident, but if they'd have put the older two in first, I would never have been able to parent the younger three, because the older child had parented the children. She was the one who had stopped them all from dying really. So because I'd had a year and a half of parenting the younger three, by the time [the older two] arrived, I was very well-established as a nurturing mother figure. And if they'd placed all five together, I think it would have been really difficult for me to replace [oldest child] as the main attachment figure (. . .) So I always say, 'If you've got a "parentified" child, don't place them first, place them second.' (Adopter 3)

Sequential placements were planned in two other cases where siblings had previously been living in separate foster homes. In one case, the oldest child was placed a week before her younger siblings, and the adopters said this worked well because it enabled her to establish herself and take on the role of a big sister. The other case involved two older siblings being placed six weeks before the youngest child. The adopter stated:

At the time we were happy with the plan, but with hindsight (. . .) I think it would actually have been better to have [the youngest child] home sooner, because a lot of the tantrums I had from [the oldest boy] were because he was missing his sister. We made a calendar for [him] to cross off each day, but he still couldn't understand why she couldn't come home sooner. I asked about this, but was told there would be no change to the plan. (Adopter 36)

It is clear from these examples that there is not a single "right" way of placing a sibling group. Adopters who had experienced a successful simultaneous placement believed that was the best approach, while those who had experienced a successful sequential placement thought that was best. Agency staff who rely on their own experience of placing sibling groups will probably also reach diverse conclusions, as very few workers will have placed many large sibling groups. It is perhaps worth noting that some LAs may have no experience of placing more than two siblings for adoption – a situation encountered by two of the adopters in our study.

Were the children able to accept their new parents?

Two-thirds (67%) of the adopters said that the children had had some difficulty in accepting them as their new parents. This was to be expected, as the children were older than most children placed for adoption, with ages ranging from under one to 11. Children who had formed strong attachments to their foster carers were understandably bereft, and sometimes they had tantrums or initially refused to let the adopters care for them, as the following statement illustrates:

The youngest one had a secure attachment to his foster carers, as he was there for three-and-a-half years and during that time they were like parents to him [. . .] The tantrums we had in the first four months! Massive. But we could understand because this little boy had been taken away from absolutely everything he loved [. . .] But we worked through it and he attached to me pretty quickly, because I was at home with him full time . . . (Adopter 17)

Children who had assumed the role of a parent to their younger siblings sometimes found it difficult to see the adopter as the person in charge. Several children rejected all the adopters' initial efforts to relate to them because they were determined to remain loyal to their birth mother, as these adopters acknowledged:

Of course, there were massive difficulties in claiming them as my own, because they were eight and six and they were not going to be claimed by anybody, thank you very much . . . Certainly my eldest was extremely guarded and remained so for very many years. (Adopter 3)

The older two (. . .) just did not understand that we were a family now. We feel they never fully believed that this was a family (. . .) They hold their mum up there. Especially in [child's] eyes, I've never been the mum . . . (Adopter 29)

These problems were sometimes exacerbated when foster carers had encouraged the children to call them "mummy" or did not allow the adopters to be directly involved in caring for the children during introductions. One adoptive mother believed that the foster carer's possessive behaviour had contributed to her son's continuing attachment difficulties:

I don't feel that she let go, and it was hard then to take him, if that makes sense. And for a long time when we brought him home, he would say, 'I don't want you, I want Nanny.' (He used to call her Nanny.) 'I want my Nanny!' And it was awful really, and I'd say the first four weeks you put him to bed and he would just cry and cry and cry, because he wanted them. (Adopter 14)

In this chapter, we have looked at how adoption agencies planned the transition and placement of siblings into an adoptive home and how these plans worked in practice. The next chapter focuses on the support the agencies provided for the children and their adopters, and whether it was adequate and effective.

Summary

- Factors taken into account by adoption agencies when planning the start of a sibling-group placement included: the need for children to settle with their new parents before starting school ideally at the beginning of term; the need for both parents to be at home for the first two weeks; and the need to avoid Christmas, any anniversaries that the children might find difficult, and Fridays, because support services would be difficult to access at the weekend.
- Adoption managers said that if there was too much unstructured time during the school holidays, new adopters could find it difficult to keep a sibling group entertained and extra support might be needed.
- Adoption staff agreed that having the foster carer bring the children to the adopters' home and then slowly withdraw could help to reduce anxiety and make it easier for children to accept the transition to their new family.
- Some children were confused or distressed by overnight stays before placement, especially if they did not want to return to the foster home.
- LA managers thought that siblings should generally be placed together to avoid any jealousy or suspicion of favouritism, but all said that how the children were placed would depend on each child's circumstances.
- Factors that might lead to sequential placements included children being re-united after living in separate foster homes; one child having particularly difficult behaviour or a big disparity in the children's ages.
- In 34 families (92%), all the children in the sibling group had been placed simultaneously, and most adopters thought this had been a good decision. Indeed, ten adopters (27%) insisted that it would not have worked if the children had been placed sequentially.
- There appeared to be no single "right" way to place sibling groups.
- Two-thirds (67%) of the adopters said that the children had difficulty in accepting them as their new parents.

13 The provision of support

This chapter considers what support is needed when sibling groups are placed with adopters and whether it is likely to be provided. We report first the views of adoption staff on what support would generally be provided by their agency for anyone adopting a large sibling group. This is followed by an account of the actual support provided to the adopters in our sample and their views on whether the support was helpful.

The adoption agencies' views on support

Taking on three or more children is a significant commitment emotionally as well as financially, so sibling group adopters are likely to need a good support package. Staff in the adoption agencies (five local authorities and nine voluntary adoption agencies) were asked what support would typically be provided to adopters taking a large sibling group.

Financial support

As regular financial support can only be provided by local authorities (LAs), we asked LA managers whether they provided a regular adoption allowance and help with furniture, essential equipment, a larger car or house extensions. Voluntary adoption agency (VAA) managers were asked about their experiences of negotiating financial support for their adoptive families.

Setting-up grants and lump sum payments

Most of the LA managers said they provided a setting-up grant to ensure that adopters had essential furniture and equipment before children were placed. The grant was usually a fixed payment per child or reimbursement for receipts up to a fixed amount. Some LA managers said they provided this for every adopter but there could be some flexibility, as described below:

We always make a grant of up to £500 per child, but (. . .) with a large sibling group it could be you'd have to pay more than that. (LA 3)

One LA had a policy of offering adopters a choice of having either a setting-up grant or an adoption allowance, but not both. The result of this policy was that more of their adopters chose the allowance. While LA managers recognised that having a large enough car to transport three or more children safely was essential, only two said they often contributed to the cost of a larger car. Perhaps this was because some adopters already had a large enough car, but there also appeared to be an expectation that adopters would be self-sufficient. Similarly, there was an assumption that many of those wishing to adopt siblings would already have a large enough house. LA managers said that sometimes they would contribute to the costs of adapting a house to accommodate three or more children, and one manager stated that her authority had paid for a loft conversion in three out of nine sibling-group adoptions. However, LAs were perhaps more likely to pay for housing alterations if they were asking an adopter to take *another* sibling. This was expressed by one respondent as follows:

I think that [paying for an extension] happens more when people have siblings and another sibling joins (. . .) If people come forward for siblings, people expect them to have the accommodation really. (LA 5)

Adoption allowances

All the LA managers said that regular adoption allowances were paid to most sibling-group adopters. Adoption allowances were usually means tested, but LAs could pay more if they considered it was necessary for the children's welfare. One manager made it clear that their approach to providing financial support was flexible:

The allowance is generally time limited, but for larger sibling groups it is more likely to be ongoing and wouldn't necessarily stop when the youngest child goes to school. (LA 1)

Four of the five LA managers thought that the amount of financial support needed to be sufficient to enable one parent to stop working in order to care for the children. However, they also stated that they were not able to do this for all sibling-group adopters. VAA managers, who typically deal with LAs all over the country, were not so confident that adequate financial support would be provided. Their staff highlighted variations in practice, what this could mean for adopters, and how they tried to deal with impervious LAs, as the following statements illustrate:

> We argue with local authorities all the time about practical things (. . .) Most adopters are very embarrassed to talk about money (. . .) Our experience is that adoption allowances are really a thing of the past. They won't get an allowance up to age 18 and may even have difficulty in getting the allowance in the first three years. (VAA 1)

> Some local authorities are like getting blood out of a stone. We would send a manager in those cases and try to get the best deal we can for the family. (VAA 3)

VAA staff thought it was important to check early on in the process what financial support would be provided, because this could affect the viability of the placement, as one manager noted:

> . . . very occasionally we have come across authorities who think you can place three or four children in the family with a zilch package, which is totally astounding (. . .) Some of our families have been quite affluent, but even so it's a huge step up to support three or four children. Sometimes we have had to withdraw at the beginning because the local authority weren't willing to provide any support. (VAA 6)

Another VAA manager deplored the increasing reluctance of LAs to pay adoption allowances and spelt out the implications for adopters and foster carers, and also (indirectly) for siblings:

. . . LAs do not want to have to pay adoption allowances and my experience is that they're means tested and so in one of the families (. . .) the adoptive mother has returned to work because the adoption allowance rate was not going to be sufficient (. . .) and of course adoption allowances are reviewed annually, so there's no security. If I was a foster carer of three children, I would have to think very seriously before I moved to adopting those three children because of the financial changes, and despite what the regulations say [it's] really difficult to negotiate good adoption allowances. (VAA 8)

There were concerns that if the unwillingness to pay adoption allowances became more widespread, only wealthy applicants would be able to consider taking a sibling group. A London-based VAA manager observed that sibling-group adopters were, in the main, 'families with financial resources'.

Practical and emotional support

Home help

Only three of the five LA managers thought that home help would be needed by sibling-group adopters, and even fewer (2) thought that it would be available. VAA managers said that they struggled to get some LAs to recognise the need for home help, even when the adopters were exhausted and struggling to cope. According to VAA staff, adopters were likely to be viewed as "a bit inadequate", if they requested home help. An LA manager explained that this issue was political as well as practical:

If you have three pre-school children, sometimes we have to do things that politically don't rest well with some people, where we might have to put in a cleaner or something very practical. That's what our adopters tell us will overwhelm you – if you haven't got help with the washing (. . .) ironing, cooking and all those things. (LA 5)

However, adopters sometimes refused to accept the offer of home help because they wanted to be self-sufficient or did not want to have a stranger coming into their home. Two VAA managers suggested different ways of trying to overcome this reluctance:

> *I think they wouldn't want [a stranger coming into their house], but if we had the capacity to perhaps pay somebody in their support network to come and do some housework, etc, that may be more acceptable. (VAA 9)*

> *I have this theory that when children are placed, people get given a book of vouchers, you know, ten hours' ironing, five hours' cleaning, and you just cash them in when you need it (. . .) I think it would be lovely to be able to do it, because I think people would then feel entitled to it (. . .) I don't think we give enough importance to the practical work that's needed for looking after three children in terms of cleaning, washing, filling the fridge. (VAA 8)*

Respite care

There was also great reluctance to provide respite care. Two LA managers said they would never provide respite care for adopters, but the remaining three acknowledged that respite care might have to be provided in extreme cases or to avoid a disruption. Respite care was thought to be inappropriate, especially at the start of a placement, because as one manager said, 'it has the feel of being like a looked after situation' with children being "shipped around". However, a VAA manager commented that respite care could be useful for sibling-group adopters who were struggling, and it did not have to include overnight stays but could be practical help provided during the day, perhaps looking after two siblings so that the adopter could have some one-to-one time with an individual child.

Support in managing contact

All the LA respondents stated that sibling-group adopters were likely to want support in managing contact arrangements, but this was not available for everyone. The following view was typical of the responses made by agency staff about contact:

We would want to encourage them to manage contact themselves. (VAA 3)

Emotional support

Staff in the adoption agencies recognised that emotional support from a social worker would usually be needed and provided. Being able to discuss issues with other sibling-group adopters could also be very helpful, and for this reason all the agencies provided adoption support groups. In addition to this, staff in three VAAs and two LAs mentioned "buddy schemes" or stated that they would put the adopters in touch with other sibling-group adopters. One LA also paid for membership of Adoption UK so that adopters could use the online message board.

Help in managing difficult behaviour

Most adoption staff thought that sibling-group adopters would need help in managing the children's behaviour and group dynamics, but despite this, a third stated that such support was only provided sometimes. This is a worrying response, as challenging behaviour can threaten the stability of a placement. We did not ask adoption staff to describe how they helped adopters to manage difficult behaviour, but a VAA social worker spontaneously offered this comment:

We do provide a high level of practical support as well as giving them practical advice. In one case, I spent a day watching an adopter who was struggling – just watching how she was interacting with the child – and I gave her some feedback. That's quite useful – calm feedback. (VAA 2)

Only one LA adoption manager said that therapy was readily available in their area. Others reported long waiting lists and problems in financing therapy. One manager said they nearly always used private therapists because Child and Adolescent Mental Health Services (CAMHS) had a long waiting list and did not appear to have much understanding of adoption issues. Another LA manager said that having a part-time play specialist made a "big difference", but there were so many children needing therapy that sometimes she was not able to respond fast enough:

> . . . although nine times out of ten she'll put her services in very quickly, there have been times when a crisis has happened and you need her quickly and she might not be able to get there for two weeks or three weeks. So sometimes that has happened and it has proved too late, it's broke down in that time (. . .) But we are luckier than some other boroughs and other agencies, because they'll have to refer out . . . (LA 4)

Support from family and friends

Repeatedly, adoption managers mentioned the need to ensure that sibling-group adopters had enough support, but it was also clear that most of them were assuming that much of this would be provided by the adopters' relatives and friends, as in the following comment:

> You have to have excellent support, and that tends to be family support, because you can't expect your friends to offer the sort of practical support that large siblings groups need when they are first placed. (VAA 2)

This VAA social worker was critical of the notion that initially adopters and children should be left alone to bond. Instead, she preferred to involve close relatives in planning the kind of support that would be needed when the children were placed. She commented:

> You know, when you have a baby, you have a midwife and a health visitor to help you. But when you place three children with adopters, the advice is, 'Back off, because these children need to attach to the primary carers. If you have too many people around the adopters, it's going to confuse the children.' Well I'm sorry, but you cannot manage the needs of three children day in day out in an isolated bubble, so if you have a grandmother who can give you two hours off, why can't she be introduced from the beginning? That's what I always ask for. (VAA 2)

Support for children placed outside the local authority area

During the first three years after children are placed for adoption, the responsibility for meeting the cost of support services remains with the children's LA, even if children are placed in an area covered by another LA. It is not unusual for additional needs to become apparent after placement, as an LA social worker acknowledged:

> ... often there's funding needed for things that become apparent when children move. Often it's maybe support around social skills, when children aren't settling and not building relationships (. . .) Maybe they need some one-to-one, and of course (. . .) they are still our responsibility when they're placed for adoption, so we would be funding and supporting education and therapy outside of [LA area]. (LA 5)

However, arranging support services for children who had moved out of the area was not always easy. VAA staff reported some arguments about which services should be provided, by whom, and for how long.

Multi-agency support

Details about the provision of multi-agency support can be found on pp 92–95.

Providing post-adoption support

Surprisingly, although VAA staff depended on LAs to pay for most support services, they were often more optimistic than LA staff that support would be provided. This may reflect the strength of their advocacy on behalf of adopters. The VAAs were also more likely to emphasise that their support was available "forever" and, while they did not want to be intrusive, they made efforts to keep in touch with their adopters, as one manager explained:

> If we don't hear from them, we contact them to ask how things are going. (VAA 3)

All the adoption managers indicated that support was available for their adopters after the adoption order. Two LA managers said that the whole range of adoption services remained available. Support was also provided through organised events such as picnics and Christmas parties, buddy groups, talks or training courses for the adopters and activities for children, including Saturday activities for older children in one agency. Two LAs arranged an annual conference with well-known speakers.

Some agencies offered an unusually wide range of continuing training and support. For example, one VAA provided an advanced Webster Stratton parenting group, a group for parents of adolescents, a joint workshop for teachers and adopters on adoptive children in schools, and story stem assessments to give adopters some insight into each child's view of family life. Another VAA offered a comprehensive programme of workshops, one-to-one counselling, direct work with children, preparation of children for contact, and support in managing their behaviour.

Adopters' views on the support provided

It is important that prior to placement adopters know what support will be available, and how to access additional support if they need it. Difficulties in obtaining support can increase the stress felt by adopters and may put the placement in jeopardy. In this sample of adopters, slightly more VAA adopters (65%) had their support plan in writing than did LA adopters (59%). However, plans were not always put into action. More than three-quarters of the LA-approved adopters (77%) stated that they did not receive expected services, in comparison with less than a quarter of the VAA-approved adopters (23%). The difference between LA and VAA adopters was statistically significant.[10]

All the adopters were asked to recall what support they had received after the children were placed with them and before the adoption order had been made. Table 13.1 sets out their responses.

Slightly more of the VAA-approved adopters had received financial support. This may be because they had adopted older and more

---

10 χ (1) = 0.744, p<0.008

Table 13.1
Support given to adoptive parents before the adoption order

	LA adopters (n = 17) %	VAA adopters (n = 20) %
Setting-up grant	88	100
Regular adoption allowance	71	85
Support in managing contact	65	63
Adoption support group	59	80
Sufficient funding to allow one adopter to remain at home	53	47
Emotional support for adopters	47	90
Home help	41	40
Support in relation to children's behaviour	35	60
Therapeutic support package	35	30
Place at nursery/playgroup	12	21
Babysitting	0	10
Respite care	0	0

challenging children or because their VAA social worker had negotiated strongly on their behalf with the children's LA.

Financial support

Four of the 37 adopters described their financial support package as generous, and it is perhaps no coincidence that these included the largest sibling groups. These adopters had been given the assurance that the adoption allowance would continue until the children left school or (in one case) university, and one had also received a very substantial payment towards the cost of buying a larger house. They commented that having enough money enabled them to spend more time with the children and also meant they were more self-sufficient and able to buy in their own support (e.g. home help), if necessary. Sometimes it was clear that their social worker had played a crucial role in negotiating the financial package, as the following illustrates:

Our social worker was just excellent . . . she was saying, 'Right, let's get help for cleaning and babysitting.' I was like, 'Well I'm the mum, I'm going to do it.' (. . .) And she was like, 'Well, you know, you're going to be adjusting and you want to make sure you can get as much time with the kids as possible and stuff.' I was really glad we had that. She made it really easy, because I didn't have to think about cleaning the house (. . .) The package was fantastic (. . .) We didn't expect any adoption allowance (. . .) we didn't expect them to buy the car. I would have managed, but it's amazing how much it just really helps to allow you to bond with the children, because it just frees up time. (Adopter 21)

However, some adopters did not find it so easy to obtain payments, as one adopter reported:

We had the settling-in grant, which did not cover the cost of the [double] buggy. They said the one we chose was too expensive. I asked if we could have something towards it – no response. They did give us money towards a car (£5,000) as ours wasn't big enough, but we practically had to beg for it and again it took months. (Adopter 12)

Even when adopters received an adoption allowance, some were still taken aback by the costs of bringing up children, as this adopter commented:

I did feel that the financial package could have been a lot more generous, because I wildly underestimated how expensive children are! (Adopter 1)

Three adopters stated that they were shocked when their LA suddenly reneged on the financial package that had been agreed prior to placement. One adoptive mother had to return to work part time, but after lengthy disputes the other two managed to get the financial package reinstated (see below).

Case example
A couple who had been matched with four siblings were assured by their social worker that the children's LA would provide an adoption allowance and would also pay for a loft conversion and a larger car. A week before they were due to meet the children, the LA was reported by the adopters to have 'backtracked on the lot', refusing to pay for anything. This was distressing for the adopters, but as the children had already been given information about them, they decided to go ahead. They went through the complaints procedure, which took many months, but gradually they managed to obtain almost everything that they had originally been promised. (Adopter 24)

Eight adopters stated that no adoption allowance had been offered. Furthermore, one of these couples received no information about welfare benefits and, as a result, they missed out on 18 months of child benefit payments, which they were unable to reclaim. The decision not to provide an adoption allowance resulted in at least one family getting into debt, but it also had adverse consequences for a sibling, as the adopter explained:

> . . . you don't like to talk about it [money], because you're afraid they will say, 'We'll find someone wealthy to have the children.' At the time we were just so relieved to have the children (. . .) Social Services have asked us if we would like to take the other [sibling], if it becomes available. My husband was adamant we couldn't afford it. (Adopter 12)

Ideally, information about what level of financial support will be provided should be given to sibling-group adopters as soon as possible after linking and matching. One couple, who were otherwise very complimentary about their adoption agency, said their only reservation was that they had to wait until a month before the placement to receive confirmation of the adoption allowance. In the meantime, they had been very worried about how they would care for the children if they did not receive an adoption allowance.

Was the allowance enough to enable one parent to stay at home?
Just under half (47%) of the sibling-group adopters received a high enough adoption allowance to enable one parent to stay at home to care for the children. Most viewed this support as essential, and one commented:

> *I could not have had these three children and had to work. It would have been impossible, so it [the adoption allowance] does provide an income of sorts to enable me to stay home and look after them.* (Adopter 5)

Although one adopter was happy to return to work part time, for others this had been a painful decision. One adoptive mother said she tried to return to work but gave up because it had such an adverse effect on the children:

> *I went back to work for the six weeks and it was complete chaos with the children . . . you know, they lost things, they didn't do their homework, and the fact that they'd come from such a chaotic background, they actually need that structure, so we do believe it's essential that one of us is at [home].* (Adopter 11)

Two couples were still in dispute with the children's authority with regard to funding for one parent to stay at home. Another adopter, who had intended to return to work part time after a year's leave, was horrified when she realised that would probably be detrimental for the children. She eventually persuaded the LA to reinstate the adoption allowance, but only after a struggle:

> *We had a huge mortgage and we were concerned about our finances, but I knew that with me going back to work it would potentially destabilise these children. So, oh my goodness, we had to fight for an adoption allowance. I really said at one stage that we were not going to go through with the adoption order until this was set up, and that didn't go down too well at all!* (Adopter 37)

Practical and emotional support

Before considering what practical support was provided, it is worth noting that a few (6) sibling-group adopters admitted to feeling frightened of what social workers might think or do if they "rocked the boat" or asked for help. These fears arose particularly in relation to financial matters and issues of competence. Two adopters had felt unable to ask their social worker for help because they were afraid of being judged or of unwanted "repercussions", as one stated:

> *I think you're awfully wary about saying anything that in any way indicates you might not be coping. So you don't say, 'Look, please God send somebody in to help me,' because you think that they're going to say, 'Well no, you're not coping,' and that's a judgement on you then. You can't cope with these children – we've made a mistake.* (Adopter 14)

Home help

Social workers could help to reduce the pressure on sibling-group adopters by providing practical support such as home help, even if it was only for two or three hours a week. Home help was provided for 16 sibling-group adopters (43%) when the children were placed, but only six (16%) continued to receive this help after the adoption order. Just over a third of adopters did not want this support, but 14 (38%) said it had been refused or not offered. Unsurprisingly, home help was offered to nearly all of the adopters who took four or five siblings. Many adopters spoke of needing home help not only because they were exhausted by the mountains of washing, but also because it enabled them to spend more time with the children. Here are comments by two adopters:

> *I didn't want it, I was determined I wasn't going to have anybody in my house cleaning my house, but then I just got so tired, I gave in.* (Adopter 8)

> *I did ask for a cleaner eventually when my ironing pile got so massive, and they did agree to pay for me to have a lady that*

came in once a week and she did three hours (. . .) While I had it, it was an absolute godsend and I couldn't have done it, so yes it was essential and I miss her terribly. (Adopter 5)

Many of the adopters (11) wished that home help had been provided. One decided to pay for an ironing service herself because she was 'up until three o'clock in the morning ironing'. Another explained the benefits of having home help, now that she was able to afford it:

I've now gone and found my own [home help] and I'm paying for it (. . .) and that is essential. That is what is actually getting us onto an even keel now (. . .) because I know that I don't have to worry about changing the beds. Once a week I don't have to worry about making tea. It's all the little things: somebody helps me get the washing done, and that means I've got the energy to give [child] the time and attention that he needs and the therapeutic parenting that he needs, well all three of them. It means that [youngest child] gets some time . . .(Adopter 27)

It was noticeable that adopters often emphasised the importance of having home help when they were dealing with difficult behaviour or had children who frequently wet the bed. One adopter who was trying to cope with all of this commented:

. . . if it would have been offered, I would have bitten their hand off! (. . .) That's the one thing that really got me down was the amount of just the washing up, just the clothes and all the rest (. . .) It just felt like a mountain to climb every day with all that lot. (Adopter 14)

It is perhaps worth noting that two adopters who received home help commented that what they really needed was help in managing the children's behaviour. Both of them said that at the beginning of the placement they felt unable to go out with the children, even to the park, because they could not control them. Mercifully, in one case relatives drew up a rota to provide support until the mother gained sufficient confidence to manage on her own.

Babysitting to give the adopters a break

Only two couples (both VAA adopters) said their adoption agency had paid for a babysitter to give them a break from looking after the children. This support was appreciated enormously, as one adopter explained:

> *We had a childminder who came three hours a month so we could go out for dinner (. . .) Oh, it was wonderful! She's remained a friend as well. We still use her or one of her grown-up daughters as babysitters.* (Adopter 30)

Being able to have a night out was invaluable to adopters who were caring for children with very difficult behaviour. Most of them had to rely on relatives or friends to babysit, as in the following statement:

> *. . . where [child] has really been playing up, at least if you can go out on a Saturday night with some friends, have a nice meal and a break from it, it helps you to put it in perspective. And we're fortunate, we've got family living nearby who are willing to help, but if you've not got that, I don't know how you would cope.* (Adopter 14)

Another adopter, whose son could not tolerate any change in his routine, could not remember when she and her husband had last had a night out, 'because obviously there are only certain people whom we can leave him with . . .' This mother had recently been diagnosed as suffering from depression.

Support from other adopters

Most of the adopters had attended an adoption support group set up by their agency and appreciated this support. Some adoption agencies ran a parallel playgroup session so that mothers could attend the group without worrying about childcare, and two adoptive fathers had attended dad's groups that met about three times a year. However, several adopters (8) did not attend because they did not have time, it was not really 'their thing', or they thought it was unnecessary, as noted in the following statement:

I would say [the adoption support group] is not needed because one of the things the girls are really adamant about (. . .) they don't want to be constantly reminded that they're adopted (. . .) like we're in some big adoption club. (Adopter 28)

A few adopters regretted the lack of an adoption support group in their area, and two had set up their own informal group. One commented that she liked being able to communicate with other adopters in her support group or through Adoption UK because she knew they would not dismiss her concerns about the children or judge her parenting.

In particular, adopters appreciated having an opportunity to meet more experienced sibling-group adopters through buddy schemes or with the help of their social worker. One adopter stated:

Our agency are very good at putting us in touch with other adopters in the area (. . .) particularly ones that have three or more and ones that still have issues going on – that are fresh rather than 'We've been doing it for five years and everything's fine'. (Adopter 2)

Respite care

Five adopters who were exhausted by their children's difficult behaviour said they would love to have respite care but it had been refused or not offered, as this comment illustrates:

Turned down on the grounds that it would introduce another person into the children's lives, even though we were down on our knees . . . (Adopter 17)

Respite care was offered to only one family in the study, and by that time it was too late to prevent the placement from disrupting, as the adopter explained:

We have had a respite care package for several months. It's a shame because we had been asking for help for years and years (. . .) Because of the level of damage [to the children], you do need respite, because if you can't retain your mental health the whole thing will collapse. (Adopter 13)

Social work support

Most of the support given to adopters came from social workers. This was provided in many ways – such as offering emotional support, helping adopters to understand children's behaviour, and advocating on the adopters' behalf with other agencies. Adopters felt very well supported when they knew they could rely on the agency (and not just the individual social worker) to respond positively. Nearly twice as many VAA adopters reported receiving emotional support from their social worker compared to LA adopters, but there were examples of good practice in both LAs and VAAs. One adopter, who described her LA social worker as 'just amazing', stated:

> . . . *no matter whom you ring within the team, everybody's aware and even if our social worker wasn't available, there was always somebody there who knew of the situation and who could offer advice . . .* (Adopter 18)

Knowing that support was available was very reassuring, and this tended to be emphasised more by VAA adopters:

> . . . *she was always there if we wanted to contact her.* (Adopter 22)

Social workers who made time to visit and who could provide support and advocacy were not only trusted by the adopters but welcomed into their home with open arms:

> *Our social worker is like a member of the family now. She provides a lot of support and has done a lot of arguing with colleagues and local authorities. I know she went and had a conversation with the educational department and CAMHS – but that's all because the adoption team in [local authority] is exceptionally good.* (Adopter 35)

However, home visits were not appreciated when adopters felt that social workers were coming to judge them rather than to offer any useful support:

... every day I think for the first week it wouldn't just be one social worker, there would be at least two of them coming here, and they would be sat on their backsides drinking tea while I flapped around the place, and I thought that was poor. I said, 'If you're going to come here, help out, make yourself a cup, even if it's just make your own cup of tea.' ... of course they're coming in to (. . .) see whether you're coping, but when you're trying to cope with three children and they're young kids, it just felt – I found it intrusive. (Adopter 14)

Other adopters found that promises of emotional support were not fulfilled (in some cases because their social worker had moved on). This left some adopters feeling very let down, although one mother recognised that the failure to provide support was probably due to budgetary constraints:

When I needed them, they weren't there (. . .) Our social worker was really keen to support us (. . .) She would come up with all these great ideas, and they would really have been great, if she could've put them into practice, but she'd go back to the office and the manager would say, 'There's not enough money in the budget.' (Adopter 36)

However, in another case it appeared that support was being withheld on ideological grounds. The adopter described her LA's approach in the following terms:

[LA] don't place threes, or they didn't, and they don't believe in threes being placed (. . .) Our current social worker is very clear that threes are not a good idea (. . .) Well, she basically hasn't supported us at all and has done what she can to shoot us in the foot, which has made life very difficult ... what was very interesting was that once we had a matching panel date for these

guys, [LA] suddenly came up with two sibling groups of three of their own that they wanted us to consider! . . . the two sibling groups they offered us were huge problems. We just looked at the basic profile and went, 'No way, we can't deal with that.' (Adopter 27)

Providing explanations

After children had been placed, they were described as often behaving in ways that adopters found hard to understand. Many adopters commented that it was difficult to know whether challenging behaviours were due to the children being adopted or were a normal part of child development. They thought it was very helpful if the children's social worker knew the children well and could provide an explanation for their behaviour. If the children's social worker was unable to do this, adoption social workers sometimes helped the adopters to piece together events and devise strategies, as one adopter explained:

The children's social worker – nothing. Our adoption social worker has been extremely good at trying to work with us through the impact of the past experiences on current behaviour, and goes on doing it (. . .) We discovered that when [child] was first here (. . .) she would play in her bedroom for hours in the middle of the night, and that's because she was left as a toddler in a cot for hours during the day with the curtains drawn (. . .) and so she didn't believe you that it was night-time. So we had to have lots of strategies for showing that it was night-time. (. . .) We don't do it now, but once [child] had gone to bed, we would get changed into our night-wear, so if you had to go to her, you were dressed as though we were in bed. (Adopter 35)

It was reassuring when social workers could look into the children's background and provide an answer, but this depended on accurate case recording. This was not available for all the children. The importance of recording events in children's files to enable others to make sense of their behaviour was highlighted in the following example given by an adopter:

[Child] kept having nightmares about being prised away from his mum, and it turns out that on the day of removal a police officer had to physically prise him out of his mother's arms – and that again wasn't in the file. It was only because the social worker at the time remembered it (. . .) and they got her to ring me and talk me through what happened that day, so that I had the knowledge to help him overcome these fears. (Adopter 36)

Providing strategies to manage children's behaviour

Some of the adopters had received assistance from their social worker in dealing with behavioural problems. The ability to explain things from the children's perspective was particularly important, as one adopter explained:

. . . the support from the adoption agency was fantastic (. . .) They provided lots of explanation about the children's behaviour – like this is the anniversary of when they were first placed in foster care – and how to deal with it. There was also a willingness to help us and a reassurance that we were doing fine. She [the social worker] always had the children in mind and I found that reassuring, because I was at times thinking, 'Poor me! Somebody help me!' and she would say, 'Well, if you see it from their point of view . . .', and that helped me to understand them. (Adopter 2)

Social workers with a good understanding of attachment issues were much appreciated by adopters who were struggling to form a relationship with their children:

[The social worker] knew all about attachment theory and she taught me quite a lot. That was (. . .) the first time that anyone had really ever explained anything like that to me – you know, this is why they do it, this is what's happening. That started me reading a lot about attachment. (Adopter 3)

Typical strategies focused on establishing daily routines and regular mealtimes to help the children to feel safe enough to begin trusting their new parents, and one adopter also described the use of visual timetables (see page 120). It is not difficult to see why routines are so important for children who have had chaotic lives, often not knowing when they were going to be fed or what would happen next. One adopter whose children all had attachment difficulties explained this as follows:

> If there's a change in routine, you've got to pay, and if you take them on holiday, you've got to pay because you've changed the routine. That's what people don't get, when you first go into it [adoption]. Adopters often adopt children and think, 'We'll go on a nice holiday,' and then of course the children go into orbit! (...) We go to the same place, same apartment, every year, because that way their anxieties are lower and we do get a bit of a break. (Adopter 3)

Although many of the children placed with the sibling-group adopters were described by their adopters as having attachment difficulties and challenging behaviour, appropriate support was not always provided. Adopters who were repeatedly told that their child's disturbed behaviour was "normal" understandably felt that they were being fobbed off. Sometimes social workers' responses left a lot to be desired, as in the following example given by an adopter who was worried about her son's violence:

> The social worker told [child] it was OK for him to hit me, because I understand that he is angry and that I can take the blows and help him understand why he is angry (...) I heard her say it! (Adopter 36)

Responding to the risk of disruption
It is worth noting that failure to provide support in dealing with difficult behaviour was a feature in both cases where the placement had partially disrupted and some of the children had returned to the care system. However, in another case, disruption was avoided by the adoption agency's prompt and effective response.

Case example

The adopters found it very difficult to manage the oldest child's attention-seeking behaviour at the same time as caring for a baby and a two-year-old. After six months, the impact on their own relationship was so serious that, despite having been happily married for many years, they thought they were going to split up. The wife phoned their VAA and they responded immediately. The social worker, her manager and a post-adoption support worker visited. The adopters thought they were going to remove the children, but instead they provided some simple measures and strategies to support the adopters in dealing with the children's behaviour. It took the adopters about a year to work through these difficulties with the children, but the placement is now stable and happy. The wife remarked, 'It's like now looking back, why did we let it get to that stage? But at the time you just don't see that.' (Adopter 32)

Sometimes when adopters were worried about their ability to love or cope with a particular child, social workers were able to defuse the situation by offering reassurance or acceptance. One adopter who was very afraid that the younger siblings might be injured by their violent older brother said it was a "huge relief" when the social worker informed him that in those circumstances only the oldest child would be removed. Another adopter described how a social worker had responded when she admitted that she did not love one of the children:

The thing that saved the placement really of the older two children was because their social worker let me off the hook, and she said a really helpful thing (. . .) I remember saying to her one day after the older kids had been with me for about six months – and I was really worried about saying it – 'I don't think I love [child]. I don't love her because there is nothing there – I don't feel anything is happening.' And I fully expected them to say, 'Right, that's it. Let's end it.' But of course instead she said, 'Well, you may never love her, and she may never love you, but what you've got is you've given her sibling relationships.' And because she said that, that took the pressure off me and I was able subsequently to form a relationship – but if she had been (. . .) blaming and cold towards me about that, I'm not sure that the placement of the older two would have lasted. In fact, I'm sure it wouldn't have done, because it was so significant that I suddenly didn't have to feel like the worst mother in the universe because I couldn't love this poor little girl who had been through all these dreadful things (. . .) I thought, 'Oh yeah, actually she's getting quite a lot out of being here.' (Adopter 3)

Remedying the effects of poor practice

Sometimes the way in which children had been treated by social workers or foster carers left them feeling very insecure and created considerable problems for the adopters. One couple described how a child who had had a bad relationship with her foster carer continually challenged her adoptive mother, thinking that she was 'going to be the same'. This was a very depressing experience for the mother and, unfortunately, her social worker 'almost laughed it off a bit'.

However, in another case where a girl had had a 'destructive relationship' with her social worker, the adopter said that her LA social worker had been 'phenomenal' in helping them to deal with the subsequent difficulties. It was only when the life story books turned up late, that this adopter realised the children had never been told why they had been removed from their birth parents. The social worker helped the adopters to do 'sort of therapy' with the oldest child 'to help her to deal with what she had learnt'. On another occasion, the social worker turned up with a student social worker and asked the child if she would mind telling the student what a social worker *should* be like. The adopter described how the child responded to this:

[Child] went on to give him about an hour's lecture about the good and bad things that social workers could do. Afterwards her confidence soared (. . .) It was almost as though all that negativity she had had from her social worker had a purpose.

She could do that with a student, and it enabled her to alter her view of social workers. (Adopter 18)

Advocating on the adopters' behalf with other services

Adopters often said they were expected to find school places themselves for their children. However, social workers who enabled adopters to obtain school places or to access educational support were very much appreciated. Being able to take the children to a nursery or playgroup sometimes provided a welcome breathing space for adopters, especially when the placement had started during the long summer holidays. Advocacy was urgently needed when staff in schools or nurseries insisted that parents had to put the children's names down months or years in advance, as an exasperated adopter pointed out:

There's no help given with finding pre-school places (. . .) 'Sorry you're on your own again.' I was phoning up pre-schools to try and get a pre-school place for [child]. 'Oh, you needed to put her name down 18 months ago.' I said, 'Look, I'm sorry, she's been placed with us for adoption. We didn't know she existed 18 months ago.' 'Well, you should have put her name down 18 months ago.' Can I go and bang my head against a brick wall, please? (Adopter 27)

In these circumstances, teachers and social workers sometimes appeared to be unaware of the regulations requiring that looked after children should be given the highest priority for admission.[11] Additional support services were also urgently needed when one child in the sibling group had more complex needs and demanded constant attention, because in these (not uncommon) circumstances the adopters often had considerable difficulty in meeting the needs of their other children. Support of this kind was rarely provided in-house and most children were referred to CAMHS.

---

11 The Education (Admission of Looked After Children) (England) Regulations 2006

Support from Child and Adolescent Mental Health Services (CAMHS)

Although there are evidence-based treatments for many child mental health problems, only about 20 per cent of children with psychiatric disorders in the general population are in contact with specialist mental health services (Meltzer *et al*, 2000). In this sample, almost half of the sibling-group adopters (18) stated that therapy had been provided for their children, usually through CAMHS. Five adopters accessed these services through their GP, and one was astonished that the GP managed to arrange an appointment within a week, when she had waited four years for a referral through the children's social worker. Quite a wide range of therapeutic interventions were described, including play therapy, theraplay, one-to-one counselling, behavioural therapy, art therapy, occupational therapy, and filial play therapy. Usually parents and children were seen together, but five children had individual sessions and three sets of parents had therapeutic support without their children. One couple said they were surprised to discover that actually it was their own behaviour that needed to change.

Many adopters said that therapy had been very helpful. For example, one adopter, whose three children had benefited from play therapy organised by their VAA, commented:

. . . they needed to learn how to be a sibling group in a sense, so how to be together. [The oldest child] started going very much into this kind of mother role again and she would tell me, you know, 'It's time to feed [younger child] now.' (. . .) So the play therapy was there (. . .) to help them come together as a group and also to help [younger child] deal with the loss of the attachment to the foster parents (. . .) All the children [took part]. I didn't take part in it at all (. . .) They loved it; they still ask for it now. They had no idea it was therapy; they just thought it was play. (Adopter 28)

For adopters who were at the end of their tether, the provision of therapy could be a lifeline and gave them "a sense of hope". One adoptive mother described how filling in mood and attitude charts was helping her oldest child to become aware that her attention-seeking behaviour was counterproductive:

> . . . her need is to have me. She absolutely and totally just wants me to herself all the time, and (. . .) she will go out of her way to get into trouble, because (. . .) she's then getting my attention and [the other two children] aren't getting it. So we're in the process at the moment of doing mood and attitude charts at all times of the day (. . .) I don't think she has any idea that to get my love and attention (. . .) she's doing it the wrong way; she can't see it no matter how much you try and explain to her (. . .) We've got these forms which we're filling in, so she can sit down with the therapist and so she can reflect and think, 'Oh blimey!' (. . .) She's taking a great interest in these forms, looking at all the boxes that mummy's been ticking on a daily basis, and (. . .) the boxes I'm ticking are anger, rage, out of control. You know, most days at some point during the day she will experience those emotions (. . .) but she's started getting better. (Adopter 5)

Sometimes having a diagnosis from CAMHS enabled adopters to obtain additional support services and a more constructive response from other professionals. When her child was diagnosed as having reactive attachment disorder, one adopter said that at last she had a "bargaining chip". She now felt able to say to teachers who were threatening to expel her son: 'Well hang on a sec. That behaviour is because of his condition, and what have you done in this school to help [child], because you've got to adapt what you do to take into account his disability because that's what inclusion is all about.'

However, gaining access to therapy was often difficult. Adopters spoke of long delays, waiting lists, misdiagnosis, and high thresholds for intervention. One couple were exasperated that despite a referral to CAMHS their son's difficulties were not considered serious enough to warrant treatment. Others said they had to "kick and scream" before therapy was provided, while some had to search for therapists themselves. Eight adopters (22%) reported that therapy had not been provided, or was not helpful, or had been provided too late. The adoptive mother of a boy who had recently returned to foster care commented:

We have had lots of therapy since and it's still not working, because I think they missed the boat. I think this should have been done probably in foster care and overlapping into placement with us. They needed attachment work very definitely. And the other thing I think should have been offered was for us to be trained in therapeutic parenting strategies. (Adopter 13)

In particular, there seemed to be an acute lack of services for very young children with severe mental health difficulties. For example, one mother said that she phoned children's services to ask for help because her five-year old son was talking about killing himself, and it took them a week to phone her back. Another adopter, whose child was self-harming, was apparently told that she was doing 'all the right kinds of things' but there was not a lot that could be done, as the child was only five years old. This adopter was eventually offered more support.

Although half of the adoptive families had received support from CAMHS, this was not always targeted at the children with the most severe problems. There was no statistical association between children's high SDQ (Strengths and Difficulties Questionnaire; Goodman, 1997) scores and the provision of therapeutic services. One adoptive mother who had moved to another area in the hope of being able to access CAMHS more easily, questioned the ability of CAMHS professionals to understand and respond effectively to attachment disorders:

I hear this over and over again with [other adopters]. It's probably the biggest problem we face – the lack of real understanding about attachment disorder in the therapeutic community and what that means for the family. I think it's really, really tough finding people who get it and can work with the family, the whole family. (Adopter 3)

Support from schools

It was very reassuring for both adopters and children if the new school ensured that the necessary support was in place to enable children to catch up or to help with speech difficulties. Learning support was greatly valued by the adopters, but often they had to be assertive to obtain it. One adopter stated:

I had a special needs teacher who came in once a week and sort of did a catch up with [child]. They gave us £500, and lo and behold [she] is now top of her class! So yeah, but that was a big battle to get that actually. (Adopter 10)

Schools could also be very helpful when individual staff offered support to adopters who were struggling with difficult behaviour. One adopter said that a teacher's intervention had helped to prevent the placement from disrupting:

If I hadn't had support from the school, I think [the placement] would have broken down, because I couldn't cope with [child] hitting and kicking me. I had rung my social worker to say, 'Come and get him today. I can't cope with him another day', but with the support of his teacher we got through it. She was the one who first offered support through the school. The school did a lot in terms of helping [child] to control his anger. (Adopter 36)

The ethos of a school could also help to improve children's behaviour. One adopter was full of praise for the way in which the headmistress not only dealt with difficult behaviour but also ensured that the children's needs were met:

[The children] go to a Catholic school which is very big on, sort of, love thy neighbour, forgiveness, etc, etc, and that has had a huge impact on all of them [. . .] in terms of forgiveness, being kind to people, sharing things . . . the headmistress has probably been one of the biggest factors in making this [placement] succeed. When [child] has had a hissy fit on his way to school, said he's going to kick me [. . .] [she] has had him in her office,

spoken to him, made him phone me up and apologise. She's made sure that his statement is absolutely tailored to his needs. She's taken on [the LA] when [they are] trying to pull money. She's made sure that her staff are fully aware of all the children's backgrounds and their needs. (Adopter 9)

However, some of the sibling-group adopters were shocked to find that the behaviour of school staff could be insensitive because they had very little understanding of adoption. They complained that some teachers automatically attributed any problem to adoption, or alternatively assumed that because the children were adopted they should be fine now. One adopter said that she had urged the school not to treat the children differently but to 'take account of the unique challenges of adoption'. In particular, she wanted the teachers to recognise that one child's attention-seeking behaviour (e.g. asking silly questions) was his way of "seeking nurture", so it was important how they responded to him.

Other difficulties reported by adopters included: not recognising that looked after children should have the highest priority for admission; delays in assessing children for a special educational needs statement (which prevented interventions such as learning support from being implemented); not using the transitional funding to provide support for a particular child; including children in publicity photographs against the wishes of the adopters; and, in the case of one school, repeatedly refusing an offer to train teachers on adoption issues. One adopter was so frustrated by the school's failure to acknowledge a child's special educational needs that she paid for him to be assessed privately, as she explained:

I paid an educational psychologist myself to get a proper assessment done on him, because people used to really mislead us and say he was capable of this, that and the other – and I knew he wasn't. So I paid for a private educational psychologist to do a report, which validated what we were saying, and then I was able to get him statemented. (Adopter 3)

181

Receiving post-adoption support

Adopters were asked what services they had received after the making of the adoption order (see Table 13.2). Only 32 families offered their views on post-adoption support; the other five families had postponed their application for an adoption order. Those five adopters were all in dispute with the children's LA about the provision of support services, particularly support with challenging behaviour and attachment difficulties, and they were refusing to apply to the court until the necessary support was provided.

There were few differences in the number or type of support services received by VAA and LA adopters after the adoption order was made. However, VAA adopters (82%) continued to report far more emotional support from their agency than did the LA adopters (22%), and again the difference was statistically significant.[12] LA adopters were also three times more likely than VAA adopters to be dissatisfied with the amount of support they had received.[13]

The families who had obtained an adoption order generally had settled into a routine with the children, and most had found ways of meeting the children's needs. After the order, almost half of the adopters were satisfied that their children did not need any therapeutic interventions, and many were confident that they could manage. Indeed, the withdrawal of support services was regarded by one adopter as a necessary part of the process, as she commented:

> . . . once the adoption happened, as I thought, it phased out. We just had to be a family, and I think that's right. You have to be normal, because if you've always got agencies involved, it makes the children feel that they're not a normal group of children. (Adopter 19)

In contrast, three adopters commented that the children's LA had abandoned them (i.e. ceased to provide support) as soon as the adoption order was made. Others were involved in protracted arguments

---

12 Fishers Exact p = 0.004
13 Fisher's Exact p = 0.007, odds ratio = 0.29

Table 13.2
Support given to adoptive parents after the adoption order (n = 32)

	Received %	Not needed %	Not provided %
Regular adoption allowance	82	9	9
Enough money for one adopter not to work	47	16	37
Further one-off payment	16	75	9
Emotional support for adopters	53	22	25
Support in relation to child behaviours	32	34	34
Therapeutic support package	31	50	19
Home help	19	38	43
Place at nursery/playgroup	13	65	22
Support with contact	47	38	15
Respite care	3	52	45

about post-adoption support and spoke about having to "fight, fight, fight" to make the LA recognise a child's needs and pay for support services. However, it is also important to note that at the time of the research interview, 81 per cent of the adopters were still receiving an adoption allowance and 55 per cent had some other form of support.

Adoption allowances are usually re-assessed every year, and this was a source of uncertainty and stress for some families, especially when payments ended. One adopter thought that the practice of paying a lower allowance for the third sibling and any further siblings explained why so few large sibling groups were adopted. Unfortunately, LAs that avoided making financial payments were sometimes also very poor at offering other kinds of support. One adopter who received very little financial help commented:

I think the whole thing was quite appalling. None of our social workers turned up in court for either hearing, and especially with the birth mother contesting, it would have been nice to have some support (...) More money would have been nice, and maybe someone who understands children to advise about their sleeping. (Adopter 12)

How helpful were the services provided?

The adopters were asked how helpful they had found the support services that had been provided. The majority thought that financial support had been the most important service provided. However, for those struggling with children's very challenging behaviour, the emotional support given by their worker and therapeutic interventions were also essential. Only three adopters rated the services they had received as not very helpful, and this seemed to be because of the quality of the service rather than the type offered. From the adopters' accounts, it appeared that most services were being effectively targeted but that the demand was higher than the supply.

Did the adopters want more support than had been provided?

When we asked the sibling-group adopters if they thought more support should have been provided, over a quarter (27%) stated that everything they needed had been put in place. Some adopters were confident that their agency would provide lifelong support, while others emphasised that they wanted to be self-sufficient, that they did not want social workers visiting, or that their own support network was sufficient. Lack of effective support in dealing with challenging behaviour and attachment difficulties appeared to cause the most distress. Some adopters repeatedly emphasised the need for practical support and strategies to help them manage children's behaviour.

It has been clear throughout this chapter that many of the sibling-group adopters had to fight for the necessary support to be provided for their children. In the next chapter we consider the personal qualities that appeared to enable these adopters to take three or more siblings and to cope with that commitment.

Summary

- All the LA managers said that most sibling-group adopters received financial support, but VAA staff were concerned that adoption allowances were becoming less common and, if this continued, only wealthy applicants would be able to adopt sibling groups.
- Most (78%) of the sibling-group adopters in this sample received an adoption allowance, but eight did not and, as a result, one family was in debt and could not afford to take another sibling. Another family missed out on 18 months of child benefit payments because they were not given any information about this.
- LA staff recognised that it would benefit the children if the allowance enabled one parent to stay at home, but they said they were unable to provide this for everyone. Only 47 per cent of the adopters received a large enough allowance to enable one parent to stay at home.
- Three adopters said their LA had reneged on the agreed support package and, although two managed to get their support reinstated, the third had to work part-time.
- Often adopters were expected to have a large enough home and car already, and agencies assumed that most support would come from family and friends. However, one LA had apparently paid for loft extensions in three out of nine sibling group placements.
- Agencies provided adoption support groups and sometimes buddy schemes, and many adopters appreciated the opportunity to talk to other sibling-group adopters.
- LAs were reluctant to provide home help, even though it helped to alleviate exhaustion and enabled adopters to spend more time with their children. This type of support was viewed as essential by many sibling group adopters, particularly those who were struggling with challenging behaviour and continual bedwetting.
- LAs were reluctant to provide respite care except as a last resort. Only one adopter received respite care and it came too late to prevent the adoption from disrupting.
- Some social workers had specialist training in attachment issues and were able to help the adopters to devise strategies for dealing

with difficult behaviour. This was valued by adopters.

- LA staff reported long waiting lists and problems in financing therapy for children. Almost half of the sibling-group adopters stated that at least one of their children had received therapy, and usually this was considered helpful. However, these services did not appear to be well targeted, as there was no statistical association between the children with the highest SDQ scores and the provision of therapeutic support. There seemed to be a lack of services for very young children with severe mental health problems, and some adopters questioned the ability of CAMHS professionals to deal with attachment issues.

- Schools could be very helpful in working with children to enable them to catch up and to improve their behaviour. However, adopters stated that: some teachers were insensitive because they did not understand adoption; schools did not always recognise that looked after children should be given priority in admissions; assessments of special educational needs were sometimes delayed; and one school did not use transitional funding for the purpose for which it was intended.

- Five adopters were refusing to apply for the adoption order until the LA provided the necessary support to enable them to cope with the children's challenging behaviour and attachment difficulties.

- Most of the sibling-group adopters who had an adoption order were still receiving a support service. VAA adopters reported greater satisfaction than LA adopters with the services they had received, but there were examples of very good practice in both LAs and VAAs. From all the adopters' accounts, services were very much appreciated and useful, but demand was higher than the supply.

14 A force to be reckoned with

What sort of person would even consider adopting a large sibling group? We did not put this question to the adopters, but looked for answers in the comments they made during the interviews and the actions they had taken during the adoption process. Again, it is necessary to emphasise that this was not a representative sample. Generally, our adopters appeared to have exactly what the adoption agencies were looking for, including a large enough house and garden. Most of them were clear from the start that they wanted more than one child. Most had experience of working with or caring for children and, if not, they made considerable efforts to remedy this. However, they were also a force to be reckoned with, as some agencies discovered later. Perhaps the best description of a typical sibling-group adopter was provided by a voluntary adoption agency (VAA) manager, who suggested they have the following qualities:

> . . . an ability to really ask questions and the ability to say, 'You haven't given me the answers that I need to have, before I make this decision' (. . .) They're pushy people, so they will be good advocates for kids, and they drive you crazy because they are! I'd much rather have them as adopters than people who actually don't do that. (VAA 9)

Determination and commitment
The most striking feature of the adopters in our sample was their determination not only to adopt a sibling group but to ensure that everything was done properly and that the children received the necessary support. They were intent on "making things happen". The vast majority (81%) described situations in which they had "put their foot down" and insisted that something should be done better or differently, e.g. demanding that life story books should be rewritten or that older children should be allowed to start school within days of being placed. The adopters were not likely to agree to anything that

they thought would be detrimental to the children, as one adoptive mother made clear:

I sat here at this table and categorically said, 'We're not doing any letterbox [contact]; they don't want it.' (. . .) I wasn't about to put the children through it. If they wanted to do it, it was different, and that was always our premise. (Adopter 24)

Usually, the adopters got their way. However, often they spoke about having to "fight" to make the local authority (LA) recognise a child's needs and pay for therapy or learning support or whatever was required. One couple managed to obtain substantial support for a child, because they 'kicked up enough of a stink'. Other ways in which the adopters signalled their determination to be taken seriously included: refusing to apply for the adoption order until the necessary support was provided; threatening to pull out if there was any more delay; insisting that it was "all or nothing" when social workers wanted to split the siblings; writing to the Director of Children's Services; making a formal complaint; taking legal action against the children's local authority; or having a meeting with a government minister to discuss their concerns.

It could be argued that, given the arduous nature of the adoption process and the complexities involved in taking a sibling group, adoptive parents have to be pushy and determined to meet the needs of their children. However, exasperated LAs could perhaps console themselves with the knowledge that these adopters were also totally committed. For example, two couples did *not* withdraw from the adoption process even when they were informed, belatedly, that a child had been sexually abused or had a serious medical condition. Another adopter clearly articulated her determination to make the adoption a success:

I was adamant from the minute I clapped eyes on them, these were our children (. . .) and if they'd let me have them, it would work. (Adopter 7)

Having a strong relationship and setting boundaries

Thirty-three (89%) of the adopters stated that they had a strong relationship or emphasised that their partner was very supportive. Some talked about needing to be "strong" in order to adopt a sibling group, and a few said that they had "become stronger" as a result of their adoption experiences:

Although individually we might have felt drained by it (. . .) we've been working as a team, so it has brought a strength to our relationship. It's an elaborate team-building exercise! (Adopter 2)

Ten adopters also emphasised the importance of being united in their approach to parenting and in setting boundaries and having regular routines as a family. Here are two of their comments:

I think your relationship as a couple is so important and the children need to see that. If you are not careful they will divide you, so you have to be united and you have to talk. (Adopter 37)

. . . they did try the challenging bit, where they tried one parent against the other, but it doesn't work with us . . . we're both together on this issue. We sit and eat as a family, we do this as a family, we have expectations and we stick to it (. . .) They're really very good, and I didn't have a cattle prod or anything! (. . .) It's all about routine; that's their expectation of the way things should be. (Adopter 15)

Adopters who did not have such a strong and united approach found caring for a sibling group much harder. One mother, who was struggling with three demanding children, spoke about 'the emotional stress of trying to work out who these children are and then work out who we were'.

Confidence and belief in their own judgement

Throughout the interviews, adopters expressed a great deal of confidence in their own abilities, and it was striking how many appeared to take it for granted that they would be able to manage a sibling group.

189

Reasons given for this confidence included having grown up in a large family, having experience of working with or caring for children, and having a strong relationship with their partner. Believing that they would receive support from their adoption agency was also a key factor for 71 per cent of VAA adopters, but only for 29 per cent of LA adopters. The attitudes expressed in the following two statements are typical:

I think the main [reason] is people having a fairly high opinion of our capabilities. (laughter) Arrogance! (Adopter 4)

It didn't occur to me that I wouldn't be able to do it. (Adopter 3)

Some of these adopters felt able to do things that people with less confidence would probably never consider – for example, putting together their own flyer and sending it to LAs, asking panel members to explain who they were, and fighting the LA (successfully) to be allowed to adopt siblings, despite becoming a single parent after the children were placed.

Remarkably, six adopters decided to go ahead with the adoption even though they had been given a gloomy prognosis about the children's behaviour or their medical prospects. These situations sometimes arose because professionals believed in giving the worst case scenario or did not really know the children. One couple did not believe the "horror stories" about the children's behaviour and concluded that the foster carer had lied in order to receive a higher fostering allowance. In other cases, it was information provided by foster carers that made adopters feel able to dismiss the negative comments of social workers or medical professionals. Here are the comments of two adopters:

Had it not been for what the foster carers were telling us and what we actually felt in our hearts, we probably would have pulled out. (Adopter 18)

[The paediatrician] painted this really bleak picture, and I think we drove back from [LA area] for the last three and a half hours almost in silence (. . .) We have been very tempted on many

occasions to send a video of [child] to the paediatrician, so she can actually see what he is like now (. . .) The paediatrician we saw hadn't actually met [child] herself. (Adopter 26)

Five of these adopters felt that their belief in the children had been completely vindicated. Indeed, one couple said they had had "no difficulties" with their group of four siblings despite the dire predictions. In the sixth case, the adopters were told that one child probably had an attachment disorder and his behaviour appeared to confirm this, but they were satisfied that therapy would be provided if necessary because their social worker had insisted that this should be written into the support package.

Knowing that they wanted a large sibling group

Twelve adopters (32%) were clear right from the start that they wanted a large sibling group and they did not change their mind. This was something that one adoption manager considered to be "slightly different" about sibling-group adopters, while another remarked:

Usually if they are going to take three siblings, they know right from the start. Sometimes they come forward saying, 'We want four children.' We have had four families doing that in the last three years. (LA 1)

Some of these adopters spoke about being "drawn to groups of three" when they looked at adoption magazines, and some found it difficult to limit the number of children they wanted or assumed that having a few more would not make much difference. Here are two of their comments:

. . . when they asked me (. . .) 'Why are you going for three children?' I said, 'Because my husband won't let me have four!' (Adopter 15)

Once you get a couple of kids, it doesn't make much difference if you have three or four or five, especially if you have early support to give you time to adjust to the routine. (Adopter 21)

Optimism and staying positive

Eleven adopters (29%) were very positive in their outlook and seemed to be able to cope with problems, such as soiling, that others might have found upsetting. For example, one couple explained that due to previous sexual abuse their oldest child had 'problems in relating to boys' and had had an unwanted pregnancy, but they spoke about her with great warmth saying they were confident that she would go to university and would 'do something amazing' with her life. Another mother was very pleased that a child who had difficulty in expressing emotion was now actually having tantrums and allowed her to have 'the odd cuddle'. These adopters were delighted by the progress their children had made, but they had learned to "go with the flow" and not to expect perfection. When asked if they had had difficulties with the children, these adopters were likely to reply, 'They are just children.' One adopter explained her reasons for adopting a large sibling group as follows:

> . . . you do think about it all very carefully, but there is an element of needing to be people who say, 'Yeah, we'll do it, we'll take it on.' My family motto is 'Do something crazy every year!' (Adopter 27)

Having a strong faith or humanitarian outlook

Eleven (29%) of the adopters acknowledged that they had strong religious or humanitarian beliefs. Seven, who described themselves as Christian, said they had "prayed a lot" during the adoption process and felt that God was guiding them or would give them strength to cope with whatever happened. Two adopters had decided not to have IVF treatment because there were 'lots of unhappy kids needing homes'. Having a humanitarian outlook sometimes made others view adoption as a vocation or some kind of obligation, as in the following statement:

> . . . there's thousands of children out there that need homes (. . .) I think the very least I could have done was to offer some children a home. (Adopter 17)

Resilience

Ten (27%) of the adopters emphasised resilience as a quality that helped them to survive the adoption process and to cope with a sibling group. Indeed, couples who had managed to resolve previous problems (sometimes including marital difficulties) had been able to convince their social worker that this was a strength, because they had worked through it together and 'could ask for help'. One couple commented:

Mother: A lot of [the adoption process] is designed to put you off.

Father: And you have to be very resilient to keep going because, you know, it would have been so easy to give up. (Adopter 8)

The adopters were a remarkable group of people, marked out by their commitment and determination. They had created a large family by adopting a sibling group, and one of the consequences of this was that their children tended to be older than those usually placed for adoption. However, it is known that older children adopted out of care are more likely to have mental health difficulties. In the main, this is the result of being exposed to abuse and neglect for long periods but it can also be the result of multiple moves in the care system. These children may also carry genetic risks and vulnerabilities. The siblings' level of mental health difficulties had not been measured at the time of placement but was measured at the time of the research interview. These findings and the adopters' own levels of mental health are described in the next chapter.

Summary

- Key characteristics of the adopters in our sample were their determination to adopt a sibling group and their commitment to making the placement a success. Many spoke about having to "fight" to ensure that their children received the necessary support. They were clearly a force to be reckoned with.
- Many of the adopters in our sample also exhibited the following notable characteristics as adopters: they had a strong relationship

and were united in their approach to parenting; they had confidence and belief in their own judgement; they knew what they wanted; they had a strong faith or humanitarian outlook; and they were optimistic, positive and resilient.

15 The well-being of the adopters and their children

In this chapter, we report on the standardised measures completed by adopters on their own mental health and the strengths and difficulties of their children.

The Strengths and Difficulties Questionnaire

The Strengths and Difficulties Questionnaire (SDQ) is a well-validated mental health screening and research instrument that measures whether children's emotional and behavioural development is problematic or within a normal range. The scale has 25 items and provides a total difficulties score as well as four subscales that indicate whether a child has problems of one or more types. These types are the four most common areas of difficulty: emotional problems (anxiety and depression), conduct problems (oppositional or antisocial behaviour), over-activity, and difficulties in peer relationships. An additional scale measures the child's strengths and shows the extent to which the child is pro-social: friendly, volunteering help and getting on well with others.

The questionnaire has been used in the general population (Meltzer *et al*, 2000), in high-risk populations such as looked after children (Meltzer *et al*, 2003), with fostered children (Sinclair *et al*, 2005) and with adopted children (Rushton *et al*, 2001; Biehal *et al*, 2010). It has also been used in countries around the world (Woerner *et al*, 2004). The SDQ can predict the presence of a psychiatric disorder but *only* when information is received from more than one person and/or combined with a clinical assessment. However, used on its own, the questionnaire *does* provide a good indication of the level and kind of difficulties children are currently experiencing.

Data and analysis

SDQs were completed by an adoptive parent for all the 119 sample children. However, the instrument has only been validated for children aged 4–15 years of age, and therefore the children outside this age range were excluded from the analysis. This gave a sample of 109 children, comprising 64 females and 45 males.

The overall level of difficulty

The SDQ produces an *overall* total difficulty score and this can sum from zero to 40. In this sample, the scores ranged from 1–33 with a mean score of 13.2 (see Table 15.1). Comparisons with the general population (Meltzer *et al*, 2000) show that the children in this sample had statistically significantly more difficulties than would be found among their peers.

Although the mean score for males was higher than that of the females in the sample, there were no statistical differences. The scores of children placed with local authority (LA) adopters were also higher than those placed with voluntary adoption agency (VAA) adopters, but again this did not reach statistical significance.

The difficulty score can be further banded into three classifications: normal, borderline and abnormal. The majority of the children were normal, i.e. falling within the responses that would be expected from a group of peers. However, over a third of the sample was in the abnormal range (see Table 15.2).

In a general population sample, one would expect to find about ten per cent scoring within the abnormal band and a further ten per cent scoring in the borderline band. Although more than a third scoring in the abnormal range is therefore higher than that found in the general population, it is lower than that found in other samples of looked after children. Research on children in foster care has found 45–55 per cent of children scoring in the abnormal range, depending on the sample taken (Meltzer, 2003; Sinclair, 2005). A comparison using t tests was undertaken of the general population and our sample subscale means. The adopted children differed from children in the general population on all the sub-scores (see Table 15.3).

Gender

There were no statistically significant gender differences in the mean total difficulty scores. However, it was striking that hyperactivity was the main area of difficulty for girls as well as boys. Hyperactivity is far more commonly reported in boys, while girls tend to score higher on emotional difficulties. The abnormal/borderline scores of hyperactivity in this sample were higher than in other samples of looked after children (Meltzer *et al*, 2003).

Age

Here we examine how the child's age was related to difficulties. Twenty-seven per cent of the youngest children were in the abnormal range, 36 per cent of the 7–9-year-olds, 59 per cent of those aged 10–12 years, and 43 per cent of those aged 13–15. Emotional problems and hyperactivity tended to increase with age. Hyperactivity was problematic for over half of the children aged 10 years or older. There were more difficulties of this kind in the 10–12 year age group than there were emotional difficulties.

Children and young people who are restless, fidgety and lacking in attention often find it difficult to maintain friendships, as peers quickly tire of this kind of behaviour. Therefore, it was not unexpected to find elevated levels of difficulties with peers. If borderline and abnormal

Table 15.1
The total SDQ difficulties score: means and standard deviations for the sample compared to British general population means

	Mean score and s.d. of sample (Male = 45, Female = 64)	British means (Male = 5153, Female = 5145)	Mean difference ±SEM[1], p-value
Total	13.2 (7.3)	8.4 (5.8)	4.8±0.47, p<0.0001
Males	15.0 (7.4)	7.8 (5.5)	7.2±0.83, p<0.0001
Females	13.4 (7.4)	9.1 (6.0)	4.8±0.76, p<0.0001

1   SEM is the standard error mean

Table 15.2
The total difficulties score

	Frequency	%
Normal	59	54.1
Borderline	11	10.1
Abnormal	39	35.8
Total	109	100

scores are considered together, peer difficulties were the main area of difficulty for all age groups.

Eight children (7% of the sample) had abnormal scores on *every* subscale (emotions, conduct, hyperactivity, and peer relationships). There were more boys in this group than girls: five boys (11% of all the boys in this sample) and three girls (5% of girls in the sample). Previous research (Howe, 1999; Rushton *et al*, 2003) has highlighted that children who are late placed are more likely to have poorer psychosocial outcomes. This is because older children are likely to have spent longer exposed to adverse environments and abusive and neglectful parenting. Surprisingly, in this study, age at placement was not associated with the total difficulties score but being the oldest sibling in the group was.[14]

The SDQ ratings are designed to pick up problems and for this reason can present a gloomy picture. However, one of the benefits of the SDQ is that it contains a subscale that asks about positive social qualities: being considerate of other people's feelings; sharing readily with other children; being helpful if someone is hurt, upset or ill; being kind to younger children, and often volunteering to help. Interestingly, despite the high levels of difficulty reported, adoptive parents were also able to identify their children's positive qualities. About 75 per cent of all the children had normal pro-social behaviours. Only a few (6) children under ten years old were identified as having abnormal responses.

---

14 Spearman's Rho = 0.220, n = 109, p<0.016

Table 15.3
Comparison of the mean scores and standard deviations of the sample children (n = 109) compared to general population norms

Area of difficulty	Females Sample n = 64	Pop n = 5145	Mean Difference ±SEM, p-value	Males Sample n = 45	Pop n = 5154	Mean Difference ±SEM, p-value
Emotions	3.1 (2.8)	2.0 (2.0)	1.1±0.3, p<0.0001	3.4 (2.7)	1.8 (2.0)	1.6±0.3, p<0.0001
Conduct	2.7 (2.4)	1.5 (1.6)	1.2±0.2, p<0.0001	2.6 (2.2)	1.7 (1.8)	0.9±0.2, p<0.0001
Hyperactivity	4.3 (2.9)	2.9 (2.4)	1.4±0.3, p<0.0001	5.4 (2.8)	4.0 (2.7)	1.4±0.3, p<0.0001
Peers	3.0 (2.0)	1.4 (1.6)	1.6±0.2, p<0.0001	3.5 (2.1)	1.5 (1.7)	2±0.2, p<0.0001

The impact of behavioural difficulties on the child and family

We used the version of the SDQ that asks additional questions about whether the child's difficulties interfered with the child's everyday life at home, their friendships, classroom learning, and leisure activities. The majority (70%) of children and young people were thought by their adoptive parents to have lives that were similar to those of their

Table 15.4
The number of children and young people with difficulties affecting their everyday life and the impact of the difficulties on their families

Difficulties of child	Burden on family None	Quite a lot or a great deal	Total
Normal	67	5	72
Borderline	7	7	14
Abnormal	4	19	23
Total	78	31	109

peers. Behavioural difficulties were recorded as having a serious impact on everyday life for a quarter of the children. However, when parents answered a question asking if the child's difficulties put a burden on the parent and the family as a whole, there was a slightly different response (see Table 15.4). Parents of four children, whose difficulties in everyday life were scored as abnormal, felt that these behaviours did *not* put a burden on themselves and their families, whereas five children whose behaviours were within the normal range were thought to put a burden on their families. This probably reflects individual differences in how behaviours are perceived and tolerated within families.

Thus far we have considered individual children's SDQ scores, but our adopters were parenting sibling groups. Although the majority (54%) of the children's scores fell within the normal range, 25 (68%) of the 37 families had at least one child in their sibling group scoring within the abnormal range. In five families all the children had mental health problems (see Table 15.5).

Table 15.5
Number of adoptive families and SDQ scores within each sibling group

	Number of families (n = 37)
No abnormal scores	12
One child with an abnormal score	10
Two or more children with abnormal scores	15
All children with abnormal scores	5

It was clear that some of the adopters were struggling to manage the children's behaviours. We therefore expected to see this reflected in the adoptive parents' General Health Questionnaire scores.

The General Health Questionnaire (GHQ) (n=37)

The GHQ assesses the respondent's current mental state and whether this is different from his or her usual state. The total possible score on the GHQ ranges from zero to 28 and allows for means and distributions to be calculated, both for the global total, as well as for the four subscales (Goldberg and Hillier, 1979). In this study, any score exceeding the threshold value of four was classified as achieving "psychiatric caseness". Psychiatric caseness is a probabilistic term, whereby if such respondents presented in general practice they would be likely to receive further attention.

The 37 adopters all completed a GHQ and their total scores ranged from zero to 26. Most (54%) of the adopters scored well within the normal range (Willmott *et al*, 2004) on all the four subscales (see Table 15.6). Seventeen adopters (46%) reached the threshold for "caseness" and eight (22%) of these scored abnormally in more than one domain. This is slightly more than would be expected in a general population sample. General population prevalence of emotional disorders has been estimated at 30 per cent in Britain (Goldberg and Huxley, 1992), with reported illness peaking in middle age and more likely to be identified in females than males (Boardman, 1987; McCrone *et al*, 2008).

Scores in the abnormal range

The adopters with abnormal scores were experiencing anxiety (19%) and severe depression (16%), with fewer reporting somatic symptoms (11%) or social difficulties (5%). High levels of anxiety and depression are reported in the general population in the UK. A report on the cost of mental health care in England (McCrone *et al*, 2008) quotes estimates of one in every 18 people suffering from anxiety disorders and one in every 38 people reporting depression. We did not ask the adopters about current medication, but one reported having been recently diagnosed as suffering with severe depression and another recorded that she was attempting to reduce her anti-depressant medication. It is worth noting that just as some mothers suffer from post-natal depression, some adoptive parents suffer from post-adoption stress or depression, especially when their expectations clash with their actual experiences (Foli and Thompson, 2004).

When the sibling group adopters' GHQ scores were compared

with the SDQ scores of their children's strengths and difficulties, it was not surprising to find that the scores in the GHQ and the SDQ were correlated.[15] There was a significant relationship between the higher adult GHQ scores and higher SDQ scores of their children. There were no significant relationships between the GHQ scores and whether the adopters had been approved by an LA or VAA, the gender of the child, the size of the sibling group, or the current age of the children.

We also asked adopters if their responses on the GHQ questionnaire were connected with being an adopter or with other unconnected life events. A few (4) said that other events such as moving house, managing their own business, family bereavements and poor physical health had led to their current feelings. Just over three-quarters (13 of the 17) of those whose scores had reached psychiatric caseness thought their elevated scores were connected with being an adopter. Thirty-five per cent attributed their poor mental health to being an adopter:

All current stresses and struggles in my life relate directly to being an adopter. (Adopter 16)

Some adopters wrote on their questionnaire that financial pressures, the huge change in lifestyle, the relentlessness of children's demands, and general fatigue had affected their mental health. One adopter wrote:

I had been a teacher [. . .] before this. None of this prepared me for the 'full on' emotional ride that three young children bring. My weight has gone up and down, my sleep habits have changed and my need for adult companionship increased. I am permanently tired even when they are at school. (Adopter 17)

Some adopters (7) also reported that their physical health had also been adversely affected. This small group of adopters reported feeling

---

15 Kendalls Tau correlation was significant at the 0.01 level two tailed (τ = .27 p<0.01)

Table 15.6
Mean and median scores and standard deviations on the four subscales of the GHQ

	n	Minimum	Maximum	Mean	Median	Std. deviation
Somatic score	37	0	7	1.65	1	1.989
Anxiety score	37	0	7	2.0	1	2.472
Social dysfunction	37	0	5	0.49	0	1.283
Severe depression	37	0	7	1.57	0	2.34

generally run down and having constant illnesses such as chest infections or symptoms of stress such as heart palpitations and hair falling out.

Scores within the normal range

Most of those scoring within the normal range stated that having children had been a benefit or had made little difference to their mental health. Eight of the 20 adopters who had normal GHQ scores attributed their good mental health and well-being entirely to becoming an adopter.

Researcher's warmth and summary ratings (n=37)

At the end of the interview, the researcher made two ratings based on all the discussion that had taken place. The first was a rating of the warmth expressed by the adoptive parent about each of the children and was on a six-point scale: none, little, some, moderate, moderately high, and high. The rating was based on consideration of the following aspects of warmth: tone of voice, expression and gestures when speaking about the child, spontaneous expressions of sympathy and concern about the child's difficulties (if any), and interest in the child as a person. Irrelevant factors in making this rating included any researcher judgement about what the parent felt; the warmth of the parent's personality; parental depression; and criticism/hostility to people other than the children. The second rating was a judgement, based on the content of the interview, of how well the placement was going.

Ratings of warmth

High warmth ratings were recorded in respect of 94 children (79%) and moderately high ratings in respect of 15 children (13%). Lower warmth ratings were recorded in respect of comparatively few children (8%). There were no statistical differences in the emotional warmth ratings of LA and VAA adopters. It was noticeable that the low warmth ratings were nearly all recorded in respect of the first and second child (the older children) in the sibling groups. Unsurprisingly, lower warmth was expressed by adoptive parents towards the three children who returned to foster care after the partial disruption of two placements. However, there were no statistical associations between children with high SDQ scores and lower parental warmth ratings. Some parents were able to express warmth and commitment to the children irrespective of their emotional and behavioural difficulties.

Ratings of how well the placement was going

The researcher rated the adoptive placements on a five-point scale: settled placement with no major problems; settled placement with some difficulties; major difficulties but adopters still committed; difficulties outweigh any positives; and, placement disrupted. It was striking that although many of the adopters were parenting children with significant difficulties, the majority of families (28) had settled placements. Two families were thought to have more difficulties than positives, and seven families had major difficulties.

For analysis purposes, the categories "settled" and "settled with some difficulties" were combined, as were "major difficulties" and "difficulties outweighing positives". This new dichotomous variable was tested against the following variables for association: LA or VAA adopter; reunited as a sibling group in the adoptive family; size of sibling group; motivations to adopt; support network; SDQ caseness; and, time in placement. None achieved statistical significance. This may have been because of low numbers, and so to try to understand why nine families were struggling we examined other possible reasons.

We considered whether the families having the most problems were parenting children with multiple difficulties as defined by having abnormal scores on at least three of the four SDQ subscales. This was not statistically significant. We also considered whether it was more likely to be the families who had two or more children in a sibling group with abnormal scores, and this was statistically significant.[16] Therefore, it was not the nature of an individual's child's difficulties but the number of siblings with difficulties that was associated with the placement not going well. It should be noted that the researcher rated seven of these nine families as still being very committed to the children.

For many of the sibling-group adopters, a key part of their commitment to the children was maintaining contact with their siblings. We examine this issue in the next chapter.

Summary

- Adopters completed a Strengths and Difficulties Questionnaire (SDQ) for each child and 109 children's questionnaires were included in the analysis.
- Over a third of children scored within the abnormal range. This is higher than would be expected in a general population sample but lower than that found in other samples of looked after children.
- The adopted children differed from the general population on all the subscales of the SDQ. There were high levels of hyperactivity reported for boys and girls. The main area of difficulty for all age groups was peer relationships. The total difficulties score increased with age, and eight children had abnormal scores on all four subscales. However, adopters were also able to identify many pro-social behaviours in their children.
- Sixty-eight per cent of families had at least one child with an abnormal score. The total difficulties score was not associated with age at placement but was associated with the child's current age. The older the child, the more likely the score was to be higher.

---

16 Fisher's exact p = 0.05

- Fifty-four per cent of adopters scored within the normal range of the GHQ. Thirty-five per cent of adopters attributed their poor mental health (anxiety and depression) to the stresses and strains of being an adopter. The adopters' scores on the GHQ and the children's scores on the SDQ were correlated. The higher the children's score, the more likely it was that the adopters' mental health was abnormal.
- At the end of the interview, the researcher made a rating of the warmth expressed by the adopters about the children. High warmth ratings were recorded for 79 per cent of the children and moderately high for 13 per cent of the children. Some adoptive parents were able to be warm and committed to their children despite the children's significant mental health difficulties.
- Seven families were rated by the researcher as having major problems, and a further two had more difficulties than positives. The number of siblings with difficulties (rather than the severity of an individual child's difficulties) was associated with the placement being rated as having major difficulties by the researcher.

16   Contact with other siblings

In this chapter, we focus on contact between the adopted siblings and their other siblings. Over three-quarters (76%) of the children in our sample had full or half-siblings who were living elsewhere, and many of the children came from very large families. Arrangements were often made to maintain or establish relationships with these children.

Receiving information about other siblings

Adopters were asked if they had received an explanation from the social worker about why the other siblings were not being placed with them. Only about half of the adopters thought that the explanation had been adequate. The reasons given to the adopters included the following: the other siblings were too old to be placed for adoption or were living happily in permanent foster care; a group placement was not considered because the siblings had never lived together; half-siblings were living with a birth parent who was able to care for them; social workers had been unable to find an adopter who was willing to take all the children; other siblings posed a risk to the children; and, grandparents had only been able to take some but not all of the siblings. One of the adopters described the situation as follows:

> *They tried to place all four children together, but the youngest child was born after the other three were put in care and was put in foster care separately. The social workers couldn't find someone for all the children and they ran out of time, because our children were in care for two years. They had always lived together. [. . .] I think [the oldest child] is still coming to terms with not living with [her baby brother].* (Adopter 2)

Half-siblings

Nearly a third of the siblings living elsewhere were half-siblings. Some of the children knew their half-siblings, as they had lived together, but other children were unaware of their half-sibling's existence. There did not appear to be the same emphasis on maintaining contact with half-siblings as there was with full siblings. In virtually all cases, the adopters had been given very little information about half-siblings. Some expressed frustration about this:

> . . . we know the birth mother was pregnant, and we've asked a number of times to find out if she's had that child or not, because if she has we need to find a sensitive way to be able to tell the girls at the appropriate time, but we still haven't been told. (Adopter 32)

Telling the children about other siblings

Many adopters mentioned how difficult it was to explain to young children about other siblings, especially if the adopters thought that the child was 'just developing his own identity' and not 'at an emotional stage' where s/he could understand and cope with the information. Some children wanted to know whether another baby would be allowed to stay with their birth mother, and the answer was not always clear. None of the adopters mentioned receiving advice on how to manage these tricky issues.

When another sibling was living with the birth parents, maintaining contact could be very difficult, and for this reason the adopters sometimes chose not to tell their children that they had another sibling. One adopter explained:

> We haven't had contact, because the birth mother has been contesting the adoption. She wanted contact with [oldest child] but not [the younger ones], and we said it was all or nothing (. . .) The children don't know they have another sibling, and I don't want to cause any more confusion. (Adopter 12)

A few adopters made it very clear that they were not keen on having any contact. These cases mostly involved half-siblings whom the children had never met, as in the following comment:

> I don't think it's relevant at all to the children to be told that they have a half-brother somewhere, because I don't see that there

will ever be the need to want to trace him for any reason at all. They don't know of his existence and he probably isn't aware of them, and I think that's the way it should stay. (Adopter 5)

However, other adopters were concerned to 'keep the door open' so that if their children decided at any stage in the future that they wanted to meet their full or half-siblings, this could be arranged. For this reason, one adoptive mother maintained a correspondence with the grandmother, because she was their last link to the two older siblings. Another mother specifically requested a contact visit because the children knew about their sister but had 'no idea what she looks like or anything'.

Requests to take another sibling

Five of the adopters had been asked if they would be willing to take another sibling, all of whom were born subsequent to the placement of the sibling group. Four couples had already refused, or were likely to do so, for the following reasons: they thought the support provided had been inadequate; it would be too complicated to explain to the children 'where number 7 came from'; and the children's authority had said that the new baby could not be placed directly with the adopters without being fostered first. One couple, who had already taken four siblings, had agreed in principle to take a fifth child: '[We] felt it was right, because he's a full sibling . . .'

Maintaining contact

About two-thirds of the sibling-group adopters initially received social work support in dealing with contact arrangements, and almost half of those who obtained an adoption order said they were still receiving help. In most cases, all that had been required was a clear explanation of how the letterbox contact system worked and advice on the content of letters to and from birth parents. For a few families, the support had been essential in maintaining face-to-face contact with other siblings who were living with a birth parent. Without social work support, contact would probably have ground to a halt in these circumstances, as two adopters explained:

I am concerned about having to manage the contact ourselves from this year. I think it's essential for the children's social worker to be there to manage [the birth relatives], because otherwise we will have to take on the social worker's role and manage them as well as looking after the children – and I'm not sure I'm prepared to do that. (Adopter 1)

I think [support] has been essential, because without them we couldn't have done it, and we didn't want to do it. (Adopter 19)

It was also clear from comments made by many of the adopters that they were sending letters to the birth parents and getting nothing back. Generally, they were concerned to protect their children from continuing rejection and disappointment, and for this reason sometimes they did not mention the letters at all to the children. Here are two typical responses:

... we've written two letters now and we've had no replies, so we're having to deal with the children's disappointment and anxiety about why haven't they had a reply. (Adopter 32)

Well, they don't even know [sibling] exists. We've sent two years of letters, we've not had anything back. (Adopter 23)

Some adopters continued to send letters to their post-adoption support team despite receiving no replies because they wanted to show that they had met their obligations and, when their children had access to those files, they wanted them to know that they had done everything they could to maintain contact. One family sent letters to the letterbox co-ordinator because they thought 'it was the right thing to do', although no arrangements had ever been made for contact.

Ongoing contact with siblings

At the time of the research interview, 15 of the adoptive families had contact with another sibling – just over half of those with siblings elsewhere. Six families had face-to-face contact and nine families had letterbox contact. Just one of these families had both face-to-face and letterbox contact with a sibling. Contact was usually once or twice a year.

Generally, the adopters described the contact arrangements as having little meaning for the youngest children in the sibling groups. They attributed this to young children having no previous relationship with the sibling and not being able to recognise them. However, sometimes contact visits triggered all sorts of feelings, especially for older children. When asked how well the contact arrangements were working for the oldest child, adopters described half as working well and half of the children as having mixed reactions. It was common for each child in the sibling group to have a different response to contact, and this could make it difficult for the adopters to manage contact visits.

There were also fears that contact would 'make such restraints on your family life that you're never going to cope'. One couple, who had been worried about the difficulty of managing more than one set of contact arrangements, took this into account when choosing their children. They were particularly concerned about the effect on their family life and explained this as follows:

Mother: . . . well, especially if we were expected to have ongoing contact with birth parents as well. You're then having two or three contacts a year and actually, having just done one direct contact with one parent, yeah, one is enough because yeah, it disrupts your family life actually . . .

Father: And normality as such.

Mother: And it sets you back, and you have to then build up again and to try and move forward again. (Adopter 6)

Whether the children themselves wanted to see their siblings was likely to determine the adopters' attitude to contact. Some children did not want to share their lives with other siblings; one girl, who had recently turned 18, had recently placed a veto on the case file to prevent her birth parents or any of her half-siblings from contacting her. However, other children really enjoyed seeing their siblings. In one case, where contact involved 'a two-hour journey there and back', the adopters were willing to do this because they realised it was important to the oldest child. Another group of siblings was very keen to meet the birth mother's new baby, and the adoptive mother helped them to send a present and recognised how much this meant to them, but she thought it was still too early for them to see their birth mother again.

While there had been some initial difficulties for the six families having face-to-face contact with siblings, it had become more of an accepted routine and the children were described as taking it in their stride. It was clear that contact was beneficial for some children, as two adopters explained:

> *It works now we have contact somewhere neutral, where there is something to do, and we keep it fairly short. We had a couple of contacts that were very difficult. We try to avoid Christmas and birthdays, so it's a bit like seeing cousins occasionally (. . .) We find it hard, but they enjoy it.* (Adopter 30)

> *The oldest child used to say, 'My mummy's had a new baby and he's dead', but he's stopped that since having contact. The second child is delighted to have a sister. The third child loves everybody, and the youngest child thinks that having contact is "cool" (. . .) They talk about their siblings quite openly and naturally, and that's the way life is for everyone (. . .) as far as they're concerned.* (Adopter 34)

Contact issues did not contribute to either of the two partial disruptions. Indeed, in one of these families contact with other siblings and birth relatives was clearly a long-standing arrangement, which was viewed very positively:

> *Loads [of contact]! We have a very natural relationship with their maternal birth family including their brother and sister. We see them probably every eight weeks. I think for all of them*

it evokes painful feelings, but they love seeing them and I think overall the relationships are healthy. (Adopter 13)

Having explored whether and how sibling relationships were maintained through contact, we report in the next chapter on how the adoption was working out.

Summary

- Just over three-quarters of the children had full or half-siblings who were living elsewhere. Only about half of the adopters thought they had received a good explanation of why other siblings had not been placed with them. Five of the families had been approached to take another sibling.
- About two-thirds of the sibling-group adopters initially received support in dealing with contact (usually letterbox contact), and almost half said they were still receiving help with contact after the adoption order. This was particularly needed for face-to-face contact involving birth relatives.
- At the time of the research interview, 15 of the adoptive families had face-to-face or letterbox contact with another sibling – just over half (54%) of those with siblings elsewhere. Agencies and adopters tended to assume that it was more important to provide information and arrange contact for full siblings than it was for half-siblings.
- Adopters thought that contact had less meaning for younger children, who often did not recognise their other siblings, but contact seemed to provoke more mixed responses in older children. Children in the same sibling group had different responses to contact. While some children were pleased to see their siblings, this was not always the case.

17 How the adoption was working out

In previous chapters, we reported on the strengths and difficulties of each child and the post-adoption support the families were receiving. We concluded the interview by asking the adopters: if they had experienced any difficulties; how the adoption had affected them and their extended family; whether they thought it was right to place the siblings together; how the children were getting on; what had been most helpful and most difficult for them; and, how they rated the services they had received. Here we report on their responses to these questions.

Had the adopters experienced any difficulties since the children were placed?

It was not surprising to find most adopters (68%) reporting some difficulties. Most new parents struggle, even when they are not taking on a whole sibling group at once. However, it is important to note that almost a third of the adopters (12) reported no difficulties or only a few minor problems. Despite adopting older children, fewer voluntary adoption agency (VAA) adopters reported major problems, but about half of *both* local authority (LA) and VAA adopters stated that their agency had helped them to resolve their difficulties.

The responses from the six adopters who had taken sibling groups of four were particularly positive: half said they had had no difficulties and only one reported major problems, which were with the school and *not* the children. This echoes positive findings about very large sibling groups and their adopters in two other studies (Smith *et al*, 2006; Glidden *et al*, 2000) but the reasons for these findings are unclear. In our study, most of the children in sibling groups of four had low SDQ (Strengths and Difficulties Questionnaire) scores, but four children (in three sibling groups) had difficulties that interfered "quite a lot" with their home life, their friendships or their classroom learning. The positive responses probably reflect the outlook of the adopters as much as the behaviour of the children, because all of these adopters expressed high warmth towards all of their children.

The behaviours identified as most difficult by the sibling-group adopters in our study were attention-seeking and challenging behaviour, attachment difficulties and "parentification". Challenging behaviours included violence, self-harm, stealing and lying, and some adopters were also concerned about low self-esteem, soiling or bedwetting. Over two-thirds (69%) of the adopters thought that the siblings were competing for their attention most or nearly all of the time. One adopter described how she and her husband had attempted to deal with this:

> . . . the biggest challenge with having three is trying to give them individual attention (. . .) but it's finding a way of being able to do that, so it feels fair (. . .) We try and do this ten-minute play thing, when we spend ten minutes playing with each of them separately, and they choose whatever they want to do. And it's all good intentions, and we start off really well and you see a real change in their behaviour, especially when things are a bit challenging, but it's really hard to keep it up. Life gets in the way. (Adopter 28)

It was not unusual to have one child who continually demanded attention with very challenging behaviour, and other siblings sometimes copied this behaviour and joined in the uproar. One adoptive mother, who described her children as being like 'three tornadoes going off one after the other', commented:

> They constantly compete for our attention, and that can be anything from going into a room and starting a fight with another sibling or just literally winding the other ones up. If you take any one of those three children out of the equation, things settle down significantly. (Adopter 13)

Six adopters (16%) had difficulty in parenting a child who had effectively assumed the parental role within the birth family. These

215

children (usually the oldest in the sibling group) had cared for their siblings, feeding them and trying to keep them safe. They were often reluctant to relinquish this responsibility, and adopters could find themselves constantly caught up in a power struggle with arguments about the best way to change a nappy or wash a child's hands. One adopter described the strategy she used to persuade her "parentified" child that she could safely hand over the care of her younger siblings:

We have to, kind of, do it in a way that – 'Right, you show me how you do it and I'll follow you.' And that way she backed off, because she thought I was doing it the right way, and obviously we made a few changes along the way, and after a matter of probably three or four weeks she gave up anyway. She was too busy playing and enjoying herself (. . .) But it was getting her to show me how to do it; it was her idea. (Adopter 23)

Sometimes, when children had experienced neglect, the adopters had to find ways of convincing them that they would not be left to go hungry. One mother commented that after clearing away the breakfast things, she always used to put out snacks straight away so her son would know 'that there was a next meal coming'.

Another issue mentioned by several adopters was their children's need to behave as though they were much younger than their actual age. One mother commented:

. . . you do sort of live a dual life. They're babies when they're at home but they're seven or eight when they're outside. [It's about allowing them] to have the experience that they've missed out on. [Child] came to us as an eight-year-old and was desperate to be younger because she could sit on dad's knee because that's what young kids do and she was too old. We said, 'Well, (. . .) you might be a bit too heavy but you're not too old.' . . . you wouldn't dream of having an eight-year-old sit on your knee outside, because it would look odd, but at home you just think, 'Well, if this is what she needs, this is the experience she needs to have at this moment . . .' (Adopter 20)

However, there were frequent occasions when a child's behaviour could not be clearly attributed to previous experiences. Many adopters found it difficult to know whether certain behaviours were due to previous experiences or were just a part of normal development:

> . . . it's always too easy to assume in this situation that a problem which has arisen with a child is due to the fact that they're adopted, and that may not necessarily be the case. Some of their problems are those problems that (. . .) all children have at some point or another, and that what's difficult to know really, not having brought up our own birth children. (Adopter 19)

Surprisingly, coping with the actual number of children was rarely mentioned as a problem; one adopter of four siblings commented that it was just getting used to buying 24 pints of milk at a time. However, caring for three or more children under school age was certainly not easy. One mother commented:

> Once you go over two, the balance of power has tipped out of your favour. There is always one hand you cannot hold. (Adopter 14)

Yet this problem was resolved in different ways by two adopters whose sibling groups both included twin toddlers. One mother had trained her oldest child to walk beside her, holding onto the side bar of the twins' buggy. The other had put safety gates on the doors, so that she could focus on feeding or changing one child without having to worry about where the other two had gone and what they were doing. This adopter also prepared lots of food in advance before the children were placed, so she did not have to spend much time cooking during the first weeks of the placement.

Conflict and rivalry in the sibling group

Just over half (51%) of the adoptive parents in our study reported arguments and disagreements between the siblings most or nearly all of the time. For most families these were not serious arguments and did not cause concern, because the adopters recognised that this was the kind of low-level bickering and teasing that occurs among siblings in most families. Some adopters had worked out how to de-escalate sibling conflict, as in the following comments:

> ... there's always a fight round the corner sort of way, but they're just squabbles. (. . .) After six months or so we will now, when there's a squabble, we just stay out of the room and it resolves itself. If things are getting a bit serious, you just offer them all a flapjack and they're like 'Oh, okay.' (Adopter 4)

> I think it's knowing when to choose your battles, isn't it? You know, shall I get involved in this or shall I leave them to bicker it out? (. . .) Providing there's no blood, we're okay. (Adopter 20)

Serious quarrels and shouting were reported less frequently: 70 per cent of the adopters said this hardly ever happened, or only sometimes. However, 30 per cent stated that quarrels and shouting were happening most or nearly all of the time. One adopter stated:

> It's low-level continual fighting. We have stopped the physical violence now. The weird thing is they actually all really have a strong bond. They all really miss each other and love each other, and their fighting is almost like an interaction (. . .) A year ago I thought this is a dreadful mistake; they don't like each other (. . .) And when I talked to them about it, it was really clear that wasn't the case – they have a strong bond, but they just have to fight and argue, because that's the way it is. And I think that can be really misleading, because if somebody came in here and did an assessment, they would think 'Oh, they don't like each other.' But they would kill to protect each other. I've seen evidence of that huge protectiveness towards each other. (Adopter 3)

Ten adopters, a third of those who had taken three siblings, found that the children played much better in pairs but the dynamics with three children could be challenging. Here are two of their comments:

They get on well if they're in pairs. Put three together and there's a bit of a disaster. (Adopter 25)

Any two of them at any time works, but you put the three in and we have trouble. They can't live with each other but they can't live without each other. It's a really difficult one – love hate. Sometimes they're great, other times they're killing each other. (Adopter 17)

Adopters were asked how much the quarrels bothered them. Although the majority (78%) did not think the quarrels were serious, the verbal disagreements bothered 28 per cent of the adopters quite a lot or very much, and in four families the quarrels nearly always resulted in a physical fight between the children. This small group of families thought the fighting was of serious concern.

The warmth and closeness of the sibling group
Although about half of the sibling groups were reported as frequently quarrelling, all the siblings were described as fairly close or very close to each other. Only one family reported that their children did not spend much time together in the home. Most spent a lot of time playing together or watching TV, and this constant contact probably triggered many quarrels. All the children were reported as going to places and doing activities together, but as many of the siblings were young, their choice of activity outside the home was likely to have been determined by their parents.

When siblings had been placed separately in foster care, there was sometimes a marked lack of warmth between them when they were re-united in adoption. For example, two brothers who had been re-united with their sister, sometimes asked: 'Does she have to live with us?' However, relationships between the children changed over time, and one adopter observed that at first if she gave the boys a biscuit, they would never ask for one for their sister, but now they did and they were 'getting really good at looking out for her'. Another mother commented that the children were very close, 'given that they didn't have a relationship at all' before they were placed together.

The effect of the placement on the adopters

Becoming adopters to a sibling group had transformed the lives of the adopters. When asked how they had been affected by having the siblings, the immediate response of almost a third (12) of the adopters was that they were 'tired all the time', and it was 'busy, busy, busy, from the minute you get up in the morning to the minute you go to sleep at night'. They talked about the pressure of trying to meet each child's different needs and having little time for themselves. One adopter was immensely grateful to her best friend, who would sometimes come and look after the children for a weekend, so that she could 'go away and go to sleep'.

Having children puts a strain on many marital relationships, and this was the case for about a quarter of these parents. Mostly this was because of the effects of tiredness. Adopters sometimes described themselves as becoming 'a bit monosyllabic' or 'grumpy', and said they couldn't remember when they last had a night out together. However, others found that the challenge of parenting a sibling group had brought them closer together. Some adopters stressed the importance of self-awareness and of reflecting on their own behaviour, as in the following statement by an adoptive father:

[The oldest child's] big thing is wetting and [wife] finds that really difficult to understand (. . .) She deals with it better now, but she just can't get her brain round the fact that [child] will quite happily stand there in wet pants (. . .) whereas I had bedwetting as a child, so it doesn't worry me so much. I have much more trouble with [the middle child's] attitude (. . .) If you tell her off about one thing, she'll just start on something else and ratchet it up until she can prove that she can outdo you (. . .) Learning to ignore it, to prevent it from ratcheting up, is my trouble, because rules are rules to me and my children know you get absolute consistency from me – and I pride myself on that, so trying, therefore, not to see some things, has taken me a long time. (Adopter 35)

The adopters thought that their lives had been transformed by the arrival of the children and sometimes 'enriched beyond measure'. Some adopters admitted that this was the hardest thing they had ever done, 'because you have to change your whole way of life', and one stated that she had 'hit rock bottom really in those first two months'. Others said that they couldn't remember what their lives had been like before, because everything 'just felt so right'. One mother, who was still dealing with a child who soiled every day, described herself as 'completely blessed', while a father said that what gave him the most joy was hearing the children laugh. Here are two more comments:

> Obviously it's a massive life change and experience, but we love the kids to bits, can't imagine life without them and the last year has just gone so quickly (...) Absolutely no regrets at all. (Adopter 12)

> Despite the fact that they are so naughty, they have given us so much and sometimes they have made us laugh till we cried. (Adopter 5)

Many adopters had struggled to find ways of coping with the children's behaviour, and in the process they had learned a considerable amount about themselves, as in the following comments:

> I can't believe how much pressure sometimes the three children have put on us and on our relationship. It has made us open our eyes and see that, but at the end of the day we're still strong enough to get through it and realise what's happening. (Adopter 32)

> ... it's that tension of trying to hold your own emotions together while they are pushing all your buttons, because they want you to shout at them. So struggling with all of that has been a learning curve. (Adopter 33)

In cases where fathers were the main carer, the children sometimes expected to be cared for by their mother but only because that was "the social norm". One father said that mothers had been hesitant to allow their daughters to come and play with his children or to come to the house themselves, while on one occasion when he was out with the children somebody had wound down a car window and shouted at him, 'Fucking loser! Get a job!' Fortunately, he and his wife had got to know people who were more "open-minded". He also commented with some satisfaction that it was perhaps easier for him to negotiate with the LA about finance because 'you get more respect' as a man and 'the general reaction tends to be "Oh, what a hero!"' Another father had been dismayed to discover that his experience as a teacher had in no way prepared him for the challenges of adopting three children. He was not the only person to reach this conclusion: an experienced social worker also found that adoption was much harder, because she could not go home to escape from problems or maintain a professional detachment from her own children.

While parenting a sibling group was always demanding, some families faced additional pressures. Five adopters had the added stress of trying to cope with the children alone; for three of them this was because their partner was serving abroad in the armed forces (sometimes in a war zone), while two had separated from their partner after the children were placed. Children in four families had made disclosures of abuse (two against their birth parents and two against an adoptive father), and there had been police investigations but no prosecutions. Where accusations had been made against the adoptive father, one placement partially disrupted, and the father in the other case left the family home. The adoptive mother in this family had the terrible uncertainty of not knowing whether her husband had actually abused the children.

The impact of the placement on the extended family

Adopting a sibling group also had a wider impact on family and friends. Almost two-thirds (65%) of the adopters reported that their own parents had responded positively to the arrival of the children. They said their parents had welcomed the children with open arms, loved them and enjoyed spending time with them. However, adopters also reported that a few friends and family were initially doubtful and did not give their wholehearted support. Here are comments by two of the adopters:

We have been really, really pleased with the response. Everyone has taken the children into their hearts and (. . .) just accepted them as part of the family. (Adopter 12)

Dad made a comment, 'You know, these kids are just going to come and take all your energy, all your money and they'll run off at 16 and get pregnant.' That was sort of his view of what was going to happen, but from the minute they met the children they fell in love with them. (Adopter 21)

The adopters were delighted when the grandparents felt able to have some or all of the children to stay overnight. One commented that her mother 'had the girls for one night and they stayed for five!' In another case, this was the perfect solution for a child who continually demanded attention, as the mother explained:

My parents have been brilliant. When we haven't managed, [child] has gone to them, and because he is on his own there, he thrives (. . .) He's an angel there because he gets what he needs – a mummy and daddy all to himself, so he's not jealous of absolutely everything I do for the other two. (Adopter 17)

However, 11 adopters (30%) reported tensions in relationships with their parents. Sometimes this was because the grandparents found it difficult to understand the challenges of adopting abused and neglected children or because they were worried that the adopters were having great difficulty in coping with the children.

In three families, relationships with extended family members were extremely difficult or had virtually broken down. The adopter whose children had made allegations of abuse against her husband stated that none of her male relatives wanted to be left alone with the children. In another family, the adopters had "fallen out" with one set of grandparents because they had treated the children "like strangers". One mother burst into tears, when she described her parents' rejection of a child with severe attachment difficulties:

My parents have washed their hands of him. They won't have anything to do with him (. . .) which is difficult because I've always been very close to my parents and they've been fantastically supportive (. . .) I think that if Social Services had helped us when we asked for help (. . .) instead of just letting it go on and on and on, that probably it wouldn't have got to this point (. . .) I can understand how they feel, because it is such difficult behaviour to cope with. It is awful, you know, he might have a row with you (. . .) and he will spit in your face . . .(Adopter 14)

The decision to place the siblings together

When adopters were asked whether the decision to keep the sibling group together was the right decision, the majority (81%) felt strongly that it had been right and that the children had benefited from being adopted together. Many emphasised how close the siblings were and how they had always been "the only constant" in each other's lives:

They are each other's family (. . .) That's why they're managing, because they weren't taken from their family – their family came with them. (Adopter 4)

One adopter stated that one of the benefits of the children being together was that the oldest child was able to provide a reality check, because she remembered the events that had happened in the birth family and could say, "No, actually . . .", if the other children reverted to fantasy. However, the benefit emphasised by most adopters was the bond between the siblings and their sense of belonging to each other, as expressed in the following interview extracts:

They have a unique bond, they have a common life experience, they have memories that only they can have and only they can share with each other. And it gives them strength, it gives them security, and it gives them a sense of being and it's their identity. (Adopter 18)

. . . they will always have each other, come hell or high water
(. . .) and it's as fundamental as that. It's knowing that you're
part of something, knowing you're not alone. It's important.
(Adopter 28)

Four adopters were not sure that the decision had been the right one, and usually this was because they thought that a child with severe difficulties 'needed to be an only child and to be given one-to-one [attention]'. Three adopters, including two who had experienced a disruption, said that placing the children together had been a big mistake. Yet even among these negative responses there was often an acknowledgement that being placed together had been beneficial for the children in some ways and they 'couldn't envisage separating them'.

It is perhaps worth noting that one adopter pointed out that the situation had changed over time and consequently her opinion had changed too:

I think it was absolutely the right thing to do [to place the
siblings together], but if you had asked me that a year ago, I
possibly wouldn't have said that (. . .) I used to think that had
[the oldest child] been placed on her own, maybe she would
have flourished more and quicker, but now I don't think that
would have been the case at all. I think it would have destroyed
her. (Adopter 1)

How were the children getting on?

There is always a temptation during a face-to-face research interview for the interviewee to sound off about anything that has annoyed or upset them. Our adopters might have felt safe to do this because the interview was conducted in their own home, they had an assurance of anonymity, and the interviewer offered no judgement on what was being said. This may partially explain the discrepancy between the high level of difficulties reported by adopters and the high number of children said to be doing quite or very well.

At the end of the interview, adopters were asked how each child

225

was getting on. The majority of the children were rated by their adoptive parent(s) as doing quite or very well (see Table 17.1). This was surprising when so many of the children had abnormal SDQ scores. However, all the children rated as 'not doing very well' or having 'lots of problems' had an SDQ total difficulties score of more than 20. This is at the severe end of the scale and is especially high in comparison with the general population, where the mean difficulties score is 8. This sample of siblings had a mean score of 13.

Table 17.1
Adopters' ratings of each child's current progress

	Quite or very well %	Not doing very well %	Lots of problems %
Eldest child	90	5	5
Second child	87	3	10
Third child	97	3	0
Fourth child	100	0	0
Fifth child	0	100	0

Many of the adopters described their children as 'blossoming' and making progress. They were making friends and were doing well at school. Indeed, some children were doing 'fantastically well' and were top of their class or had 'gone up six levels last year, which has never been heard of'. Even a child with serious attachment difficulties was said to be 'an absolute star at school'. The adopters were very pleased when the children enjoyed going to school and were happy there, as in the following statements:

> They're all getting on very well. They are behind at school but we know why. They all love school. I had a three-year-old wanting to go to school yesterday – she couldn't understand why she couldn't go! (Adopter 7)

> . . . that's one thing the teachers always comment on – such happy children, and they are genuinely happy. (Adopter 26)

Some children had clearly adapted very well to their adoptive families, understood the boundaries set by their new parents, and were a source of delight. It was very satisfying for adopters when the children were happy, secure and able to enjoy the stability and normality of their new lives, as shown in the following interview extracts:

> They respond really well to us (. . .) They're good at adhering to rules and (. . .) I think it makes you realise when you meet up with other kids how lucky we are (. . .) I love their characters; they're very different but their characters are great. (Adopter 22)

> They have responded well to being parented . . . they relish the stability and routine (. . .) We don't allow them to run riot just because they're adopted (. . .) I think it's just about the consistency and the stability. Things that are important to them are things like having their meals (. . .) to know it will be a good meal, to know that they'll enjoy it, to know that we get to school on time, that they're not going to be late, because they used to be late a lot. The older two remember that. They don't want to be late to school, so they respond well to me saying, 'Come on or we'll be late,' and we get there and it's all fine. So it's just I suppose responding to everything being what it wasn't before. (Adopter 24)

However, some adopters also rejoiced in the fact that their children now felt safe enough to be naughty, as one mother explained:

> [Child] is going through the stage of being an absolute terror, because he's secure. You know, he very much was trying to do the right thing and hardly ever getting into trouble, and now he is just doing normal stuff . . . (Adopter 18)

Although the children still had difficulties, some of the more severe behaviours were becoming less frequent, or had stopped altogether (e.g. self-harming or compulsive eating). However, sometimes children still needed lots of reassurance, as in the following example:

She has to know who's picking up. Even if we're walking the dog in the park, she has to be within about three foot of my leg. She does worry that she's going to be abandoned, but apart from that she's blossoming really. She was very underweight, very tiny, but she's now caught up. (Adopter 23)

It was also apparent that some children or young people would have ongoing difficulties, as one adopter explained:

... he's a lovely young man. If he walked in here and you didn't know any of his background, you'd just say, 'Oh, isn't he lovely,' and he is – but his learning problems, his lack of social skills, very young interaction, and of course now at high school that's becoming a big issue, because friends are like 'Idiot!'pushing him away and he doesn't understand why ... (Adopter 16)

What had the adopters found most helpful during the adoption process?

When the adopters were asked what had helped them most, the majority immediately named the person or agency that had given them the most support. Almost a third (12) identified their own social worker, and it was clear they particularly valued having an experienced social worker whom they could trust, especially when they encountered difficulties. Here are two of their comments:

Her experience and her generosity in time and in knowledge was exceptional. She held our hand all the way through it, and she was really honest with what she thought, what she felt, and what she knew. (Adopter 28)

There were several times when we both felt if we hadn't had her [the social worker] we might have given up. (Adopter 30)

Several adopters (five VAA-approved adopters and one LA adopter) said they felt very well supported, not just by their social worker but by the entire adoption agency. Again, the VAA adopters felt reassured that their agency was 'always going to be there' to provide support. A few other professionals (such as a counsellor and two health visitors) were also mentioned as providing crucial support and making helpful interventions.

Adopters had also found it helpful to speak to other adopters through buddy schemes, support groups, or the message boards at Adoption UK, as one commented:

> . . . one thing our worker was very good at, she put us in touch with other adopters, so I've got quite a network of adopters across the area (. . .) people who understand. (Adopter 31)

Surprisingly, only four adopters mentioned friends and relatives as being very helpful, but that may have been because the main focus of the interview was on adoption agency practice. A few made it very clear that they depended on friends and relatives for support, as one explained:

> [The local authority] did offer support (. . .) and I turned them down, because I've got a strong friendship, I've got a strong family, and I'd rather have that kind of support . . . (Adopter 16)

A few adopters (3) remembered particular training sessions or work-shops where they learned specific skills or strategies to manage the children's behaviour. Two adopters with a child who was a danger to him/herself or others were very relieved to have received training or instruction in how to restrain the child safely. One adopter described a course on 'safe handling de-escalation skills', which had enabled her to restrain her daughter without hurting her in any way when the child was trying to throw herself out of a window. She emphasised that it was crucial to know that she was not hurting her child, because 'children with attachment problems are very over-sensitive to touch'. Apparently this adopter only had to use these skills twice and 'actually it turned into a hug' and 'changed the dynamics of the relationship'. The other adopter admitted that at one stage she was 'frightened to come home', because she could not control a five-year-old boy who could not manage his emotions and was 'repeatedly hitting, kicking biting'. She commented that thanks to a colleague they had found 'a way of holding him to keep him safe and us safe, which has been a revelation'. It was an indication of progress that they had not had to use this technique 'for a few weeks'. As these were clearly extreme situations, it was worrying that both of these adopters had to find appropriate training themselves. The third adopter described why a trauma recovery course provided by the adoption agency had been very helpful:

> I would say the trauma recovery course actually (. . .) because we could identify our children with what they were saying, and suddenly the penny dropped (. . .) We could identify and develop strategies and how we could work with those issues . . . (Adopter 37)

Three very self-sufficient adopters commented that the most helpful thing was their own experience or the support they provided for each other. One couple made it clear in the following statement that they had prepared themselves thoroughly before even starting the adoption process:

> ...we knew this was going to be hard, and we basically tested every aspect of our relationship and knew that it would survive the things that were to come . . . we've always been very clear on how we were going to approach this, and in a sense I think the most helpful thing about making the adoption work for us has been that resolve and the willingness to just put everything behind it. You know, we've both made sacrifices (. . .) and we do them willingly and never ever have we thought, you know, we didn't think about this beforehand. (Adopter 4)

Other things identified as helpful by the adopters included: having time together as a family; receiving an adoption allowance or ongoing support; the foster carer being very positive about the adoption; and, the children being well prepared so they called their new parents "mummy" and "daddy" from the start. However, for one adopter who had apparently been told her allowance would be stopped if she "made a fuss", obtaining the adoption order was the most helpful thing because now she 'didn't have to fear social services any more'.

What had the adopters found most difficult during the process?
When we asked the sibling-group adopters what they had found most problematic, 16 (43%) expressed their frustration at the amount of paperwork and bureaucracy involved in the adoption process. This was not just time consuming but also emotionally draining, as one adopter made clear:

> Emotionally (. . .) it's wading through the paperwork, the bleak paperwork, and everybody saying, 'The issues are . . . The risks are . . .' and still going forward with hope and faith. (Adopter 2)

The length of time that everything had taken was also a major issue. One adopter finally issued an ultimatum to the children's LA: 'If you don't do it by this date, we are pulling out.' Another was adamant that delays could have been avoided by better organisation:

> The bureaucracy – dealing with the paperwork and meetings (. . .) was a complete and utter shambles, and we were just pulling our hair out, because it just seemed to us that (. . .) we were never going to get them home (. . .) A meeting in [the children's LA] was postponed because the foster carers couldn't go, and they didn't hold it again for another 12 weeks. No baby-sitter was offered to help look after the children, so the foster carer could go to the meeting (. . .) The reason the foster carer didn't come down here was that nobody paid for her to come. They should get that sorted. (Adopter 7)

Over a third (14) of the sibling-group adopters had encountered various problems with social workers or managers. They complained about: the pessimism and negativity of social workers; 'being fobbed off by social workers'; decisions being made behind the scenes; conflicting reports; the failure to provide life story books; and, agencies not accepting responsibility for providing support. One couple stated that it was only when they made a complaint to Ofsted that they got their own social worker. Another adopter highlighted the need for clear explanations, saying that it was pointless for social workers to ask, 'What support do you need?', when adopters had no idea what support was available.

However, for some adopters the main challenge was simply having the stamina to keep going and not allowing themselves to feel overwhelmed by the children's needs. This was emphasised by an adopter who had taken five siblings:

> You don't have time for each child, and some of these children's needs are so huge (. . .) You can go to bed at night and think, 'I know so-and-so's unhappy, and I haven't had time even to have a proper conversation with her today.' (. . .) It's a huge feeling of disempowerment really. You think, 'I'm never going to meet this child's needs.' (. . .) If you actually do stop and think, it can be very overwhelming. It is quite important not to stop and think, just keep going. And then you get – of course, you get the little rewards, as things start falling into place. (Adopter 3)

In a case where the placement had partially disrupted, the adopter felt this could have been avoided if appropriate support had been provided years before instead of during a recent crisis. She commented that the biggest problem was:

> . . . the lack of training for us and recognition that parenting these kids requires completely different strategies. We could have made an enormous difference if we had had the knowledge that we have recently acquired, because it would have allowed us to parent. (Adopter 13)

How did adopters rate the service provided by the adoption agency?

Adopters were asked to look back at the service they had received from their adoption agency and from the children's LA and to rate these services on a five-point scale ranging from poor to excellent. Although the adopters had given examples of very good practice from workers in both types of adoption agency, twice as many VAA adopters (85%) as LA adopters (47%) rated the service they had received as excellent or good. The services provided by the children's social worker were rated even lower: only a third of the adopters rated the service provided by the children's LA as good or excellent. Even within the same LA, the rating was higher for the adoption worker than for the children's social worker. Surprisingly, the VAA adopters (50%) were more likely to give a higher rating to the children's social worker than were the LA adopters (12%). This may be because their own adoption worker had advocated strongly on their behalf.

Adopters' suggestions for improving the service

At the end of the interview, we asked the sibling-group adopters if they wanted to add anything else and several took this opportunity to offer us their views on how adoption services could be improved.

Several adopters expressed concern that potential adopters could 'easily go away thinking I don't want to do that at all', because the adoption process takes so long, social workers 'give you a lot of negative information', and it's like a 'never-ending series of hurdles'. There was a suggestion that adoption agencies could speed-up the process by getting adopters to fill in details about themselves on Form F. One couple questioned why adopters should have to go through the same procedure again if they wanted to adopt more children. Another adopter commented:

> . . . it's a shame because there are so many kids out there who need good families (. . .) I'm sure that social workers can tell a lot quicker if a family is right or not right. (Adopter 23)

The adopters' views were very much based on their personal experiences. One adopter who had successfully adopted a large sibling group after being turned down by her own LA suggested that one way of ensuring this did not happen to other potential adopters would be to introduce a national adoption scheme. She emphasised in the following comment that this would help to establish a consistent standard of service:

I think there are people like us out there who are able to do it, but the system just knocks them back. The fighting they have to do to get things. I would like to see, I think the idea has been mooted by Adoption UK about having a national adoption scheme so you don't get local authorities who have many different agendas, different budgets, different priorities (. . .) So yeah, to have national consistency (. . .) If you had a national organisation, you wouldn't have places like [LA] saying to me, 'We don't need any more adopters.' (. . .) Presumably a national scheme would say, 'We're taking on anybody that wants to adopt and nationally we must be able to find a child to match that.' (Adopter 24)

Insufficient funding was highlighted as another deterrent by one adopter, who thought LAs were more likely to prioritise funding for children in the care system than for adoption support. She commented:

I think that's the main problem to be honest. That's why people do not adopt more than three (. . .) because the support isn't there. But they haven't got the budget to do it (. . .) I got a much lower adoption allowance for [the youngest child] simply because she is the third sibling, even though she has more needs. (Adopter 36)

Several adopters were concerned that adoption was not promoted well enough. In particular, one mother said she passionately believed that lots of people could adopt sibling groups, 'if they were helped to open their eyes to that possibility'. Having benefited from life coaching herself, she thought that might help other adopters 'to take more control' in the adoption process.

Support was the key issue for adopters who had children with challenging behaviour. One suggested that 'all adopted children should automatically come with a CAMHS referral'. Another thought that someone should work with you and say, 'Right okay, [child] has this condition. Let's help you now as a family [to] access the help that you need.' There was also a suggestion that the social worker should accompany the adopter to the school to explain the needs of a child with an attachment disorder. Another mother, who often had to care for the children for long periods by herself, said she would really appreciate being able to go 'somewhere like a family centre or a drop-in centre', where she could have a coffee and talk to someone while the children could run around and let off steam. That would help her 'not to feel so alone'.

It was striking that sometimes the improvements in practice suggested by the sibling-group adopters would not have been so difficult or expensive to provide. For example, an adopter whose three children had all been living in separate foster homes thought that the introductions would have been much easier if the social worker had asked the foster carers to bring the children to a place where they could play. Similarly, there was a suggestion that whenever a sibling group was placed, the LA should 'send somebody in for the first three weeks to do your ironing for you' – not a big commitment, but one that might have made a big difference.

However, one adopter thought that the failure of LAs to provide adequate support should be directly attributed to the legislation on adoption. She commented:

> . . . the problem with the legal situation is that legally after adoption they have to assess needs [but] they don't have to do anything about it. And you just sit there and go, 'What planet was somebody living on, when they wrote this up?' (. . .) It feels like there's that attitude throughout everything . . . It's just this sense that there's no joined-up thinking. They talk about all these agencies working together – my hat! (. . .) [Child] was having speech therapy up in [LA]. It had taken him two years to get to the top of the list (. . .) Had to go back to the bottom of the list when he moved down here with us. (Adopter 27)

Would they recommend adopting a sibling group to others?

Adopters were asked whether they would advise other prospective adopters to adopt a sibling group. Almost two-thirds (65%) of the adopters said they would do so, and indeed three had already done so. Surprisingly, adopters' perceptions of the services they had (or had not) received from social work agencies often made no difference to their view. An adopter, whose placement had partially disrupted, commented:

> Yes, go for it, sibling group, single, whatever – but whatever you decide, how many children you want, stick to your guns. Don't get swayed. That's the advice we have given [to friends who are thinking of adoption]. (Adopter 29)

Several adopters said their adoption agency had asked them to talk to a group of prospective adopters about their experiences of adopting a large sibling group, and they had all gladly agreed to do this.

This chapter concludes the reporting of the research findings. The adopters had provided rich accounts of the adoption process and their lives with the children. In the final chapter, we draw conclusions about the practice issues and general themes raised by this study.

Summary

- Adoption had brought major changes to the parents' lifestyle. While a third of the adopters said that they were tired all the time and a quarter said that having the children had put a strain on their marital relationship, others highlighted ways in which having the children had enriched their lives. Some emphasised the importance of self-awareness and reflection.
- About half of the children quarrelled constantly. This was usually just low-level bickering, but four families were concerned that quarrels often turned into fights. However, the children were also very close to each other and most spent a lot of time together. The majority (81%) of adopters strongly believed that the right decision had been made to keep the siblings together.

- The difficulties mentioned most frequently by the adopters were challenging behaviour, attention-seeking, attachment difficulties, and having a "parentified" child. These problems were compounded by having to meet the needs of every child within the sibling group. Five adopters had faced the additional stress of parenting for long periods on their own. Post-adoption support had been essential.
- The most helpful support for most adopters had come from their own social worker, and some felt supported by the entire agency. They had also found it helpful to speak to other sibling group adopters.
- Almost two-thirds of adopters reported that their relatives had responded positively to the children and accepted them as part of the family. However, in about 30 per cent of adoptive families, tensions were reported with extended family members.
- Adopters had been frustrated by the length of time the adoption process had taken, the bureaucracy and the form-filling. They complained about pessimistic workers, being fobbed off, conflicting reports, the failure to provide life story books, and LAs' reluctance to accept responsibility for providing support and explaining what support was available.
- Adopters described examples of good practice from workers in LAs and VAAs. However, twice as many VAA adopters rated the service they had received as excellent or good in comparison with the LA adopters. The service provided by children's social workers was rated the lowest.
- Adopters reported that most of their adopted children were making progress. Many were described as "blossoming" and some of the more severe behaviours were becoming less frequent, or had stopped. The children who were not doing well and had lots of difficulties had scored 20 or more on the SDQ total difficulties score (general population mean is 8).
- Almost two-thirds of the adopters stated that they would recommend adopting a sibling group to others.

18 Conclusions

The aim of this study was to enhance understanding of the experience of adopting a large sibling group by seeking the views of adopters and adoption staff. Specifically, the study explored the motivation of sibling-group adopters, variations in the practice of adoption agencies, the experiences of the adopters, and the rewards and challenges of adopting a large sibling group. Large sibling groups are defined here as three or more siblings.

Sample and method

Fourteen adoption agencies – five local authority adoption (LA) teams and nine voluntary adoption agencies (VAAs) – were recruited, all of whom had had three or more siblings placed with their adopters in recent years. Agency staff agreed to be interviewed. To recruit adoptive parents, the 14 agencies sent letters to their sibling-group adopters inviting them to take part in the study. Publicity through Adoption UK also elicited responses from other sibling-group adopters. The final sample of 37 came from England, Wales and the Isle of Man. These families had a total of 119 children and young people placed with them: 30 groups of three siblings, six groups of four and one group of five.

Face-to-face semi-structured interviews (usually lasting 1.5 hours) were conducted with adoption managers in the LAs and VAAs and with the sibling-group adopters. The interviews looked at the whole adoption process and explored the practices of the adoption agencies and the experiences of the adopters, including what they found helpful and unhelpful. All the adopters completed the General Health Questionnaire (GHQ28) and also a Strengths and Difficulties Questionnaire (SDQ) for each of their children. Quantitative data were analysed in SPSS and qualitative data in NVivo.

The children and adopters

All the children had been placed with two parents, including one female same-sex couple. Nearly all the adopters were childless couples. All the adopters were white, which provides further evidence of an acute national shortage of prospective adopters from minority ethnic communities (Selwyn *et al*, 2010). There were five sets of twins, and this very high incidence within a sample of 37 sibling groups may partially reflect the difficulties that the birth parents faced in coping with twins in the early years – a difficulty that would also confront three adopters, whose twins were under age three at placement.

The children had been placed on average a year later than most children who are placed for adoption in England. Nearly twice as many children were over the age of four when they were placed with VAA approved adopters compared to those placed with LA adopters, and the difference was statistically significant. Possible reasons for this delay include: a reluctance to use VAA placements because of the inter-agency fee; the huge volume of paperwork involved in sibling-group adoptions; difficulty in finding adopters willing to take three or more children; and, the time taken to convince all the relevant professionals that a sibling placement will work.

Two of the sibling-group placements had partially disrupted in recent months, and as a result three children were now living with foster carers.

Almost half of the children (17 of the 37 sibling group) had *not* been living together in foster care prior to their adoptive placement. This suggests that it is not easy to find foster carers willing to take large sibling groups. Moreover, maintaining sibling relationships when the children are living separately requires effort and commitment in terms of contact arrangements. It is crucial that LAs consider how large sibling groups can be kept together in the care system, because siblings who are initially placed apart are likely to remain apart.

Only two adopters in this sample had fostered the children before adopting them. These adopters were interviewed despite not meeting our eligibility criteria (see pp 30–31). They had both been caring for the children for nine years or more, and fostering was part of the required procedure under the previous legislation. As American research (Rosenthal *et al*, 1988; Rosenthal and Groze, 1992) suggests that outcomes are better for special needs adoptions (including sibling groups) when the children are adopted by their foster carer, consideration should perhaps be given to ways of enabling foster carers to adopt sibling groups.

Why are so many sibling groups not placed together for adoption?

We know that most looked after children have siblings (Ivaldi, 2000), and legislation requires LAs to place these children together so long as it is in their best interest and is practicable. Yet comparatively few sibling groups are placed together for adoption. There are 27 VAAs in England, and although VAAs have considerable expertise in finding adopters for children who are "hard to place" (a category that includes large sibling groups), only 17 were known to have had any large sibling groups placed with their adopters in the three years from 1 January 2006 to 31 December 2008. The proportion placed with LA-approved adopters was even smaller. In our sample of five LA adoption agencies, sibling groups accounted for only 2–6 per cent of the authority's adoption placements. In the revised Adoption Statutory Guidance (Department of Education, 2011) the emphasis placed on some of the requirements (e.g. Chapter 3, paragraph 19) suggests that the Government believes LAs should be doing more to make it practicable to place large sibling groups for adoption.

Professional resistance to placing large sibling groups for adoption

It is often considered very difficult to find adopters who will take three or more siblings. However, our research suggests that at least some of these difficulties are created by LA policies and the beliefs of individual professionals. Similar findings have been reported in other studies (Avery, 2000; Lowe *et al*, 2002; Biehal *et al*, 2010). At the most basic level, if social workers and other professionals do not believe it is possible or advisable to place large sibling groups for adoption, that mindset will inevitably affect the decisions they make. The adopters in our sample provided three examples of this kind of thinking:

- A guardian recommended that four siblings should be split, with two remaining in long-term foster care, because s/he thought it would be impossible to place them together for adoption, *even though approved adopters were waiting specifically for these children*.
- One couple, who said they were the first to adopt three siblings in their LA, complained that they had received very little support from their LA and attributed this to a belief within the adoption team that placing large sibling groups was not advisable.
- Another couple reported that a VAA social worker had been very sceptical about the viability of sibling-group placements – and for this reason they chose to go elsewhere.

In these cases there appeared to be an assumption that taking three or more siblings would destabilise the placement, but our research showed that the adopters who experienced the greatest difficulties were not those who took larger sibling groups but those who had two or more children with serious behavioural problems.

Similar pessimism appeared to lie behind the "worst case scenario" approach that several of our adopters criticised. While it is important for adoption agency staff to be honest and realistic with prospective adopters, the situations described often seemed to suggest prejudice or stereotypical thinking or perhaps an attempt to disclaim liability for whatever might happen. In these cases, adopters who had been given a very gloomy prognosis decided to trust their own instincts, or sometimes reassurances provided by foster carers, and usually the dire predictions had proved unfounded. However, they were concerned that other prospective adopters might be dissuaded by such a pessimistic approach and, as a consequence, siblings might lose their chance of being adopted together.

Hopefully, this research might help to convince sceptical social workers, managers and individual professionals that it is actually possible to place large sibling groups for adoption and that with appropriate support these placements can work well.

Rejecting or not considering potential sibling group adopters

Five of the 37 sibling-group adopters had initially been turned down by their own LA but went on to adopt through another agency. Only one of these five couples subsequently had a sibling-group placement that partially disrupted, and the reasons for the disruption did not appear to be linked to the reason for their initial rejection. It is worth examining the reasons why these applicants were rejected.

A couple who had successfully adopted four siblings reported that staff in their own LA had rejected their application because they did not need any more adopters at that time. Another couple said their LA had advised them to contact a VAA because they lived too close to the city centre and, if the LA placed children with them, there was a danger that they might encounter the birth parents. In both these cases it was clear that staff in the LAs concerned were only interested in placing their own looked after children and did not want to engage in exchanging adopters with other LAs. When an LA does not view adoption as an inter-agency activity, some prospective adopters will inevitably be turned away and might never adopt. This approach also severely limits the number of adopters who can be matched with the authority's looked after children. When so many children are waiting for adoption and when the personal, social and financial costs of keeping children in the care system are so high, it is unacceptable that LAs should squander the good will of prospective adopters in this way.

Other sibling group adopters said they had been rejected by their LA because: they had a partner working in the armed forces; they were a same-sex couple; or they were thought to have psychological problems because they wanted to adopt rather than have a birth child. There is no inherent reason why people in these categories should be unsuitable to adopt a sibling group. However, if one member of a couple is serving in the armed forces, the other parent might have to cope on their own for long periods of time and therefore a substantial support package may be needed.

Not considering certain kinds of people for a sibling group placement

In this study, all the children were placed with two parents and nearly all were placed into households where no other children were living. The only exception to this was the family who adopted two groups of four siblings. Clearly the adoption agencies were generally seeking to place sibling groups with childless couples. Research highlights the potential dangers of placing siblings into families with biological children, especially when they are close in age (Wedge and Mantel, 1991; Quinton *et al*, 1998). Nevertheless, it should be noted that these risks can be diminished by insisting on a wider age gap, careful assessment of the siblings' needs, and skilful preparation of the adopters and the children already living with them. One adopter in our study became a single parent after the children were placed and continued to care for them single-handedly for five years before re-marrying. This, however, would not have been possible without a generous financial support package.

Money (or the lack of it) appeared to be the reason that many potential sibling-group adopters were not even considered. For example, one LA manager acknowledged that there was pressure on social workers to find adopters in-house because often there was not enough money in the budget to pay the inter-agency fee required by VAAs. This problem was also highlighted by VAA managers. If LAs re-structured their budgets to ensure that money was available to pay for VAA placements, it is likely that more sibling groups could be placed and LAs would not have to meet the infinitely higher costs of keeping siblings long term in the care system.

While some LAs in our study actively looked for ways of financially enabling adopters to take on a sibling group (e.g. by paying for house extensions), others were hoping to find couples who *already* had a large enough house and garden and a high enough income to support three or more siblings. This was particularly problematic in London, where the high cost of property meant that homeowners often did not have sufficient bedrooms for three or more children and both partners often had to work in order to pay the mortgage. However, some of the barriers to finding suitable adopters for sibling groups were self-inflicted: one LA wanted their adopters to be able to provide a separate bedroom for each child regardless of their age and gender, even though many children in ordinary families share bedrooms.

Providing the basics

When we asked the five LA respondents what makes a difference when trying to recruit adopters for a sibling group, they emphasised the importance of providing very good information, having a social worker who really knows the children, and offering a support package to reassure adopters that they will be able to manage.

Responding to potential sibling group adopters

Like most people, prospective sibling-group adopters want to be valued. In all probability they will have spent a long time thinking about adoption before they approach an adoption agency. While it is important to assess adopters and test the strength of their commitment, adoption social workers who do not respond positively or encourage adopters to realise their own potential are unlikely to establish good working relationships. Most of the sibling-group adopters in our study based their choice of adoption agency on whether they liked the attitude of the staff, and because of this eight adopters who had initially approached LAs subsequently adopted through a VAA instead. Prospective adopters who had announced their wish to take three or more siblings also felt frustrated when adoption agencies had a standard assessment procedure for all prospective adopters and social workers persisted in talking about 'the child' throughout their assessment.

It is important to be aware of the ways in which assumptions may also prevent a sibling group from being placed. For example, it was clear that the adoption agencies in our study were looking for *childless* couples to adopt sibling groups, and many adoption staff may not have been willing to consider the family in this study who had already adopted four siblings and wanted to take another sibling group. Fortunately, their social worker was very open minded, but even so it took a long time to persuade the LA to consider this and the adopters said it would have been so easy for them to give up. In another case, the children's authority were said to be very reluctant to match four siblings with adopters who had very little childcare experience, but nobody else came forward for these children so finally they approved the match. Both of these adoptions are stable and happy, but these placements might never have been made if the adopters had not had a very supportive social worker and a flexible LA.

Providing good information

Less than a third of the sibling-group adopters were satisfied with the information provided, and many complained that information was missing or was provided very late in the adoption process. They wanted to be fully informed about medical issues, sexual abuse, behavioural problems, the extent of any learning difficulties, and the possible long-term effects on the children of exposure to drugs or domestic violence. It is often difficult to know how the development of a child will be affected by adverse experiences and if the birth parents refuse to provide information there may be considerable gaps in what is known about the children. Also, prospective adopters do not always take in the full implications of the information they are given when emotions are running high (Selwyn *et al*, 2006). However, in two cases it appeared that adverse information about the children had been withheld until the introductions (i.e. when the adopters already felt committed to the children). Even worse, in a further two cases the adopters stated that key information had only come out after the placement had partially disrupted. This underlines the findings of previous studies (Evan B. Donaldson Institute, 2004; Selwyn *et al*, 2006) that failing to provide adequate information was implicated in the disruption of adoptive placements. LA staff who fail to provide all relevant information about the children and their birth family will be in breach of their obligations under the Adoption Agencies Regulations 2005 (section 17). It should also be noted that at least one council has been sued for not providing essential information (*The Guardian*, 17.10.02).

Surprisingly, six adopters stated that they did not know why the children had been removed from their birth parents, and one thought this lack of knowledge was because of a "dogma" in Children's Services that the birth family should not be criticised. These adopters were justifiably concerned that this might eventually undermine their relationship with the children. Indeed, problems have arisen when children have had contact with birth parents and have not been told the reasons for their removal (Loxtercampe, 2009). On a more positive note, all of the adopters who had attended a child appreciation day (38%) said this had been helpful, and some emphasised that it had given them an insight into what their children had experienced and what they were like.

Having a social worker who knows the children very well

The adopters really appreciated social workers who could describe the children in detail and explain what they had experienced and how this had affected them. They were also quick to recognise and distrust social workers who did not know the children well, and were effectively giving them second-hand information. Often social workers were put in this position through no fault of their own, for example, if the LA had a very high turnover of children's social workers or if it was standard practice in their LA for different social workers to handle different parts of the adoption process. In at least one authority, the pressure on social workers was increased further by the fact that a sibling group counted as only one case, even though all the necessary forms and assessments had to be completed for each individual sibling.

There will always be a need for LA managers to ensure that children's social workers have the necessary skills and sensitivity to relate well to the children they serve. Three of the adopters in this study found it very frustrating to have to depend on social workers who did not appear to like children generally and who did not relate well to their children in particular. While VAA social workers can question the way in which a child's social worker is handling the situation, often it is difficult for other LA social workers to complain about the poor practice of a colleague. In these circumstances, the Whistleblowing Arrangements Code of Practice (BSI British Standards, 2008) may be helpful, but managers also need to take responsibility for identifying these issues.

Offering a support package

In most large families, children are born one at a time and parents have the opportunity to establish a relationship with each individual child and gradually build up their parenting skills. In contrast, nearly all of our adopters took on an entire sibling group simultaneously and had to gain the trust and acceptance of each child at the same time as responding to the needs of children at different stages of development, and coping with any emotional or behavioural problems that might arise due to their previous adverse experiences. This is a huge undertaking, and for many of our adopters a crucial factor in deciding to do this was the promise of "life-long" support from their VAA.

Most adopters said that the financial support provided by the children's authority was the most important part of the support package. However, for those struggling with children's very challenging behaviour, emotional and practical support and therapeutic interventions were also essential. It is worrying that many sibling-group adopters said they had to fight to obtain the necessary support for their children.

Why was it difficult for the sibling group adopters to obtain certain kinds of support?

As LAs pay for much of the support given to adopters, especially in the first three years after placement, there is concern that many LAs may cut their adoption budgets due to the current financial crisis. We can only hope that LA managers recognise the need to prioritise adoption support services so that children do not remain in long-term foster care unnecessarily.

Financial support

In this study, a social worker in the LA that had placed most sibling groups observed that it was easier to attract sibling-group adopters now that they were able to advertise that an adoption allowance would be attached to the placement and that ongoing support would be provided. Most of our adopters stated that the financial support they had received was essential in enabling them to take three or more children. However, only 47 per cent of our adopters received sufficient funding to enable one adopter to stay at home with the children. It should also be noted that eight sibling-group adopters did not receive an adoption allowance, and at least one of them had experienced debt problems. We share the concern expressed by some VAA managers that if LAs become more reluctant to provide adoption allowances, large sibling groups will only be adopted by wealthy applicants, their chances of living together will diminish, and the costs of keeping them in care will increase.

Support from relatives and friends

Adoption agency managers generally said that they expected sibling group adopters to have a good support network. Despite this, when asked what they had found most helpful, only three of our adopters identified the support provided by relatives and friends. This may have been because the interview had focused on the practice of adoption agencies. However, it was clear that many adopters were unable or unwilling to rely on relatives for day-to-day support, and it is important that adoption social workers should be aware that such support is not always provided.

The new grandparents were usually delighted to welcome the children into their family, but some had difficulty in understanding the children's behaviour or were worried about the adopters' ability to cope, and the adopters did not always find their involvement helpful. There are various ways in which adoption agencies can help relatives and friends to understand the children's needs and to provide appropriate support. For example, one VAA allowed grandparents to attend a course on trauma, loss and recovery, while another ran a workshop for close friends and family of the adopters and also involved close family members in planning the provision of support.

Contentious issues – home help, respite care and babysitting

It does not cost a large amount to pay for someone to help with cleaning, washing and ironing for perhaps three hours a week, and this can help to reduce exhaustion and make the bonding process easier by enabling an adopter to spend more time with the children. In spite of this, the LAs were generally reluctant to provide a home help; VAA staff stated that adopters who requested home help were sometimes thought to be inadequate; and, in one LA it was considered politically unacceptable to offer such support. Yet it was often the mountains of washing and ironing that the sibling-group adopters found overwhelming, and a refusal to provide home help could make them feel uncertain about their ability to cope with other problems such as the children's difficult behaviour. The benefits of providing home help for sibling-group adopters in the first two or three months appear to outweigh the costs. However, the resistance was not all one sided. Some of the sibling-group adopters were reluctant to ask for home help or to have a stranger coming into their house. Agency staff suggested ways of overcoming such resistance, including giving adopters a book of vouchers for a certain number of hours of washing and ironing or offering to pay for someone within the adopters' support network to come and help with the housework.

LAs were even more reluctant to provide respite care, and we were told by a VAA manager that questions might be asked about the commitment of any adopter who requested this. Concerns were also expressed that children placed in respite care might feel as though they were still looked after. In this study, respite care was only provided for one family when it was too late to prevent the placement from disrupting. However, a VAA manager pointed out that respite care did not have to involve overnight stays. For example, providing practical help during the day could enable the adopter to spend time with an individual sibling and to become more confident in parenting a sibling group.

There was also a value in the adopters themselves being able to spend time alone together, and the two couples who received a babysitting allowance so that they could go out once a month for a meal both appreciated this enormously. Indeed, the 2005 Adoption Support Services Regulations 3.3 state that local authorities can provide assistance in cash specifically for this purpose. This kind of support is relatively inexpensive, yet it can make a real difference to a sibling-group adopter who is feeling overwhelmed and struggling to cope.

Helping adopters to deal with emotional and behavioural problems

Many of the sibling group adopters encountered problems such as continual attention seeking, challenging behaviour, attachment difficulties, and having a "parentified" child. Experienced social workers, who could offer emotional support, explain things from a child's perspective, access additional support services and help to devise strategies for defusing difficult situations, were highly valued by the adopters. In families where one child continually demanded attention with very challenging behaviour, additional support services were essential to ensure that the adopters would be able to meet the needs of all the siblings. We would suggest that adoption staff bear in mind the finding that the number of siblings with difficulties, rather than the severity of an individual child's difficulties, was associated with almost a quarter of the placements rated as having major problems. Clearly families with two or more "difficult" children need urgent support.

Adopters particularly appreciated social workers who helped to prepare them for meeting the needs of the *specific* children who were going to be placed with them. Typically, this involved the social worker accompanying the adopters to the child appreciation day, asking about any matters that needed to be explored, and subsequently providing the adopters with detailed notes explaining what kind of behaviour might be expected from each child. The best example of this in our study was a social worker with specialist training in attachment issues who emphasised the crucial importance of routines and explained how the adopters could reinforce this by getting the children to draw pictures (a visual timetable) of what they were going do each day (see page 120). It is frequently assumed that only mental health professionals can work with children who have attachment problems, but the intervention provided by this social worker was so effective that the adopter informed us that she no longer had any problems.

Support from CAMHS

Almost half of the sibling-group adopters stated that at least one of their children had received therapy, and most thought that this had been helpful. However, LA staff reported long waiting lists and problems in financing therapy for children, and sometimes there was a very long wait (in one case four years) before children with severe behavioural problems were seen by a CAMHS professional. As this is clearly a scarce resource, it is worrying that there was no statistical association between the children who received therapeutic support and the children who had the greatest difficulties according to the SDQ scores. Some respondents also raised questions about whether CAMHS professionals had a good understanding of attachment difficulties and adoption issues and whether they knew how to treat very young children with serious mental health problems.

Mental health difficulties posed a threat to the continuity and stability of some of the placements in our study. Within our sample of 37 sibling-group adopters, five couples had postponed applying for the adoption order because they saw this as the only way of putting pressure on the children's authority to provide appropriate support for children with challenging behaviour and attachment difficulties. The two families whose placements had partially disrupted had also been struggling to cope with children with severe behavioural problems and attachment difficulties. As CAMHS are not always able to respond to the urgent needs of adoptive families, perhaps adoption agencies should seek to ensure that at least one member of their social work team has specialist training in attachment issues and can help to prepare and support adopters to respond effectively to children with attachment difficulties. However, there is also a clear need for a specialist mental health service for looked after and adopted children, and perhaps this should be addressed at a national level, as suggested by Tarren-Sweeney (2010).

Some general observations on adoption agency practice

This study found many examples of good practice. While adoption allowances were needed by nearly all of the sibling-group adopters, it was striking that many of the adopters' descriptions of effective practice and support did not involve excessive expenditure. Often what was critical was an understanding of the children's needs, careful planning and preparation to ease the adoption process, a willingness to be flexible, and an ability to respond quickly and appropriately when adopters were struggling to cope with children's behaviour or feeling overwhelmed. A key factor was the attitude and approach of social workers and their adoption agency – how they welcomed prospective adopters, the experience, openness, encouragement and realism that they brought to the task, and a commitment to placing large sibling groups together in the right family whenever possible. The promise of "life-long" support was crucial for many VAA adopters, and LAs might be more successful in attracting adopters if they were able to offer a similar pledge.

Unfortunately, we also found examples of bad practice such as concealing the full extent of the children's difficulties and reneging on agreed support plans. Some poor practice was due to lack of training (e.g. allowing only three days for introductions) or rigidity of approach, such as a refusal to alter a plan that was not working well. However, in five cases adoption social workers appeared to be motivated by their agency's financial considerations rather than the best interests of the children or the adopters, because adopters reported being manipulated or pressurised into taking more children than they had intended. It should be noted that most adoption agencies were very careful not to do this. Perhaps the most serious malpractice was the failure to provide appropriate advice and support for five adopters who were struggling with the children's challenging behaviour and attachment difficulties.

This suggests a need to employ a therapist or provide more specialist training for adoption social workers.

It was often apparent from the comments of agency staff and sibling-group adopters that social workers wanted to control the whole process of adoption. While this can aid planning and reduce delay, sometimes practice appeared to be unnecessarily restrictive. For example, was there any need to insist that an adopter could only read the Child Permanence Report in the Children's Services office? Why should adopters not be shown children's profiles before being approved? While agency staff were understandably cautious about showing prospective sibling-group adopters photos of babies – they had to be sure that adopters wanted all the children – was there any justification for insisting that one couple should make their choice before being shown any photographs of the children? The reported reluctance of some LAs to allow VAA social workers to view the children's files *before* placement could also make it difficult for social workers to prepare sibling-group adopters effectively to meet the specific needs of their children. (It is worth noting that adoption files are exempt from the Data Protection Act 1998, and under the 2005 Adoption Agencies Regulation (42.2) an adoption agency 'may provide such access to its case records and disclose such information in its possession, as it thinks fit for the purposes of carrying out its functions as an adoption agency'.)

However, the main impression emerging from the study is one of inconsistent practice, not only between LAs and VAAs, but also within each sector. There were huge variations in the amount of financial support offered to the sibling-group adopters. While some LAs appeared to be actively looking for ways to enable adopters to take three or more siblings (e.g. by providing an adoption allowance and paying for a house extension), others clearly expected the adopters to have a large enough house and income already. Similarly, there were considerable variations in the provision of practical and emotional support.

This variation may be due to a lack of clarity in the legislation and regulations on adoption support. Under the 2002 Adoption and

Children Act (s.2(6)) adoption support services are defined as counselling, advice and information and any other services prescribed by regulations. The 2011 Adoption Statutory Guidance (Chapter 9) contains a table headed 'People to whom adoption support services must be extended: ASR 4', which sets out the various services for which an agency adoptive child and his/her adoptive parents are 'entitled to be assessed'. However, this is qualified by the following statement:

> *ASR 4 sets out the persons to whom the local authority must extend adoption support services. That is not to say that every service must be supplied to each person in the category, rather that the local authority is obliged to ensure that these services can be made available if an assessment shows that they are needed.* (Adoption Statutory Guidance, 9.6)

These words are clearly intended to protect LA budgets from being overwhelmed by excessive demands. However, they also absolve LAs from the obligation to provide the support assessed as necessary for individual families. It is very worrying that five of our respondents who had children with challenging behaviour and attachment difficulties had refused to apply for an adoption order, because they saw this as the only way of exerting pressure on the children's LA to provide the necessary support.

The comments of VAA managers in our study indicated that LAs were becoming increasingly reluctant to provide adoption allowances. This could severely limit the chances of large sibling groups being adopted, as it will become even more difficult to find prospective adopters who feel able to take three or more children without adequate support. Ironically, keeping the children in foster care is likely to be much more expensive.

It is unacceptable that there should be such huge inconsistency in the standard of service and support offered by adoption agencies and that the opportunity to adopt or be adopted should vary so much from one area to the next. A national adoption scheme might help to ensure that prospective adopters who can offer a loving home are not turned away and that their assessed support needs are actually met.

The need for further research

Children in almost half of the sibling groups had been placed in separate foster homes before being reunited in adoption. This raises interesting issues about recruiting foster carers for sibling groups, organising contact and preparing separated siblings for adoption. We were surprised to find that there was no statistical association between children being separated in foster care and the level of difficulties experienced by their adopters. We expected to find that reunited siblings would pose more difficulties. However, this is a small sample and we were unable to explore this issue in depth. Nor did we have the time or resources to seek the views of children on their experiences of being adopted with their siblings. We hope that future research will be able to explore these issues with the full participation of children who have been adopted with their siblings.

American research also suggests two further issues that could be usefully investigated in the UK. If belonging to a sibling group being jointly photolisted for adoption in New York state *increases* the probability of adoption with each additional child in the sibling group speeding up the adoption by approximately 3.2 months (Avery and Butler, 2001), why does the opposite appear to be true in the UK and what can be done to reverse this? Also, if adoptions of four or more siblings are *less* likely to disrupt than adoptions of smaller numbers of siblings in the US (Smith *et al*, 2006), is this also true in the UK, as the positive responses of adopters of sibling groups of four in our study might suggest?

Looking to the future

The findings of our study suggest that people who are willing to adopt three or more siblings tend to have remarkable determination, commitment and generosity of spirit. These adopters should be valued, encouraged and given all the support they need, particularly in the first year of the placement. Adoptive families represent the best chance of securing a better future for many large sibling groups who are in the care system waiting for a new family.

References

Aldridge M. J. and Cautley P. W. (1976) 'Placing siblings in the same foster home', *Child Welfare*, 55:2, pp 85–93

Argent H. (2008) *Ten Top Tips for Placing Siblings*, London: BAAF

Averett P., Nalavany B. and Ryan S. (2009) 'An evaluation of gay/lesbian and heterosexual adoption', *Adoption Quarterly*, 12:3(4), pp 129–151

Avery R. (2000) 'Perceptions and practice: agency efforts for the hardest to place children', *Children and Youth Services Review*, 22:6, pp 399–420

Avery R. J. and Butler J. S. (2001) 'Timeliness in the adoptive placement of photolisted children: the New York State Blue Books', *Adoption Quarterly*, 4:4, pp 19–46

BAAF (2008) *BAAF response to the CAMHS review*, London: BAAF

Baker K. (2006) 'Understanding violent and antisocial behaviour in children and adolescents', *Current Paediatrics*, 16, pp 472–477

Bank S. and Kahn M. (1982) *The Sibling Bond*, New York: Basic Books

Barth R. P., Berry M., Yoshikami R., Goodfield R. K. and Carson M. L. (1988) 'Predicting adoption disruption', *Social Work*, 33:3, pp 227–233

Barth R. P. and Brooks D. (1997) 'A longitudinal study of family structure and size and adoption outcomes', *Adoption Quarterly*, 1:1, pp 29–56

Baumrind D. (1971) 'Current patterns of parental authority', *Developmental Psychology*, 4:1, Part 2, pp 1–105

Baydar N., Brooks-Gunn J. and Furstenberg F. F. (1993) 'Early warning signs of functional illiteracy: predictors in childhood and adolescence', *Child Development*, 64, pp 815–829

Beckett C., Castle J., Groothues C., Hawkins A., Sonuga-Barke E., Colvert E., Kreppner J., Stevens S. and Rutter M. (2008) 'The experience of adoption (2): the association between communicative openness and self-esteem in adoption', *Adoption & Fostering*, 32:1, pp 29–39

Beckett C., Groothues C. and O'Connor T. (1998) 'Adopting from Romania: the role of siblings in adjustment', *Adoption & Fostering*, 22:2, pp 25–34

Benton B. B., Kaye E. and Tipton M. (1985) *Evaluation of State Activities with Regard to Adoption Disruption*, Washington, DC: Urban Systems Research and Engineering

Berridge D. and Cleaver H. (1987) *Foster Home Breakdown*, Oxford: Basil Blackwell

Biehal N., Ellison S., Baker C. and Sinclair I. (2010) *Belonging and Permanence: Outcomes in long-term foster care and adoption*, London: BAAF

Biehal N. and Wade J. (1996) 'Looking back, looking forward: care leavers, families and change', *Children and Youth Service Review*, 18:4(5), pp 425–445

Bifulco T. (2006) 'Summary information about ASI-AF', *Lifespan Research Group*, Royal Holloway, University of London

Bigner J. J. and Jacobsen R. B. (1989) 'Parenting behaviours of homosexual and heterosexual fathers', *Journal of Homosexuality*, 18, pp 173–186

Bilson A. and Barker R. (1992-93) 'Siblings of children in care or accommodation: a neglected area of practice', *Practice*, 6:4, pp 307–318

Boardman A. (1987) 'The General Health Questionnaire and the detection of emotional disorder by general practitioners: a replicated study', *British Journal of Psychiatry*, 151:pp 373–381

Boer F., Versluis-den Bieman H. J. M. and Verhulst F. C. (1994) 'International adoption of children with siblings: behavioral outcomes', *American Journal of Orthopsychiatry*, 64:2, pp 252–262

Boer F., Westenberg P. M. and Ooyen-Houben M. M. J. (1995) 'How do sibling placements differ from placements of individual children?', *Child and Youth Care Forum*, 24:4, pp 261–268

Boneh C. (1979) *Disruptions in adoptive placement: A research study*, Boston: Department of Public Welfare, Office of Research Evaluation

Boronska T. (2000) 'Art therapy with two sibling groups using an attachment framework', *Inscape*, 5:1, pp 2–10

Bressan P., Bertamini M., Nalli A. and Zanutto A. (2009) 'Men do not have a stronger preference than women for self-resemblant child faces', *Archives of Sexual Behavior*, 38:5, pp 657–664

Brody G. H. (1998) 'Sibling relationship quality: its causes and consequences', *Annual Review of Psychology*, 49, pp 1–24

Brody G. H. and Stoneman Z. (1994) 'Sibling relationships and their association with parental differential treatment', in Hetherington, E. M., Reiss, D. and Plomin, R. (eds.) *Separate Social Worlds of Siblings: The impact of nonshared environment on development*, Hillsdale, NJ: Lawrence Erlbaum Associates, Inc

Brodzinsky D. M., Schechter M. D. and Henig R. M. (1992) *Being adopted: The life-long search for self*, New York: Doubleday

Brooks D., Allen J. and Barth R. P. (2002) 'Adoption services use, helpfulness, and need: a comparison of rublic and rrivate agency and independent adoptive families', *Children and Youth Services Review*, 24:4, pp 213–238

Bryant B. and Crockenberg S. B. (1980) 'Correlates and dimensions of prosocial behavior: a study of female siblings with their mothers', *Child Development*, 51, pp 529–544

BSI British Standards (2008) *Whistleblowing Arrangements: Code of Practice PAS 1998*, London: BSI British Standards

Buhrmester D. and Furman W. (1990) 'Perceptions of sibling relationships during middle childhood and adolescence', *Child Development*, 61:5, pp 1387–1398

Byng-Hall J. (1995) *Rewriting Family Scripts: Improvisation and systems change*, New York: Guilford Press

Caffaro J. V. and Conn-Caffaro A. (2005) 'Treating sibling abuse families', *Aggression and violent behavior*, 10:5, pp 604–623

Cicirelli V. G. (1980) 'A comparison of college women's feelings toward their siblings and parents', *Journal of Marriage and the Family*, 41:1, pp 111–118

Cicirelli V. G. (1989) 'Feelings of attachment to siblings and well-being in later life', *Psychology and Aging*, 4:2, pp 211–216

Conger R. D. and Conger K. J. (1996) 'Sibling relationships', in Simons, R. L. (ed.) *Understanding Differences between Divorced and Intact Families: Stress, interaction, and child outcome*, Thousand Oaks, CA: Sage

Connidis I. A. and Campbell L. D. (1995) 'Closeness, confiding, and contact among siblings in middle and late adulthood', *Journal of Family Issues*, 16:6, pp 722–745

Courtney M., Skyles A., Miranda G., Zinn A., Howard E. and George R. (2005) *Youth who Run Away from Substitute Care*, Chicago: Chapin Hall Center for Children

Cox M. J. (2010) 'Family systems and sibling relationships', *Child Development Perspectives*, 4:2, pp 95–96

Crea T. M., Barth R. P., Guo S. and Brooks D. (2008) 'Behavioral outcomes for substance-exposed adopted children: fourteen years postadoption', *American Journal of Orthopsychiatry*, 78:1, pp 11–19

Cunningham A. and Baker L. (2004) *What about ME! Seeking to understand the child's view of violence in the family*, London, Ontario: The Centre for Children and Families in the Justice System

Dance C., Ouwejan D., Beecham J. and Farmer E. (2010) *Linking and Matching: A survey of adoption agency practice in England and Wales*, London: BAAF

Deater-Deckard K. and Dunn J. (2002) 'Sibling relationships and social-emotional adjustment in different family contexts', *Social Development*, 11:4, pp 571–590

Deloitte (2006) *Commissioning Voluntary Adoption Agencies: An independent review*, London: DCSF

Department for Children, Schools and Families (2009) *Children Looked After in England (including adoption and care leavers) Year Ending March 31st 2009*, London: DCSF

Department for Education (2010) *Statistical First Release 2009–2010*, London: DfE

Department for Education (2011) *Adoption Statutory Guidance, Adoption and Children Act 2002, first revision February 2011*, London: DfE

Downey D. B. (1995) 'When bigger is not better: family size, parental resources, and children's educational performance', *American Sociological Review*, 60:October, pp 746–761

Drapeau S., Simard M., Beaudry M. and Charbonneau C. (2000) 'Siblings in family transitions', *Family Relations*, 49:1, pp 77–85

Dunn J. (1987) *The Beginnings of Social Understanding*, Cambridge, Mass.: Harvard University Press

Dunn J. (1993) *Young Children's Close Relationships: Beyond attachment*, California: Sage

Dunn J., Deater-Deckard K., Pickering K. and Golding J. (1999) 'Siblings, parents and partners: family relationships within a longitudinal community study', *Journal of Child Psychology and Psychiatry*, 40, pp 1025–1037

Dunn J. and Munn P. (1986) 'Sibling quarrels and maternal intervention: individual differences in understanding and aggression', *Journal of Child Psychology and Psychiatry*, 27:5, pp 583–595

Dunn J. and Plomin R. (1990) *Separate Lives: Why siblings are so different*, New York: Basic Books

Dunn J., Slomkowski C. and Beardsall L. (1994) 'Sibling relationships from the preschool period through middle childhood and early adolescence', *Developmental Psychology*, 30:3, pp 315–324

Dunn J. and Stocker C. (eds.) (1989) *The Significance of Differences in Siblings' Experiences Within the Family*, Hillsdale, NJ: Erlbaum

Edwards R., Hadfield L., Lucey H. and Mauthner M. (2006) *Sibling Identity and Relationships: Sisters and brothers*, Abingdon: Routledge

Erich S. and Leung P. (2002) 'The impact of previous type of abuse and sibling adoption upon adoptive families', *Child Abuse and Neglect*, 26:10, pp 1045–1058

Evan B. Donaldson Institute (2004) *What's Working for Children: A policy study of adoption stability and termination*, New York: Evan B. Donaldson Institute

Family Futures (2007) *Siblings – Together or Apart? A Family Futures' Training*, London: Family Futures Consortium Ltd

Farmer E. and Parker R. (1991) *Trials and Tribulations: Returning children from local authority care to their families*, London: HMSO

Farmer E. and Pollock S. (1998) *Sexually Abused and Abusing Children in Substitute Care*, Chichester: John Wiley and Sons Ltd

Felson R. B. and Rosso N. (1988) 'Parental punishment and sibling aggression', *Social Psychology Quarterly*, 51:1, pp 1–18

Festinger T. (1986) *Necessary risk: A study of adoption and disrupted adoptive placements*, New York: Child Welfare League of America

Finkelhor D., Ormrod R. K. and Turner H. A. (2007) 'Re-victimization patterns in a national longitudinal sample of children and youth', *Child Abuse and Neglect*, 31:5, pp 479–502

Finkelhor D. and Turner H. (2006) 'Kid's stuff: the nature and impact of peer and sibling violence on younger and older children', *Child Abuse and Neglect*, 30:2, pp 1381–1399

Fogelman K. R. (1975) 'Developmental correlates of family size', *British Journal of Social Work*, 5:1, pp 43–57

Foli K. J. and Thompson J. R. (2004) *The Post-Adoption Blues: Overcoming the unforeseen challenges of adoption*, New York: Rodale Press

Folman R. D. (1998) '"I Was Tooken": How children experience removal from their parents preliminary to placement into foster care', *Adoption Quarterly*, 2:2, pp 7–35

Fratter J., Rowe J., Sapsford D. and Thoburn J. (1991) *Permanent Family Placement: A decade of experience*, London: BAAF

Furman W. and Buhrmester D. (1985) 'Children's perceptions of the qualities of sibling relationships', *Child Development*, 56:2, pp 448–461

Gass K., Jenkins J. and Dunn J. (2007) 'Are sibling relationships protective? A longitudinal study', *Journal of Child Psychology and Psychiatry*, 48:2, pp 167–175

Glidden L. M., Flaherty E. M. and McGlone A. P. (2000) 'Is more too many?', *Adoption Quarterly*, 4:1, pp 67–80

Glover M. B., Mullineaux P. Y., Deater-Deckard K. and Petrill S. A. (2010) 'Parents' feelings towards their adoptive and non-adoptive children', *Infant and Child Development*, 19, pp 238–251

Gnaulati E. (2002) 'Extending the uses of sibling therapy with children and adolescents', *Psychotherapy: Theory, research, practice, training*, 39:1, pp 76–87

Goldberg D. and Huxley P. (1992) *Common Mental Disorders: A bio-social model*, Abingdon, Oxfordshire: Routledge

Goldberg D. P. and Hillier V. F. (1979) 'A scaled version of the General Health Questionnaire', *Psychological Medicine*, 9, pp 139–145

Golombok S., Spencer A. and Rutter M. (1983) 'Children in lesbian and single-parent households: psychosexual and psychiatric appraisal', *Journal of Child Psychology and Psychiatry*, 24:4, pp 551–572

Goodman R. (1997) 'The Strengths and Difficulties Questionnaire: a research note', *Journal of Child Psychology and Psychiatry*, 38, pp 581–586

Groze V. (1986) 'Special-needs adoption', *Children and Youth Services Review*, 8, pp 363–373

Gustafsson P. A., Engquist M. and Karlsson B. (1995) 'Siblings in family therapy', *Journal of Family Therapy*, 17:3, pp 317–325

Hafford C. (2010) 'Sibling caretaking in immigrant families: understanding cultural practices to inform child welfare practice and evaluation', *Evaluation and Program Planning*, 33, pp 294–302

Hamilton-Giachritsis C. E. and Browne K. D. (2005) 'A retrospective study of risk to siblings in abusing families', *Journal of Family Psychology*, 19:4, pp 619–624

Harris I. D. and Howard K. L. (1985) 'Correlates of perceived parental favoritism', *The Journal of Genetic Psychology*, 146, pp 45–56

Harrison C. (1999) 'Children being looked after and their sibling relationships: the experiences of children in the working in partnership with "lost" parents research project', in Mullender, A. (ed.) *We Are Family: Sibling relationships in placement and beyond*, London: BAAF

Haskey J. and Errington R. (summer 2001) 'Adoptees and relatives who wish to contact one another: the Adoption Contact Register', *Population Trends*, London: Office for National Statistics, 104, pp 18–25

Hawthorne B. (2000) 'Split custody as a viable post-divorce option', *Journal of Divorce and Remarriage*, 33:3(4), pp 1–19

Head A. and Elgar M. (1999) 'The placement of sexually abused and abusing siblings', in Mullender, A. (ed.) *We Are Family: Sibling relationships in placement and beyond*, London: BAAF

Hegar R. (1986) *Siblings in Foster Care*, DSW dissertation, Tulane University

Hegar R. (1988) 'Sibling relationships and separations: implications for child placement', *Social Service Review*, 62, pp 446–467

Hegar R. L. (2005) 'Sibling placement in foster care and adoption: an overview of international research', *Children and Youth Services Review*, 27:7, pp 717–739

Hegar R. L. and Rosenthal J. A. (2009) 'Kinship care and sibling placement: child behavior, family relationships, and school outcomes', *Children and Youth Services Review*, 31, pp 670–679

Heptinstall E., Bhopal K. and Brannen J. (2001) 'Adjusting to a foster family: children's perspectives', *Adoption & Fostering*, 25:4, pp 6–16

Herrera C. and Dunn J. (1997) 'Early experiences with family conflict: implications for arguments with a close friend', *Developmental Psychology*, 33, pp 869–881

Hetherington E. M. (ed.) (1988) *Parents, Children, and Siblings: Six years after divorce*, Oxford: Oxford University Press

Hetherington E. M., Henderson S. H., Reiss D., Anderson E. R., Bridges M., Chan R. W., Insabella G. M., Jodl K. M., Kim J. E., Mitchell A. S., O'Connor T. G., Skaggs M., J and Taylor L. C. (1999) 'Adolescent siblings in stepfamilies: family functioning and adolescent adjustment', *Monographs of the Society for Research in Child Development*. Society for Research in Child Development

Hill A. (2003) 'Issues facing brothers of sexually abused children: implications for professional practice', *Child and Family Social Work*, 8:4, pp 281–290

Hines D. A., Kantor G. K. and Holt M. K. (2006) 'Similarities in siblings' experiences of neglectful parenting behaviours', *Child Abuse and Neglect*, 30, pp 619–637

Holloway J. S. (1997) 'Outcomes in placements for adoption or long term fostering', *Archives of Disease in Childhood*, 76:3, pp 227–230

Hollows A. and Nelson P. (2006) 'Equity and pragmatism in judgement-making about the placement of silbing groups', *Child and Family Social Work*, 11:4, pp 307–315

Howe D. (1999) 'Disorders of attachment and attachment therapy', *Adoption & Fostering*, 23:2, pp 19–30

Howe N., Petrakos H., Rinaldi C. M. and LeFebvre R. (2005) '"This is a bad dog, you know . . .": Constructing shared meanings during sibling pretend play', *Child Development*, 76:4, pp 783–794

Hughes D.(September 2009) NICE Expert paper: EP15 – LAC 8.4a Siblings Together <http://www.nice.org.uk/nicemedia/live/11879/47439/47439.pdf> accessed 13.09.2011

Iacovou M. and Berthoud R. (2006) *The Economic Position of Large Families*, London: Institute for Social and Economic Research

Isaacs S. (ed.) (1941) *The Cambridge Evacuation Study: A wartime study in social welfare and education*, London: Methuen

Ivaldi G. (2000) *Surveying Adoption: A comprehensive analysis of local authority adoptions 1998-1999*, London: BAAF

James S., Monn A. R., Palinkas L. A. and Leslie L. K. (2008) 'Maintaining sibling relationships for children in foster and adoptive placements', *Children and Youth Services Review*, 30, pp 90–106

Jenkins J. (1992) 'Sibling relationships in disharmonious homes: potential difficulties and protective effects', in Boer, F. and Dunn, J. (eds.) *Children's Sibling Relationships*, Hillsdale, NJ: Erlbaum

Jones M. and Niblett R. (1985) 'To split or not to split: the placement of siblings', *Adoption & Fostering*, 9:2, pp 26–29

Jurkovic G. J. (1997) *Lost Childhoods: The plight of the parentified child*, New York: Brunner Mazel

Kadushin A. and Seidl F. W. (1971) 'Adoption failure: a social work postmortem', *Social Work*, 16, pp 32–38

Kagan R. M. and Reid W. J. (1986) 'Critical factors in the adoption of emotionally disturbed youths', *Child Welfare*, 65, pp 63–73

Kaniuk J. (1988) 'Post-placement support or learning to live with your decisions', *Adoption & Fostering*, 12:3, pp 23–28

Kaplan L., Ade-Ridder L. and Hennon C. (1991) 'Issues of split custody: siblings separated by divorce', *Journal of Divorce and Remarriage*, 16:3(4), pp 253–274

Kempton T., Armistead L., Wierson M. and Forehand R. (1991) 'Presence of a sibling as a potential buffer following parental divorce: an examination of young adolescents', *Journal of Clinical Child Psychology*, 20, pp 434–438

Kendrick C. and Dunn J. (1983) 'Sibling quarrels and maternal responses', *Developmental Psychology*, 19:1, pp 62–70

Kim J. Y., McHale S. M., Osgood D. W. and Crouter A. C. (2006) 'Longitudinal course and family correlates of sibling relationships from childhood through adolescence', *Child Development*, 77:6, pp 1746–1761

Kitzmann K. M., Cohen R. and Lockwood R. L. (2002) 'Are only children missing out? Comparison of the peer-related social competence of only children and siblings', *Journal of Social and Personal Relationships*, 19:3, pp 299–316

Knipe J. and Warren J. (1990) *Foster Youth Share their Ideas for Change*, Washington, DC: Child Welfare League of America

Kominkiewicz F. B. (2004) 'The relationship of child protection service caseworker discipline-specific education and definition of sibling abuse: an institutional hiring impact study', *Journal of Human Behavior in the Social Environment*, 9:1(2), pp 69–81

Kosonen M. (1996a) 'Maintaining sibling relationships – neglected dimension in child care practice', *British Journal of Social Work*, 26, pp 809–822

Kosonen M. (1996b) 'Siblings as providers of support and care during middle childhood: children's perceptions', *Children and Society*, 10:4, pp 267–279

Kosonen M. (1999) "Core" and "kin" siblings: foster children's changing families', in Mullender, A. (ed.) *We are Family: Sibling relationships in placement and beyond*, London: BAAF

Kowal A. K., Krull J. L. and Kramer L. (2006) 'Shared understanding of parental differential treatment in families', *Social Development*, 15:2, pp 276–295

Kramer L. and Baron L. A. (1995) 'Parental perceptions of children's sibling relationships', *Family Relations*, 44, pp 95–103

Kramer L. and Conger K. J. (2009) 'What we learn from our sisters and brothers: for better or for worse', in Kramer, L. and Conger, K. J. (eds.) *Siblings as agents of socialization. New Directions for Child and Adolescent Development*, San Francisco: Jossey-Bass

Kunz J. (2001) 'Parental divorce and children's interpersonal relationships: a meta-analysis', *Journal of Divorce and Remarriage*, 34:3, pp 19–47

Laviola M. (1992) 'Effects of older brother-younger sister incest: a study of the dynamics of 17 cases', *Child Abuse and Neglect*, 16, pp 406–421

Leathers S. J. (2005) 'Separation from siblings: associations with placement adaptation and outcomes among adolescents in long-term foster care', *Children and Youth Services Review*, 27, pp 793–819

Leung P., Erich S. and Kanenberg H. (2004) 'A comparison of family functioning in gay/lesbian, heterosexual and special needs adoptions', *Children and Youth Services Review*, 27, pp 1031–1044

Linares L. O., Li M. M., Shrout P. E., Brody G. H. and Pettit G. S. (2007) 'Placement shift, sibling relationship quality, and child outcomes in foster care: a controlled study', *Journal of Family Psychology*, 21:4, pp 736–743

Linares L.O. (2006) 'An understudied form of intra-family violence: sibling-to-sibling aggression among foster children', *Aggression and Violent Behavior*, 11 pp 95–109

Loehlin J. C., Horn J. M. and Ernst J. L. (2010) 'Parent–child closeness studied in adoptive families', *Personality and Individual Differences*, 48:2, pp 149–154

Logan F., Morrall P. and Chambers H. (1998) 'Identification of risk factors for psychological disturbance in adopted children', *Child Abuse Review*, 7:3, pp 154–164

Lord J. and Borthwick S. (2008) *Together or Apart? Assessing brothers and sisters for permanent placement*, London: BAAF

Lowe N., Murch M., Bader K., Borkowski M., Copner R. and Lisles C. (2002) *The Plan for the Child: Adoption or long-term fostering*, London: BAAF

Lowe N., Murch M., Borkowski M., Weaver A., Beckford V. and Thomas C. (1999) *Supporting Adoption: Reframing the approach*, London: BAAF

Loxterkampe L. (2009) 'Contact and truth: the unfolding predicament in adoption and fostering', *Child Psychology and Psychiatry*, 14, pp 423-435

Ludvigsen A. and Parnham J. (2004) 'Searching for siblings: the motivations and experience of adults seeking contact with adopted siblings', *Adoption & Fostering*, 28:4, pp 50–59

Macaskill C. (1988) *Safe Contact? Children in permanent placement and contact with their birth relatives*, Lyme Regis, Dorset: Russell House Publishing

Maclean K. (1991) 'Meeting the needs of sibling groups in care', *Adoption & Fostering*, 15:1, pp 33–37

Martin J. L. and Ross H. S. (1995) 'The development of aggression within sibling conflict', *Early Education and Development*, 6:4, pp 335–358

McCrone P., Dhanasiri S., Patel A., Knapp M. and Lawton-Smith S. (2008) *Paying the Price: The cost of mental health care in England to 2026*, London: The King's Fund

McGuire S., Dunn J. and Plomin R. (1995) 'Maternal differential treatment of siblings and children's behaviour problems: a longitudinal study', *Development and Psychopathology*, 7, pp 515–528

McHale S. M., Updegraff K. A., Jackson-Newsom J., Tucker C. and Crouter A. C. (2000) 'When does parents' differential treatment have negative implications for siblings?', *Social Development*, 9, pp 149–172

McKay S. (2010) *The Effects of Twins and Multiple Births on Families and their Living Standards*, Birmingham: University of Birmingham

McPheat G., Milligan I. and Hunter L. (2007) 'What's the use of residential childcare? Findings from two studies detailing current trends in the use of residential childcare in Scotland', *Journal of Children's Services*, 2:2, pp 15–25

McRoy R. G. (1999) *Special Needs Adoption*, New York: Garland Publishing

Meltzer H., Gatward R., Goodman R. and Ford T. (2000) *Mental Health of Children and Adolescents in Great Britain*, London: The Stationery Office

Meltzer H., Gatward R., Goodman R. and Ford T. (2003) *The Mental Health Needs of Looked After Children*, London: The Stationery Office

Miller J. A., Jacobsen R. B. and Bigner J. J. (1981) 'The child's home environment for lesbian vs. heterosexual mothers: a neglected area of research', *Journal of Homosexuality*, 7:1, pp 49–56

Mullender A. and Kearn S. (1997) *"I'm Here Waiting" – Birth relatives' views on Part II of the Adoption Contact Register for England and Wales*, London: BAAF

Nandy S. and Selwyn S. (2011) *Spotlight on Kinship Care: Using Census microdata to examine the extent and nature of kinship care in the UK, Part 1 of a two-part study on kinship care*, Bristol: University of Bristol, School for Policy Studies, Hadley Centre for Adoption and Foster Care Studies

Neil E., Cosser J., Jones C., Lorgelly P. and Young J. (2010) *Supporting Direct Contact after Adoption*, London: BAAF

Nelson K. A. (1985) *On the Frontier of Adoption: A study of special-needs adoptive families*, Washington, DC: Child Welfare League of America

Nix H. (1983) 'Sibling relationships in older child adoptions', *Adoption & Fostering*, 7:2, pp 22–28

Noller P. (2005) 'Sibling relationships in adolescence: learning and growing together', *Personal Relationships*, 12, pp 1–22

Norris-Shortle C., Colletta N. D., Cohen M. B. and McCombs R. (1995) 'Sibling therapy with children under three', *Child and Adolescent Social Work Journal*, 12:4, pp 251–261

O'Leary S. and Schofield F. (1994) 'The right of siblings to live together', *Practice*, 7:1, pp 31–43

Ofsted (2010) *Children's Care Monitor: Children on the state of social care in England*, Reported by the Children's Rights Director for England, London: Ofsted

Office for National Statistics (2001) *Census 2001*, London: ONS

Office for National Statistics (2007) *Birth Statistics FMI*, London: ONS

Padilla-Walker L. M., Harper J. M. and Jensen A. C. (2010) 'Self-regulation as a mediator between sibling relationship quality and early adolescents' positive and negative outcomes', *Journal of Family Psychology*, 24:4, pp 419–428

Penn R. and Lambert P. (2002) 'Attitudes towards ideal family size of different ethnic/nationality groups in Great Britain, France and Germany', *Population Trends 108*, National Statistics. Lancaster: University of Lancaster, Centre for Applied Statistics

Pike A., Coldwell J. and Dunn J. (2006) *Family Relationships in Middle Childhood*, London: National Children's Bureau

Platt L. (2002) *Parallel Lives? Poverty amongst ethnic minority groups*, London: Child Poverty Action Group

Quinton D., Rushton A., Dance C. and Mayes D. (1998) *Joining New Families: A study of adoption and fostering in middle childhood*, Chichester: John Wiley and Sons Ltd

Radford L., Corral S., Bradley C., Fisher H., Bassett C., Howat N. and Collishaw S. (2011) *Maltreatment and victimization of children and young people in the UK: NSPCC research findings*, London: NSPCC

Rao P., Ali A. and Vostanis P. (2010) 'Looked after and adopted children: How should specialist CAMHS be involved?', *Adoption & Fostering*, 34:2, pp 58–72

Richmond M. K., Stocker C. M. and Rienks S. L. (2005) 'Longitudinal associations between sibling relationship quality, parental differential treatment, and children's adjustment', *Journal of Family Psychology*, 19:4, pp 550–559

Rosenthal J. A. and Groze V. K. (1992) *Special Needs Adoption*, New York: Praeger

Rosenthal J. A., Schmidt D. and Conner J. (1988) 'Predictors of special needs adoption disruption: an exploratory study', *Children and Youth Services Review*, 10:2, pp 101–117

Rushton A., Dance C., Quinton D. and Mayes D. (2001) *Siblings in Late Permanent Placements*, London: BAAF

Rushton A., Mayes D., Dance C. and Quinton D. (2003) 'Parenting late-placed children: the development of new relationships and the challenge of behavioural problems', *Clinical Child Psychology and Psychiatry*, 8:3, pp 389–400

Rushton A. and Monck E. (2009) *Enhancing Adoptive Parenting: A test of effectiveness*, London: BAAF

Ryan S. D., Hinterlong J., Hegar R. L. and Johnson L. B. (2010) 'Kin adopting kin: in the best interest of the children?', *Children and Youth Services Review*, 32, pp 1631–1639

Sanders R. (2004) *Sibling Relationships: Theory and issues for practice*, Basingstoke (England) and New York: Palgrave Macmillan

Schechter M. D. and Bertocci D. (1990) 'The meaning of the search', in Brodzinsky, D. and Schechter, M. (eds.) *The Psychology of Adoption*, New York: Oxford University Press

Scholte R. H. J., Engels R. C. M. E., de Kemp R. A. T., Harakeh Z. and Overbeek G. (2007) 'Differential parental treatment, sibling relationships and delinquency in adolescence', *Journal of Youth and Adolescence*, 36:5, pp 661–671

Selwyn J., Quinton D., Harris P., Wijedasa D., Nawaz S. and Wood M. (2010) *Pathways to Permanence for Black, Asian and Mixed Ethnicity Children*, London: BAAF

Selwyn J. and Sempik J. (2010) 'Recruiting adoptive families: the costs of family finding and the failure of the inter-agency fee', *British Journal of Social Work*, 40:4, pp 1–17

Selwyn J., Sturgess W., Quinton D. and Baxter C. (2006) *Costs and Outcomes of Non-infant Adoptions*, London: BAAF

Sheehan G., Darlington Y., Noller P. and Feeney J. (2004) 'Children's perceptions of their sibling relationships during parental separation and divorce', *Journal of Divorce and Remarriage*, 41:1(2), pp 69–94

Shlonsky A., Bellamy J., Elkins J. and Ashare C. J. (2005) 'The other kin: setting the course for research, policy and practice with siblings in foster care', *Children and Youth Services Review*, 27, pp 697–716

Shlonsky A., Webster D. and Needell B. (2003) 'The ties that bind: a cross-sectional analysis of siblings in foster care', *Journal of Social Service Research*, 29:3, pp 27–52

Simmonds J. (2010) 'The making and breaking of relationships: organizational and clinical questions in providing services for looked after children?', *Clinical Child Psychology and Psychiatry*, 15:4, pp 601–612

Sinclair I., Wilson K. and Gibbs I. (2005) *Foster Placements: Why they succeed and why they fail*, London: Jessica Kingsley Publishers

Smith M. C. (1996) 'An exploratory survey of foster mother and caseworker attitudes about sibling placements', *Child Welfare*, 75:4, pp 357–375

Smith S., McRoy R., Freundlich M. and Kroll J. (2008) *Finding Families for African American Children: The role of race and law in adoption from foster care*, New York: Evan B. Donaldson Adoption Institute

Smith S. L., Howard J. A., Garnier P. C. and Ryan S. D. (2006) 'Where are we now? A post-ASFA examination of adoption disruption', *Adoption Quarterly*, 9:4, pp 19–44

Staff I. and Fein E. (1992) 'Together or separate: a study of siblings in foster care', *Child Welfare*, 75:4, pp 357–375

Stanley N., Riordan D. and Alaszewski H. (2005) 'The mental health of looked after children: matching response to need', *Health and Social Care in the Community*, 13:3, pp 239–248

Stansfield W. D., Carlton M. A. and Matthew A. (2007) 'Human sex ratios and sex distribution in sibships of size 2', *Human Biology*, 79:2, pp 255–260

Stocker C., Dunn J. and Plomin R. (1989) 'Sibling relationships: links with child temperament, maternal behavior and family structure', *Child Development*, 60, pp 715–727

Stocker C. and Youngblade L. (1999) 'Marital conflict and parental hostility: links with children's sibling and peer relationships', *Journal of Family Psychology*, 13, pp 598–609

Stormshak E. A., Bellanti C. J., Bierman K. L. and Group C. P. P. R. (1999) 'The quality of sibling relationships and the development of social competence and behavioral control in aggressive children', *Developmental Psychology*, 32:pp 79–89

Stormshak E. A., Bullock B. M. and Falkenstein C. A. (2009) 'Harnessing the power of sibling relationships as a tool for optimising social-emotional development', *News Directions for Child and Adolescent Development*, 2009:126, pp 61–77

Suitor J. J., Sechrist J., Plikuhn M., Pardo S. T., Gilligan M. and Pillemer K. (2009) 'The role of perceived maternal favoritism in sibling relations in midlife', *Journal of Marriage and the Family*, 71:4, pp 1026–1038

Sulloway F. J. (1996) *Born to Rebel: Birth order, family dynamics, and creative lives*, New York: Pantheon

Tancredy C. M. and Fraley C. R. (2006) 'The nature of adult twin relationships: an attachment-theoretical perspective', *Journal of Personality and Social Psychology*, 90:1, pp 78–93

Tarren-Sweeney M. (2010) 'It's time to re-think mental health services for children in care, and those adopted from care', *Clinical Child Psychology and Psychiatry*, 15:4, pp 613–626

Tarren-Sweeny M. and Hazell P. (2005) 'The mental health and socialisation of siblings in care', *Children and Youth Service Review*, 27:7, pp 697–716

Tasker F. and Golombok S. (1995) 'Adults raised as children in lesbian families', *American Journal of Orthopsychiatry*, 65:2, pp 203–215

Thomas C., Beckford V., Lowe N. and Murch M. (1999) *Adopted Children Speaking*, London: BAAF

Thorpe M. B. and Swart G. T. (1992) 'Risk and protective factors affecting childen in foster care: a pilot study of the role of siblings', *Canadian Journal of Psychiatry*, 37:9, pp 616–622

Timberlake E. M. and Hamlin E. R. (1982) 'The sibling group: a neglected dimension of placement', *Child Welfare*, 61:8, pp 545–552

Toman W. (1993) *Family Constellation: Its effects on personality and social behavior*, New York: Springer Publishing Company, Inc

Triseliotis J., Feast J. and Kyle F. (2005) *The Adoption Triangle Revisited*, London: BAAF

van IJzendoorn M. H., Juffer F. and Poelhuis C. W. K. (2005) 'Adoption and cognitive development: a meta-analysis comparison of adoption and nonadopted children's IQ and shcool performance', *Psychological Bulletin*, 131:2, pp 301–316

Vivona J. M. (2007) 'Sibling differentiation, identity development, and the lateral dimension of psychic life', *Journal of the American Pscyhoanalytic Association*, 55:4, pp 1191–1215

Voice (2004) *Start with the child, Stay with the child, A blueprint for a child-centred approach to children and young people in public care*, London: National Children's Bureau

Volling B. L. (ed.) (2003) *Sibling Relationships*, Mahwah, NJ: Lawrence Erlbaum Associates

Ward M. (1984) 'Sibling ties in foster care and adoption planning', *Child Welfare*, 63:4, pp 321–332

Ward M. (1987) 'Choosing adoptive families for large sibling groups', *Child Welfare*, 66:3, pp 259–268

Ward M. and Lewko J. H. (1988) 'Problems experienced by adolscents already in families that adopt older children', *Adolescence*, 23:89, pp 221–228

Washington K. (2007) 'Research review: sibling placement in foster care: a review of the evidence', *Child and Family Social Work*, 12, pp 426–433

Webster D., Shlonsky A., Shaw T. and Brookhart M. A. (2005) 'The ties that bind II: reunification for siblings in out-of-home care using a statistical technique for examining non-independent observations', *Children and Youth Services Review*, 27, pp 765–782

Wedge P. and Mantel G. (1991) *Sibling Groups and Social Work: A study of children referrred for permanent substitute family placement*, Aldershot: Avebury Academic Publishing Group

Weisner T. S. and Gallimore R. (1977) 'My brother's keeper: child and sibling caretaking', *Current Anthropology*, 18:2, pp 169–190

Whipple E. E. and Finton S. E. (1995) 'Psychological maltreatment by siblings: an unrecognised form of abuse', *Child and Adolescent Social Work Journal*, 12:2, pp 135–146

Whiting J., B and Lee R. E. (2003) 'Voices from the system: a qualitative study of foster children's stories', *Family Relations*, 52:3, pp 288–295

Wiehe V. R. (1996) *The Brother/Sister Hurt: Recognising the effects of sibling abuse*, Brandon, VT: Safer Society Press

Willmott S., Boardman J., Henshaw C. and John P. (2004) 'Understanding GHQ28 and its threshold', *Social Psychiatry and Psychiatric Epidemiology*, 39, pp 613–617

Winter K. (2010) 'The perspectives of young children in care about their circumstances and implications for social work practice', *Child and Family Social Work*, 15, pp 186–195

Woerner W., Fleitlich-Bilyk B., Martinussen R., Fletcher J., Cucchiaro G., Dalgalarrondo P., Lui M. and Tannock R. (2004) 'The strengths and difficulties questionnaire overseas: evaluation and applications of the SDQ beyond Europe', *European Child and Adolescent Psychiatry*, 13:supplement 2, pp ii47–ii54

Wolke D. and Skew A. (2011) 'Bullied at home and at school: relationship to behaviour problems and unhappiness', in McFall, S. L., Garrington, C., Buck, N., Laurie, H. and Nolan, V. (eds.) *Understanding Society: Early findings from the first wave of the UK's household longitudinal study*, Colchester: Institute for Social and Economic Research

Wrobel G. M., Grotevant H. D. and McRoy R. G. (2004) 'Adolescent search for birthparents: who moves forward?', *Journal of Adolescent Research*, 19:1, pp 132–151

Wulczyn F. and Zimmerman E. (2005) 'Sibling placements in longitudinal perspective', *Children and Youth Service Review*, 27:7, pp 741–763

Yahav R. (2007) 'The relationship between children's and adolescents' perceptions of parenting style and internal and external symptoms', *Child: Care, Health and Development*, 33:4, pp 460–471

Yeh H. C. and Lempers J. D. (2004) 'Perceived sibling relationships and adolescent development', *Journal of Youth and Adolescence*, 33:2, pp 133–147

Zill N. (1996) 'Parental schooling and children's health', *Public Health Reports*, 111:1, pp 34–43

Zimmerman R. B. (1982) 'Foster care in retrospect', *Tulane Studies in Social Welfare*, 14, pp 1–125

Zukow-Goldring P. (ed.) (2002) *Sibling Caregiving*, Mahwah, NJ: Erlbaum

Resources for siblings

Siblings Together: An initiative set up by Delma Hughes to promote positive contact between siblings who have been separated by the care system. Runs holiday camps where siblings can spend time together, taking part in a wide range of creative and adventure activities. Aims to build foundations for continued contact and to educate social workers about the importance of sibling family contact. Email: delma@siblingstogether.co.uk Tel: 020 7231 6925, Mobile: 07899 89 2745, Address: 320 Southwark Park Road, London SE16 2HA.

Siblings United Shaftesbury Young People: An organisation that works to improve outcomes for children in care, and organises summer camps for separated brothers and sisters to spend time together. Tel: 020 8875 1555, Address: C0/o Linda Jones, Royal Victoria Patriotic Building, John Archer Way, London SW18 3SX, www.shaftesbury.org.uk

Rethink Siblings: New online national network for siblings to share experiences and get support. Set up by Rethink mental health charity. www.rethink.org/siblings

'Sibs': Generic website for siblings of disabled people. Produces information sheets and regular newsletter, runs workshops and will take calls from siblings. www.sibs.org.uk

Index